THE BEATLES, FOOTBALL
AND ME

THE BEATLES, FOOTBALL AND ME

A Memoir

Hunter Davies

headline
review

Copyright © 2006 Hunter Davies

The right of Hunter Davies to be identified as the Author of
the Work has been asserted by him in accordance with the
Copyright, Designs and Patents Act 1988.

First published in Great Britain in 2006
by HEADLINE REVIEW

An imprint of HEADLINE BOOK PUBLISHING

1

A CIP catalogue record for this title is available from the British Library

ISBN 0 7553 1402 6

Typeset in New Baskerville by Avon DataSet Ltd,
Bidford-on-Avon, Warwickshire

Printed and bound in Great Britain by
Mackays of Chatham plc, Chatham, Kent

Headline's policy is to use papers that are natural, renewable and
recyclable products and made from wood grown in sustainable forests.
The logging and manufacturing processes are expected to conform
to the environmental regulations of the country of origin.

HEADLINE BOOK PUBLISHING
A division of Hodder Headline
338 Euston Road
London NW1 3BH

www.reviewbooks.co.uk
www.hodderheadline.com

Acknowledgements

Thanks to Steve Matthews for his encouragement in publishing the Carlisle years; to Val Hudson for supporting the whole story; to Roger McGough for letting me reproduce two of his verses; and to Margaret, my dear wife, the best thing that ever happened to me . . .

Contents

Introduction

It's pretty presumptuous, writing your memoirs. I can't say I was asked to do it, that they needed to be done, that publishers were beating a path to my door, that the world awaited my inside story on myself. In fact when my wife and children heard what I was planning, they each said the same thing. Oh no, spare us.

I haven't witnessed any of the grand public events of my lifetime from the inside, only outside looking in, so I can't offer any unique insights or first-hand accounts of the political, social or economic events of my times. And I haven't even tried. That's not been the point. In my own private life, nothing truly remarkable has happened, and the awful things, when they did happen, have been awful things which have happened, alas, to hundreds of thousands of others.

I have by chance met some well-known people, but only in the way of work, being paid to do so, which is cheating really, fame by association. So have hundreds of other hacks. Nothing special there. If you start name-dropping about people you've met because that was your job, it looks pathetic, showing off. That's the first danger.

The second danger, once you start, is becoming self-important, imagining that your life, your thoughts, are in fact important. God, I hope that hasn't happened. The very best I would like to achieve is being vaguely interesting and, now and again, passably amusing.

The final danger is becoming self-obsessed. That's been the hardest trap to avoid. Having decided to write about me, there is little escape from me. In all the books I have done, even those about other people, some of them totally self-obsessed, I have been able to leaven it by bringing in other people, other thoughts, or poking fun. Going on and on about me and my life all the time, a task I set myself, it's been very difficult to avoid becoming obsessed by self. Of course, by saying I tried to avoid being self-obsessed, that's a sure sign of self-obsession.

So why did I do it? Catharsis, that's what people often say when they decide, unbidden, to unload themselves. They found it therapeutic, so they maintain, to explore where they have come from in order to find out who they are and now they can move on, which on the whole I think is bollocks. I've learned nothing about myself in doing this book, except how lucky I have been, which I knew already, and what a lousy memory I have for people's names and dates.

Fortunately, as I've travelled through life, since 1960 I have carefully kept endless files of memorabilia, letters, documents, photographs, some of them going back to birth and childhood. Most of them are of pure domestic, family, personal or work interest, but I grandly entitled these files MY LIFE and have them arranged decade by decade.

I suppose the first reason for doing the book is it's what I do. I have gone through life, once I stumbled upon writing, which was by sheer chance, committing words to paper. Even when some of those ordinary awful things happen to me, as one did last year, I find myself thinking, while I'm hardly out of the ambulance, hmm, I'll get 1,000 words out of that, perhaps 5,000 if I do all the side-effects.

So it seemed a natural thing for me to do, from where I am sitting, and it didn't worry me that I had nothing important or earth-shattering to write about it. I've always been fascinated by the ordinary. I take trivial things very seriously. And with serious things, my inclination is to be trivial.

Secondly, I like to imagine there are other ordinary people out there who will find it of interest, just for ordinary reasons. I've always liked the idea of someone trying to get to grips with the narrative of their life, whoever they are, telling us their story in a straightforward chronological order.

There is a fashion for ordinary people to write the story of their ordinary life and, on the whole, I enjoy them. Two years ago, I did a little book (*Strong Lad Wanted for Strong Lass*) about growing up in Carlisle, for a Carlisle publisher, and purely for a Carlisle audience. It got more letters for a book than I've had for years. And no, they didn't all say boring, boring.

I'm a judge each year of the Lakeland Book of the Year awards and we get an increasing number of retired farmers or old miners who sit down and tell us about their life. Very often they have had a wartime experience, finding themselves suddenly transported from Burgh by Sands to Burma. Even out there, their experiences have usually been ordinary, as far as wartime memoirs go, but of course not to them.

I didn't serve the Queen, or the King, not even as a National Serviceman, so you are spared all that, but I do clearly remember the war, as millions of others do. To the modern generation, having any prewar memories, which I can roughly manage if I concentrate hard, makes you positively ancient. These memories will get rarer as the world trundles on. It was when my children started asking me about my memories of the Sixties, as if they were equally prehistoric, that I realised life was going on at far too fast a trundle.

Being seventy in 2006, that's what's really done it. Well, that's my main excuse. It just seemed neat, a good time to do it, look back, get it all down before it's too late and I haven't the energy left to cool my porridge or switch on my old Amstrad. Three score and ten, it's quite a long spell, I think, and I am very surprised and thrilled to have got here, roughly in one piece, more or less.

Anyone who has lived through any or all of these last seventy years will often have thought that what they were doing and thinking was special to them, in their own location, at that precise time, but with age, you realise you were part of the herd, that other people, in other places, at the same time, were thinking and doing very much the same. It's these ordinary things we can identify with, as much as the extraordinary. So ordinary life is one of the things I'm offering, plus a few famous people, dragged in . . .

Hunter Davies, London, 7 January 2006, his birthday

Chapter One

Falling off a Bus

I was born on 7 January 1936 at Thornhill maternity hospital in Johnstone, Renfrewshire, Scotland. So it says on my birth certificate, but I have no memory of Johnstone and have never been back since. I'm told, but can't remember it, that I used to stand at the gate of our house in Inchinnan Road and tell all the passers-by, whether they wanted to hear it or not, all the things happening in our house. Nothing has changed, really.

My earliest memory is of being pushed in my pram through crowds and mud to see the launch of the *Queen Mary* at John Brown's shipyard on the River Clyde. What a great day, a proud event for millions of Scottish people as Scottish-built ships were famous throughout the world, so every Scot believed.

Now I look up the dates, I see that the *Queen Mary* was in fact launched in 1934, so some confusion there. Could it have been the *Queen Elizabeth* which was launched in 1938? Possibly, but I doubt it. This memory of going to a launch is a received one. I was only told about it later by my mother. It was probably the launch of some minor ship, but I adopted it, convincing myself I was there on a great national occasion.

Both my parents were Scottish. My mother, Marion Brechin, came from Motherwell and my father, John Hunter Davies, from Cambuslang. My mother's parents lived in a council house on the Bellshill Road in Motherwell and I spent many holidays with them. I didn't like their house, just an upstairs flat really, and my grandfather never spoke. He just sat, silently whistling, a constant hissing noise that never turned into a tune, while he unravelled knots in balls of string, smiling to himself. Now and again, he did play Ludo with me. My grandmother Brechin was small and fierce, always fussing about my vest, making me wash my hands whenever I sat down to look at the photographs in her big, glittery *Daily Express* book about the Royal Family.

Opposite their house was The Bing – an overgrown spoil heap from a disused coal mine – on which I played with the Wallace boys from the Buildings further down the Bellshill Road. These were older council blocks, tenements, with brutal outside concrete landings and communal wash houses in the back yard. I preferred the Buildings to my grandmother's flat because they were always full of children running about, skipping, playing football, with mothers shouting from the landings for them.

My grandfather Brechin had been on the railways, ending up as an engine driver, which my mother told me was a very good job, people were proud of it, especially as it gave you free travel. They hardly travelled anywhere, so to me it didn't seem much of an advantage. And if his job had been so good, why were they living in a pokey, very cold, one-bedroom council flat?

My Davies grandparents, over in Cambuslang, seemed much posher, higher class. They owned their own house on the Hamilton Road, with a garden. They had books in the house and an attic room and a hole-in-the-wall bed in the main living room. This was just an alcove, filled by a double bed, hidden behind a screen, typical of many Scottish homes of the time. They also had a clothes pulley suspended from the ceiling in the living room which I loved pulling up and down.

My father's sister Jean had been to Glasgow University, and had become a teacher at Hamilton Academy. His brother Alex was also a teacher. Another brother Jim, despite working as a rent collector and at various other jobs, was really a poet and playwright, so I was led to believe. He did have a play produced at the Byre Theatre in St Andrews which everyone in the family went to see. It was a biblical play, called *The Hands of Esau,* written in the Scots dialect. When I got a bit older, he insisted on reading it out to me. It seemed to go on for hours. I couldn't understand a word and eventually I fell asleep, which rather hurt him.

Grandfather Davies had been some sort of engineer, probably little more than a fitter, upper working class, not professional class, but the Scottish education system had always been better, more enlightened, more open to all classes than in England and so several of his children had received higher education in the 1930s and done quite well for themselves.

Except for my dad. He had left school at fourteen. But unlike my Motherwell relatives, who were blue-collar workers, he became a white-collar worker, a clerk attached to the Air Force.

At the time of my birth, he was still serving in the RAF. I have several photos of him in uniform, one of them with the Duke of Hamilton, who was his commanding officer, sitting in the front row, so he told me, and also snaps of him in an RAF football team.

It was through the RAF he met my mother Marion. She also had left school at fourteen and she became a maid, serving in the house of a Church of Scotland minister. One of the guests when she was there, whom she brought tea in bed, was the Rev Eric Liddell, the well-known Scottish runner whose life was portrayed in *Chariots of Fire.* So that's the first famous name, rather worked in.

She then got a job as a waitress in the NAAFI in Perth where my father happened to be stationed. I always sensed my father's family rather looked down on my mother socially. She certainly felt inferior to the teachers in his family, especially his sister Jean, who seemed to my mother to be so clever, so organised, having a career and running a family, with her house always immaculate. My mother, poor soul, could never be said to have run an immaculate house.

While we were still living in Johnstone, with my father still in the RAF, my mother had twins, Marion and Annabelle who were born in 1939. My father was carried shoulder-high round the station, as if it had been a triumph for him personally.

Not long afterwards, in 1940, we moved to Carlisle where my younger brother Johnny was born in 1941. My father had been posted to 14 MU in Carlisle, an RAF Maintenance Unit. By this time he was a civilian, but working with the RAF as a wages clerk.

One of my earliest Carlisle memories is of going with him in some sort of RAF jeep, guarded by two uniformed RAF men, while we travelled round some RAF stations, taking the wages. I thought it was very exciting, the first time I had ever been in any sort of motor vehicle. We stopped somewhere, possibly a pub, while the RAF types listened to the Grand National on a radio. We never had a car in our family, nor – surprisingly – did any of my Cambuslang relatives, though we always looked upon them as rich.

In Carlisle we lived at 25 Deer Park Road on the St Ann's Hill estate. It was a newly built 1930s council estate, and rent was collected by the council every week. The fathers of almost all my friends worked at the nearby 14 MU which had been established in 1938 when the RAF took over the old Kingstown Aerodrome. Thousands of people worked there at the time, spread over several sites to the north of the city. It supplied the whole of the RAF with various sorts of parts, hence all the hangars, warehouses and men who called themselves storemen.

There were apparently seven such Maintenance Units spread around the UK, all classified as secret, and each had a complete range of stock, in case any of them got hit during an air raid. At the height of the war, in 1945, there were 4,300 people employed at Carlisle's 14 MU – 784 uniformed airmen and the rest civilians. A good half of the workers were women, who were replaced by men in the postwar years. It even had thirteen miles of its own railway track.

I assume our part of the estate had been built to serve 14 MU, or that's what it became, for the MU was the focal point of our lives. As children we would go to sports days and similar events held at 14 MU. During the war, it was well guarded, seemed very hush-hush and important, as if real war work was being done there. I was never aware of any bombs falling on Carlisle during the war, but we could hear the German bombers flying overhead, on their way to Glasgow or Belfast. There was a rumour once that a Jerry plane had come down at Kingstown and I went with some other boys to look for it in Kingmoor Woods. We never found it.

My best friend was Reggie Hill who lived in the next street, in Fraser Grove. I was told later, while still living in Carlisle, that all the streets on our estate were named after 1930s Carlisle doctors – and that Fraser Grove got its name from Dr Fraser, the father of George MacDonald Fraser, the author of *Flashman*, who went to Carlisle Grammar School. The connection has always amused me, and I've often repeated it as a fact, without really knowing, so for the sake of this book I wrote to George MacDonald Fraser in the Isle of Man, where he now lives, to ask if it was true.

'There were four Dr Frasers in Carlisle before the war,' so he replied. 'My father "Dr Willy", my uncle "Dr Allan", and two who were no relation, Kenneth and Mark. Kenneth was the Medical Officer and I think Fraser Grove was named after him.

'Altogether, there have been eleven Dr Frasers in Carlisle. I should have been the twelfth, but wasn't, thank heaven.'

Reggie Hill, my friend, was known as Toddles. Even at the age of five and six, he didn't like his mother or his family calling him by that name. I presume it started because as a toddler he toddled along. I would call him Toddles, just to annoy, but not for very long as he soon grew much taller than me and could therefore beat me up.

We started at the same time at Stanwix Primary School about a mile away in what is today still seen as one of the posher parts of Carlisle. At the time, and for many years, it was the nearest primary school to our estate, so we had to go there, but we always felt a social divide, that the ones who actually lived in Stanwix were the elite who lived in houses owned by their parents, with their own doorbell and a garage, sometimes even a car to go in it, while we were the council-house scruffs.

I suppose my mother must have taken me to Stanwix School in the early weeks, but I was soon going on the bus myself, along with Reggie and the other kids from the St Ann's Hill council estate. No one would let kids of five or six go on buses on their own today, or even walk to school unattended, but it was normal at the time, what everyone did. Reg and I would be out for hours, raking round the estate, mucking around in the allotments behind Caird Avenue, going into the new council houses being built at Briar Bank and climbing on the scaffolding, playing endless games on our own in Kingmoor Woods or in the surrounding fields, building dams, paddling in streams. All memoirists of the 1940s and 1950s have such rosy images of unattended play, but we did, we did.

One day, when I was about seven, Reg and I were waiting for the Ribble bus to take us home after school. We let several buses pass us because we wanted to come home on the Dummy, which was a smaller bus, a funny-shaped one, as if it had been cut in half. It was the same price, just another Ribble bus, for the public at large, not confined to school children. We just liked it better.

We got on, with a gang of other kids, who also liked this bus, so naturally there was a lot of pushing and shoving as we all tried to get to the back. Being there, up against the back door, was the place to be.

As the bus was going down a steep cobbled hill, it always got up a good speed, which added to the excitement. The emergency door with a big handle at the back of the bus was not to be touched by anyone, but suddenly it flew open. Some kids had probably been tampering with it, or perhaps Reg and I had touched it. I don't think it was the fault of the Ribble bus company. But the result was that Reg and I fell out together – right into the path of a lorry which was following behind the bus.

Somehow, the lorry managed to avoid us, swerving and braking in order to stop itself running over us. That was what we were subsequently told. The fall from the bus, probably going at forty miles an hour, had rendered us both immediately unconscious. I knew nothing about anything until I woke up in hospital.

It was only many years later, when I grew up, supposedly, that I ever wondered what our mothers must have been put through. Neither of us had a phone or a car. It was the arrival of a policeman at each of our houses which informed our mothers that there had been a road accident and that we were both lying in the Carlisle Infirmary. Presumably they then had to catch a bus to town, to find out how we were.

I don't know how long I was in there, or what the injuries were, but we knew we had had a very lucky escape. What a loss to literature that would have been. Toddles is now Reginald C. Hill, one of our most distinguished and best-selling crime writers, author of the Dalziel and Pascoe books, winner of the Gold Dagger and many other awards. That makes three well-known names, already.

When we returned to Stanwix School, Reg and I rather traded on our notoriety for the rest of the term, as it made us known by the older classes. It became a bond between us, something we had gone through together.

But then, not long afterwards, our friendship was broken. In 1943, when I was aged seven, my father got another posting. He was being moved back over the border to Scotland. Reg and I promised to write to each other. We probably did, for a few weeks, but then the correspondence petered out and Carlisle began to fade from my mind.

Chapter Two

Fighting Hitler

We moved to Dumfries in 1943. I had no idea why. Were my parents homesick and wanting to return to Scotland? Was my father offered a better job? He was still doing the same thing, as far as I was aware, working as a wages clerk attached to the RAF. He probably had no choice. It was wartime, so you did what you were told.

We lived in a house called Nancyville on the Annan Road, which sounds quite smart, as opposed to a council estate, but we didn't have the whole house, just rented part of it. The ground floor had been a shop but the front window had been boarded up and in it lived a disabled Polish airman. He'd had some sort of war injury, his face all burned, and looked rather frightening. We could hear him at night, banging around downstairs.

In the night could also be heard Peter, our cat, the first and only time I can remember having a family pet. Peter had disappeared in the fields behind our house for some weeks, presumed lost for ever, then returned one night half dead, dragging a trap in which his foot had been caught. One leg had to be amputated, but he lived on for many years, managing with three legs and a stump. The noise he made at night was a soft pad pad pad, followed by a thump of his gammy leg.

We only had two bedrooms. My parents slept in one while we four children slept in the other. Our bedroom was at the front and at night it was illuminated by the military convoys going along Annan Road towards England. The headlights would waken one of us, who would start talking, and wake all the others.

As the oldest, I would say out loud, 'One Two Three, no more talking, goodnight.' If anyone spoke after that, I had to say it all again. Strange how such a piddling, pointless little thing has stayed in my mind all these years.

Each evening before bed, our mother made us say our prayers which always ended with 'And please God, look after all our soldiers, sailors and airmen.' I went to Noblehill Primary School, just along the Annan Road, which was very handy and didn't need a bus. I fell in love there with a girl called Mary Ferguson. That's what it felt like. She was in my class, dark-haired, pretty, and lived not far away.

At school we did a lot of knitting, each of us doing a square which would then be stitched together by the teacher to make blankets for our brave soldiers, sailors and airmen, whom God was busy looking after. Poor sods. My blanket square was always full of holes and taggles and wouldn't have kept anyone warm and safe. We saved waste paper to help fight Hitler and the 'Nazzies', the ones not keeping our boys safe. I was never clear how waste paper helped. Was it thrown at the Nazzies or turned into paper bombs? There were drawings in the comics showing piles of waste paper which we had saved and when the piles got to a certain height, they were marked 'Berlin'. That didn't make it any clearer, unless the piles of paper were for walking on.

We knew all about Hitler. He had a funny moustache, did a silly walk with one hand in the air, and had only one ball. As a child in the war, I don't remember Hitler as a scary figure, more a figure of fun. We knew nothing about the concentration camps. We were more worried about Spies, people secretly watching what we were doing, who were usually thought to be old people we didn't like anyway, especially the ones who told us off.

In Dumfries, as in Carlisle, we had black-out curtains on our windows at home and a metal shelter under the kitchen table. We were issued with gas masks and ration books which bought very little. We never tasted real chocolate or proper sweets, just pretend sweets, made of what tasted like cardboard. My mother gave us what she said was mashed banana, which tasted quite nice, and we said yes, we like bananas, not knowing that they were mashed parsnips. Now and again, my father came home from work with a tin of fruit cocktail, containing bits of real fruit: what a treat that was. He'd got them from some American servicemen at his RAF station, so he said, though it might well have been via the black market.

Even more special was to get hold of real chewing gum, which again needed contact with Americans. I managed this at first hand, or first fingers. Convoys of American troops often passed along the Annan Road, throwing up clouds of dust. I would stand for hours by the side of the road, giving them the V for Victory sign. I couldn't manage on my own to form my fingers in the right arrangement, so my mother would do them for me, then I would rush out of the house and stand there, waving frantically at the Yankee jeeps and trucks till eventually one would throw out a packet of chewing gum. Other kids would appear from nowhere and we'd all scramble and fight each other in the gutter to grab the treasure. 'Got any gum, chum?' I can still hear myself shouting the words, with a Scottish accent of course.

Being at war seemed normal and ordinary. How life was, would always be. I had no memory of any prewar life. I heard stories of people eating real oranges, real bars of milk chocolate, but couldn't believe it. Orange to us came in a bottle, thick stuff, which the clinic provided. Eggs were always dried. Our wartime comics were all skimpy, printed on cheap nasty paper with very few pages. One of my Cambuslang uncles gave me one of his prewar comics which was so fat, with masses of pages and cartoons. I couldn't believe comics could ever be like that. But of course we needed paper for fighting Hitler.

At school one day, the teacher asked all those whose fathers were prisoners of war to stand up. When they did, they were all given food parcels. I was so jealous. I rushed home and complained loudly to my father that it wasn't fair, why wasn't he a prisoner of war?

There was an Italian prisoner of war camp not far away. We would often see them, in trucks or in groups, being taken to work in the fields. They wore light brown tunics and light brown trousers. I remember the colour, despite being colour blind, because my mother bought me a little tunic jacket to wear which was almost the same colour. Kids at school shouted after me, Eye Tie, Eye Tie.

I got into one real fight in the playground, after someone had been calling me names. Perhaps for having come from England, rather than looking Italian. On that particular day, I'd had a terrible attack of asthma and felt awful, very weak, hunched and wheezing. I didn't have the energy for a fight, but this kid went on and on, pushing and pulling me, calling me names, till in the end, in anger and frustration, I managed to summon up courage and strength I never knew I had and flew into this kid like a wild animal, scratching and punching, screaming and shouting. Every other kid in the school had gathered round as the cry of 'Fight Fight Fight' had echoed round the playground. In the end, he backed away, frightened by what he had unleashed.

I always had asthma as a child. I can't remember not having it. Like the war, it had always been with me, a fact of my life. My mother and father both smoked, but I have never held that against them. Most grown-ups did. I once overheard my grandmother Davies complaining that my mother had smoked over my cot, but I didn't understand the significance.

Doctors prescribed various medicines, none of which ever gave much relief. There was a nasty powder I had to set fire to and inhale, which was supposed to help breathing, but it never did. Then there was a red rubber ball thing into which you put medicine and then squeezed it, and the spray went into your throat. I was given an allergy test, my arm covered with scores of pin-pricks, like stamp perforations, but they didn't find any allergies, except dust.

One long summer holiday I was sent with my grandmother Brechin to the Highlands, to a croft belonging to some distant relatives. The clean, fresh, Highland air was supposed to help my asthma. I did feel stronger and bigger, but this was mainly because on this croft were living two or three foster kids from the Glasgow slums, very small and scrawny. I'd always felt a midget, compared with Toddles, I mean Reggie, but for once I felt big.

I hated being with my grandma. On the train there and back she insisted on telling total strangers that I had very bad asthma. She made me wear a special silk vest, next to my bare little chest, saying it would help my breathing. It did feel good, cool, clean and soothing.

During the war, I spent another summer with my grandmother Davies in Glasgow at the very height of the bombing. I loved looking up at the enormous barrage balloons which were tethered in bits of open space, often just at the end of streets, held on ropes, but allowed to float in the sky. The most exciting part was rushing out of the house when the sirens sounded, to take cover in the Anderson shelter in the garden. I would peer out at the night sky all lit up, hear the drone of Nazzie bombers heading for the Clyde shipyards, watch the sudden flashes of flames, hear the ack-ack guns trying to find the bombers, then would come a series of enormous explosions.

I enjoyed being in Glasgow in the middle of the bombing. It never struck me, till many years later, that it was a strange thing to do, sending a child from the safety of semi-rural Dumfries, where no bombing took place, to the centre of the Glasgow blitz. I think it was because my mother was ill, suffering from varicose veins. When she was in hospital, my father couldn't cope, and all fathers were useless in those days, so we were spread around relatives and neighbours.

Another time, when she was ill, I was for several weeks in charge of my younger sisters and brother, cooking for them and getting them to school. All I cooked was toast and boiled potatoes, which they hated, as I forced them to clean their plates. I must have been aged only eight or nine at the time. I also ran messages for neighbours, going on the bus into Dumfries with their shopping lists and ration coupons to buy their groceries. They would pay me a few pennies which I spent on marbles, comics or pretend sweets.

The first time I tasted real bananas was in Dumfries towards the end of the war. I was playing football in Noblehill Park when a cry started up amongst a group of kids nearest the road, then spread around the whole park. 'The Co-op's Got Bananas! The Co-op's Got Bananas!' Every kid took up the chant and then dashed from all corners of the park to run towards the Co-op. The word Co-op was pronounced 'Cope', as if it was one word. I didn't quite understand it at first when we moved from Carlisle. Every customer was allowed only a small amount, so back at home, mothers would solemnly cut up a banana into small pieces and hand it round. I remember being disappointed. Real bananas did not taste anything like parsnips.

At Noblehill School, I was quite high up in the class, except when it came to handwriting. I was constantly having to write out lines of letters and words over and over again. However careful I was, however long I took, my handwriting was still appalling. I was quite good at most lessons, for a boy, but of course the top of the class was always dominated by the girls. They seemed to fill the first five places in every subject, though the higher up the school we got, the more boys began to come through.

I have got one of my Noblehill report books from 1945–6, and it shows my class numbered forty-four pupils and during that year, I came eleventh, fifth and fourth in the class. At Stanwix Primary, there had been forty-nine in my class. I have only two reports from Stanwix and each one says 'Rather talkative'!

When I got to the age of eleven, and into the top class, I was led to believe I would be going on to Dumfries Academy, the secondary school for the so-called cleverer children. That seemed to be what was expected. In Dumfries, the equivalent of the Eleven-Plus was taken at twelve and called the Qualifying.

But in 1947, before I had even sat the entrance exam, we were on the move again – back to Carlisle. My father was returning once again to 14 MU. I don't know whether he chose to move back, or he had to. I just woke up one day and was told we were off.

My mother, sisters and brother went on the train while I travelled in the furniture van with my father. He sat at the front, with the driver, while I was at the back, with our meagre items of furniture. I was so excited when we set off. Being able to travel in any sort of car, even an old van, was looked upon as a special treat for children in the 1940s. I had been allowed to, being the oldest, attracting much jealousy from my sisters and brother.

As the journey proceeded, and we got out into the country, going faster and faster, I began to feel sick, with all the bumping, and very cold with sitting in the open air, exposed to the wind. And also a bit scared. I realised I could not communicate with my father and the driver, should anything go wrong, such as another vehicle banging into us or being thrown right out of the van when we went over a particularly nasty bump in the road.

When we eventually reached our new home in Carlisle, I managed somehow to clamber out of the back of the van – and then was violently sick. Not an auspicious start to what became my life proper in Carlisle.

Chapter Three

Life at the Creighton

We had returned to St Ann's Hill in Carlisle, moving into 28 Caird Avenue, in the next street to where we had previously lived, the end of a little terrace of four houses. It backed on to the old allotments which had been used during the war by local people but now, two years after the war, had been allowed to grow wild and unattended. The ground was bumpy and over-grown, good for hiding in and games, with just enough flattish open space to play football. I soon made a hole in our back hedge for quick access.

I made contact again with my old friend Reggie, still living in Fraser Grove, and returned to my old school, Stanwix Primary. Although we had been away no more than four years, I had acquired a Scottish accent, so was immediately known as Scottie in the playground. I also found sums hard to understand. I had been good at them at Noblehill, but now in my class at Stanwix, when reciting our times-tables, and being cross-examined on them, I couldn't get the hang of it. For some reason, they were recited in a different way from Scotland, yet of course they were the same. So much of learning was by rote, the whole class reciting the same things aloud, over and over, so you picked up things parrot fashion, without quite understanding them.

It slowly began to dawn on me that the class had divided itself into little cliques. The children going to Carlisle Grammar

School and the Carlisle and County High School were forming their own little circles, cutting themselves off socially and intellectually from the also-rans, the second-class citizens, the ones who apparently had not passed the Merit, which was what Carlisle's Eleven-Plus exam was called.

In Dumfries, I had not yet sat my exam, but in England, the top class at all primary schools had already taken their Eleven-Plus and each child had recently been informed of the results and knew where they were going – not just for the next five years, but for life. If you didn't go to the grammar school, your chances of any further education, and therefore a good job in life, were nil. That was it, for ever.

I didn't quite understand what was going on, the system, the terminology, the names of the schools people were talking about, or the long-term implications, but I was aware that some sort of important divisions had taken place, which was why the chosen children were already segregating themselves. My parents knew even less about the system than I did. My mother, in all her years in Carlisle, never really understood Carlisle anyway, the names of places, streets and institutions.

But either she or someone at Stanwix School must eventually have alerted the education authorities to the fact that I had not been allocated to a secondary school. The Grammar School was full, so she was told, and had a reserve list, so that was it. I would have to go to Lowther Street, one of the secondary moderns.

One day I found myself sitting in the headmaster's office at a big school called the Creighton School in Strand Road. I had been set my own little exam. I can't remember what sort of questions there were, but I remember it being strange that I was on my own. After my little exam paper, the head asked me what I wanted to do in life and I said be a professional footballer. I had taken the question to be about my fantasy job in life, not what I expected to be. It must have struck him as amusing, this small, weedy, asthmatic child having such an ambition.

I don't remember his reply, or being told the result of my exam, but in September 1947, I started at the Creighton School.

I wore a dark blue blazer and a red and blue tie, a proper uniform, which appeared to make it a cut above the secondary schools which had no uniform.

I've just looked up my school reports from the Creighton School. On the front of my report book it says 'HUNTER DAVIES'. Inside I am sometimes E. H. Davies, Edward Hunter Davies and even Edward Hunter-Davies. (We did actually have a double-barrelled boy in our class, Norman Heeley-Creed, but his was genuine.) I have gone through life with this problem, and seldom reveal that Hunter is not strictly my true, first christian name.

I was christened Edward Hunter Davies, the Hunter bit being a long-established family name, hence my father, John Hunter Davies. He was always called John but for some reason, right from birth, I was always known as Hunter. Why they didn't put it as my first christian name, I'll never know.

It came as a big surprise the first time I learned the truth. I was at Stanwix School and a school nurse was looking for nits and she said, 'Edward, come here.' I looked around, wondering who the Edward was. We didn't have an Edward in the class, soppy name, so I was getting ready to giggle. I was hauled out in the end, still refusing to believe it was me.

This kept on happening throughout my school life. All teachers and pupils would know that I was called Hunter, but on official forms, like medical reports, the Edward would suddenly pop out, some bossy nurse trying to be matey and personal would say it out loud and I would hate her.

I now love being called Hunter. Partly because I've never met another person with it as a first name, apart from in the USA, where surnames as first names are common. But it still leads to confusion the first time I give it, in hotels or restaurants, where it gets written down as David Hunter. Once people have got it right, they tend to remember it. Usually, I deny I have or ever had another first name.

The Creighton School seemed to be half way between the Grammar School and a secondary modern, where all the Eleven-

Plus failures went. Not thickos, exactly, but obviously not quite up to the standard of the brain box boys who had passed for the Grammar or the brain box girls who went on to the High School. There was a sister school to the Creighton called the Margaret Sewell, in an adjoining building, which was the school to which my twin sisters went. My younger brother Johnny, when he came to the Eleven-Plus, did not make any reserve lists and was shunted off to Kingstown School.

Carlisle's tripartite system, with three layers of secondary schools, was an unusual arrangement, so I realised many years later. In most towns, there were only two. I have also just discovered, which I never knew at the time, just how few children aged eleven did pass the Merit in Carlisle in the 1940s and 1950s: 12½ per cent went to the Grammar and High, the next 12½ per cent to the Creighton and Margaret Sewell, while the vast majority, some 75 per cent, were consigned to the secondary moderns. I felt a gulf between the Creighton and the Grammar, so the next gap, between the sec mods and the chosen few, must have seemed enormous. The Creighton not only had a uniform, but did French and played rugby, three signs that the school had pretensions. One half of the school, the A-stream, could go on to take the General Certificate of Education O-levels at sixteen, but there was no Sixth Form. Everyone, whether they had passed any sort of exam or not, left the school and started work at either fifteen or sixteen.

I was lucky, in a way, that in Carlisle such a school as the Creighton existed, but intellectually and socially, we knew we were inferior to the Grammar. Down the road at the Grammar, so I learned from Reggie and other friends who had gone there, masters wore gowns, indicating they had degrees, which very few had at the Creighton, and Greek, Latin and German were taught as well as French. Their classes had strange names, like the Fifth Remove, and school work got marked not in numbers or percentages but with Alpha Minus or Beta Plus Plus. Their building appeared venerable and ancient, covered in ivy, while our school was red brick and modern.

Many of the male teachers had recently come out of the Forces, having done short-term teacher-training courses which were made simpler and quicker after the war to encourage men into teaching. Most of them seemed to have passed few exams themselves, judging by the lack of letters after their names on the speech-day programmes. I never ever heard our French teacher speak French. I suspected he had never sat a French exam, but had simply been roped in to teach it, as no one else would do it. He would make us read aloud, and tell us if our pronunciation was good or bad, without any French ever passing his own lips.

The ogre, the teacher everyone feared and loathed, was Mr Garrigan who taught Maths. He was small, ugly, bespectacled, very sarcastic. I had only been at the school a few months when he called me out for some reason and made some catty comment about my accent, asking where I had come from. I said Dumfries. He asked which part. I said the outskirts of Dumfries. 'I never knew Dumfries had skirts.' A really stupid, obvious, banal joke, but of course the whole class laughed uproariously, keeping in with Garry, enjoying my discomfort, glad that they were not being picked upon. I used to dread his lessons so much that I often bunked off, sitting in the drying room of the cloakroom in the dark, along with a few other pathetic specimens, in order to miss his lessons, shaking in fear in case we got found out.

He seemed to me a poor teacher, who ruled by fear and ridiculed anyone who was slow or stupid or simply had failed to understand the theorems he had explained so badly. About the third year, it all began to dawn on me, which I think was thanks to me, not him. It just suddenly seemed to make sense and I actively enjoyed doing algebra and geometry, something I had never expected.

For the first year, I turned up for games, which meant rugby, even though I was always put with the weedy, the overweight or the sickly, the ones who were forced to play amongst themselves behind the goals while the games teacher devoted himself to the thugs and morons who played on the proper pitch. I still had terrible asthma, always wheezing and puffing, so in the end, I got a medical certificate from the doctor and for the rest of my career at the Creighton I was permanently excused games.

I still did gym which was enough of an ordeal. In the showers, bigger kids would flick wet towels at you, which really did hurt, and then very soon, as we went up the school, they were flaunting their pubic hair and their big willies, walking up and down the showers displaying themselves. One trick was to pull their cock back between their legs to make it look as though they had a hairy fanny, then pretend to speak in a girl's voice, asking if anyone fancied them. This was all very embarrassing and humiliating for pathetic specimens like me, with not a pubic hair in sight, far less a willy you could do anything with.

I was still in short trousers till I was at least fourteen, perhaps even fifteen, which was another source of humiliation. Boys, even quite big boys, all wore short trousers in those days and woollen socks which hung at half mast, like Just William's. Having bare legs in the winter was agony. I was always getting my thighs chafed, partly through not wearing underpants and the pee dripping when I went to the lavatory. I didn't know why I didn't have any underpants. I did get them now and again for Christmas, from aunts in Scotland, along with vests, which I always considered the most useless presents ever.

By the third year at the Creighton, several boys who had appeared normal and in fact quite eager in the first year had given up on school, just messed around in class or absented themselves from lessons, stole things and committed various minor acts of vandalism. I was fascinated by them. I half admired their bravery and bravado, even though I knew that most things they did were really stupid. I was such a scaredy pants, keeping in with authority, being polite to teachers, doing what I was told. They seemed to get such a buzz, such excitement, out of stealing from shops, such as Dinkies from Woolies, then giving them away. They tended to be the bigger, more sexually advanced boys, but not always the most stupid. I was very friendly with one called Vinny who was just as good as me at lessons in the first two years, till he gave up, maintaining he was being picked upon, so what was the point?

When Teddy Boys came in, Creighton had its fair share, some of them headcases with razors who would hang around the Town Hall after school, looking for rivals to beat up. There was a ginger-headed one I was terrified of, who'd left school, or been expelled, who used to hang around the school entrance in his brothel creepers, drape jacket, greased back DA haircut, swinging his chain, looking for any goody-goodies to thump if they happened to look at him the wrong way, or even just looked at him.

The stars of the school, the ones most admired, were of course the sports stars, as they always were and always will be at every secondary school, for boys as well as girls, at least up to a certain age. The clever ones, the swots in our class, were the neat fuckers. Their essays and sums were always immaculately presented while their technical drawing work, a subject I hated, was stunning.

I said 'fucker' there, but at the time I didn't. I don't remember using such obscene or profane language as a schoolboy, nor did most other people, even the thugs and thickos. Swearing was minimal, the f and c words rarely used, even amongst close friends. Talking dirty and crude, that was different and very common. By the third and fourth year, dirty books like Hank Jansen's were being passed around, or drawings and photos of naked women which had been torn out of *Health and Efficiency*. Sexual things were constantly talked about, but the language used was slang rather than four-letter swearing. A girl was a tart, bewer or bint, her vagina was a minge, boys boasted how they were going to fin some tart and get a sticky finger. Most of it fantasy talk of course.

Chapter Four

Father Frets

When I was about twelve, and had not long started at the Creighton, my father began staggering. He would come home from the Redfern, the pub nearest to our house in St Ann's Hill, holding on to the gates and hedges in Caird Avenue to steady himself. Naturally, the neighbours assumed he was drunk. He went out only once a week to the Redfern, on Saturday with some of his friends from 14 MU, and didn't really drink a lot. We never had drink in the house, except at Christmas when my mother would buy a bottle of VP British Sherry and a bottle of Egg Nog. She kept the bottles in the cocktail cabinet in our front parlour and would offer a glass to visitors over Christmas time or more usually New Year's Day. Being Scottish, Hogmanay mattered more to us than Christmas Day.

'Cocktail cabinet' and 'parlour' make our council house seem ever so smart, but lots of people had cocktail cabinets, made of shiny cheap wood with glass doors, in which one's best ornaments would be kept. My mother's treasures included three little brass monkeys crouched in different poses, to represent See no Evil, Hear no Evil and Speak no Evil. She also had a pair of brass candlesticks and two fancy coloured glass goblets which were kept purely for show, as if they were precious objects, family heirlooms handed down. I think they had been prizes won at some fairground at Troon or Rothesay when my parents had been courting. I always wished my father had gone for the goldfish instead.

Also in this parlour, which was the little front room to the left of the front door, was a piano. A very old, beat-up one, which no one could play, though my sisters had for a time been sent to lessons at sixpence an hour.

Over the following year, my father's staggering got worse, and his hands began to shake as well. No one seemed to know what was the cause and it began to make him very bad tempered. I had a tremendous row with him once over a piece of fretwork which he had insisted I help him with. He was not at all handy in the house, no more than I was, but got it into his head that he would make some book-ends, despite the fact that we owned very few books. The half a dozen we had were cheap medical books and gardening books, bought with tokens through the *Daily Express*.

He'd bought a fretwork saw and I had to hold the wood, while he sawed away, following a plan of the book-ends to be. Because of his shaking hands, the saw kept on slipping, and he blamed me, shouting at me for being clumsy and stupid. He had begun to shout at me a lot, mainly telling me to 'pipe down', complaining that my voice gave him a headache. I was a noisy child, I was aware of that, and at school I was always being told off for being too talkative. Fifty-odd years later, my wife still tells me to sit down, stop fidgeting, why can't I be still, stop nattering, keep quiet, like a normal person?

In the end, with shouting at me, and his hands shaking, he split the special piece of fret wood, making it useless. He threw it at me, and the saw, blaming me for what had happened, then he sort of collapsed on the floor as his legs gave way.

I thought it was just his bad temper, not that there was anything wrong with him, so I slammed out of the kitchen door, saying that was it, I was off, and never coming back. I reappeared a few minutes later, stepped over him as he still lay on the kitchen floor, went upstairs and packed some clothes in a big hankie. I slung it over my shoulder, like Dick Whittington, and stormed out again, saying they would never see me again, goodbye. The twins, who had had to watch this scene, were in tears, and my little brother Johnny was very upset, the three of them thinking it was true. I was running away for good. My mother might also have been in tears, not fearful of me running away, but fearful of what was really wrong.

It took some time for multiple sclerosis to be confirmed, after various tests, different explanations and several false hopes. When it was diagnosed, its progress was rampant and his physical deterioration very quick. He was discharged from 14 MU and given an ugly clock as his leaving present.

He was soon unable to get up the stairs to his bedroom so a single bed was put in the front parlour and the piano removed. When he went out, which he did for about another year, he had to be pushed in a wheelchair. I often had to do it, being the oldest and biggest, and I hated it. Not just the shame of having an invalid father, but it was hellish to push, as he was so heavy and the wheelchair so clumsy. He liked being pushed up to the pub where he would sit outside while people would bring him the odd pint, if he was lucky.

Outside, in public, he was cheerful and friendly, waved to people getting off the bus, even when he couldn't quite see them as his eyes began to deteriorate as well. At home, inside the house, he grew more and more bad tempered, throwing his meals at my mother, if he didn't happen to like what she had made for him.

One of my jobs was to fill in his football pools for him and then on Saturdays at five o'clock, sitting with him as we listened to 'Sports Report' on the radio, filling in the scores in the *Daily Express*, then checking how many draws he had got on the treble chance. None was usually the answer, or not enough to win anything. I would be blamed for his lack of success, that I'd got the scores wrong. Every Saturday now, when I hear that familiar tune which introduces 'Sports Report', and then listen to the voice of James Alexander Gordon reading out the results, I think of my father.

On Sundays, I would read out to him the quiz from the *Sunday Post*, as he prided himself on being good at general knowledge. I moaned and groaned at having to do these little jobs, which was unfair, as I got off so lightly. My mother received the brunt of his bad temper and did most of the looking after as did my sisters, when they got a bit older. My sister Marion was particularly good with him. When he'd thrown down his meal, she would tell him off, threaten him with no more food, and he would say sorry.

Of course I felt sympathy for him. Someone who had been so fit and active and sociable, made immobile in his forties, but at the time I was more interested in my own life. He hadn't after all been such a big presence in my life, as far as I could remember. Perhaps he had been ill for far longer than I realised. And yet, at the same time, it seemed sort of normal, how life was, that was what happened, and we just got used to it. I don't recall thinking our life was much different from those around us on the estate.

My father got no help from anyone, and hardly any medical treatment or other forms of care and support. For a while, once a month or so, an ambulance came and took him to the Cumberland Infirmary for physio, but he hated it and it did him no good and they soon gave up. Once a year he went for a week to some sort of residential home at Grange over Sands, respite care for my mother, to give her a break, but he hated that as well. The moment my mother appeared at his bedside he would mutter, 'Get me the hell out of here.'

No nurses came to help bathe and clean him, although he was a heavy man, hard to manoeuvre, or to attend to his sores which soon started with lying in bed all day. My mother didn't have a hoist or a stair lift or an invalid's shower or any of the other facilities which such invalids are entitled to today, supplied by the National Health or other agencies. There was of course no MS Society. He had just been dumped in our parlour and forgotten by society. If any help did exist, my mother didn't know about it.

His friends and neighbours, such as they were, the people

with whom he used to go to the pub, ceased to visit. Some of them had been promoted, moved to a better area, able to buy their own house. Not long before he took ill, my father had been before some sort of Civil Service board and emerged as a Higher Executive Officer. That might have been why we moved back to Carlisle, with the prospects of promotion. Perhaps there would have been more advancement to come, had he not got MS.

As for money, I don't know how my mother managed. I presume when he retired through ill health, he got some sort of pension, but my mother had four young children to provide for through their most expensive years. Her total income was about £3 a week, £1 of which went on rent. She never moaned or complained. If the topic ever came up, she would say, 'Oh, lots of money, I've got lots of money.' Which was a total lie.

Every Monday there was pandemonium in our house, as if Monday was a surprise, she had not seen it coming. We all needed bus money and dinner money to get to school, and she never had enough, or never had the right change. Chairs would be overturned, drawers emptied as the twins and I ran round the house, searching for any lost pennies.

We paid for our school dinners, as I can remember handing in the money each Monday morning. There might have been some embryonic system of income support, or free school meals for households with no wage earners, but no one told my mother how to apply. She didn't understand about the English Eleven-Plus exam, or how the Ribble buses operated, and she got lost going down town, so how could she cope with the suits at Carlisle City Council Social Services Department? She had other things on her mind. Apart from my father's condition, she herself was in poor health.

Her escape was reading. Although we didn't own any books, apart from the handful of reference books, there were always library books lying around. Each week she got out the maximum number, all of them novels. She loved Somerset Maugham, Galsworthy, A. J. Cronin and, best of all, Dickens. I can see her now, standing at the kitchen stove, stirring the mince, which was slowly drying out and about to burn, turning over the pages of *Nicholas Nickleby* or *Oliver Twist*, reading aloud her favourite bits and laughing to herself. She usually read standing up, having so little time in her life to sit down. No wonder she had problems with her varicose veins. Every year, she re-read all of Dickens, and all her other favourite authors.

She hardly ever sat with us at the table but remained in the kitchen, bringing plates backwards and forwards. Usually mince and potatoes, sometimes potatoes on their own, often just toast. The teapot was permanently stewing. 'I've heard tea is very good for you,' she would say, pouring out her twentieth cup of the morning.

In the kitchen itself was the coal-hole, a dark little concrete pantry with its own door. The coalman had to walk through the kitchen with the bags of coal on his back, then empty them inside the coal-hole, which meant there was instantly coal dust everywhere. The coalman had a horse and cart as many delivery people did in the 1940s and 1950s. The fruit and veg man also had a horse. My mother would make me rush outside when she saw any horse manure as she'd heard it was good for the garden. I was always embarrassed, picking up horse shit, which was a waste of time anyway as there was nothing growing in our garden.

Next to the kitchen was an outside wash house with a gas boiler tub which had to be lit for the water to be heated. She would soak and then thump the clothes with a wooden dolly, scrub them on a wash board, wring out the water with a hand wringer, then hang the washing out on the line. We had no drying facilities, apart from a clothes-horse which would be draped in front of the coal fire. The steam and mist from the damp clothes, allied with the smoke from our fire which never drew properly, would make me choke the minute I entered the room. Our street was always dusty anyway with the soot from the railway engines at Kingmoor railway sidings.

Hot water for the bathroom was heated by some sort of back boiler behind the coal fire, which was very inefficient.

Traditionally the working classes of the time had one hot bath a week. I can't remember having any. I hated our bathroom, so cold, damp, cheerless. There was no heating in the house, apart from the coal fire. When I was really ill with asthma, and forced to stay all day in my bed in my horrible bedroom which I shared with Johnny, my mother would bring up a tray of hot coals and put them in my little fireplace and let the downstairs fire go out. She couldn't afford two fires.

I loved the sight of the hot embers arriving and the little fireplace being lit, suddenly making my bedroom marginally comfortable, slightly warm and passably attractive. I would sit up and turn over the pages of my stamp album, looking into each stamp, imagining lives in all the different countries, or study the pages of my football album, where I had stuck in photos of my favourite players, till slowly, my wheezing would subside and perhaps even stop. I discovered quite early on, without exactly working it out, that while all the medicines and potions failed, if only I could take my mind off my wheezing, somehow distract it, my body would start to recover. By then, the fire would be totally out, and the room freezing, but with luck I would have fallen asleep.

Our bedroom floor was covered in linoleum. In winter time, it would be absolutely freezing, so you devised a system of somehow getting from under the blankets straight into your clothes, without touching the lino, otherwise your bare feet would be left there, stuck for ever to the lino.

This was our house in Carlisle in 1950, normal life, so I assumed, for everyone. Writing it down now makes it sound more like 1850. At the time, I didn't write it down or remark on it or even think about it. And if asked about it, I would have said I'm having a very happy childhood, thank you very much.

Chapter Five

Fun and Games

Slowly, through the 1950s, families around us got electric immersion heaters in their water tanks, which provided reliable hot water. They put extra sockets in the rooms, so electric fires could be plugged in. The more affluent acquired a fridge, a phone and a TV. We never had any of these things, until the 1960s. In 1953, for the Coronation, there was one local family with a TV. My sisters, being friends of theirs, were allowed to stand in their front garden, looking through the front window to catch a glimpse of the lovely Queen.

My father's income had come to a halt, so there were no improvements, refurbishments or DIY being done. But we did have a radio, which was the main source of entertainment for most families of the 1950s. Throughout most of my childhood and teenage life it was connected to the overhead light bulb socket in the living room, the only way it could be plugged in, which was highly dangerous, as the wires became frayed with constantly being pulled in and out. We couldn't of course have a light on while listening to the radio. I quite enjoyed listening in the dark with my mother to the Saturday play or 'Paul Temple'.

My father loved 'ITMA', and would repeat all the popular phrases and smile, but I was never a fan, couldn't see why it was thought so funny. Perhaps I was too young. It was aimed more at my parents' generation. I didn't think much of 'Educating Archie' either and found the idea of a ventriloquist on radio very strange. When the 'Goon Show' started, I adored it, copied all the silly voices, as all my friends did, while my father couldn't see the joke at all.

My mother did her best with the house, despite having no money. Most of her energies went into repainting the kitchen walls which she did constantly, always in lurid colours with cheap paint, end-of-line pots bought in Woolworths. The pots would usually run out after one wall, or half a wall, so midway up a wall, deep purple would turn into bright green. The kitchen walls were bare brick, unplastered, so the effect of the paint was to make them glaring and brutal. You could see visitors shielding their eyes when they entered the back door. I was supposed to do the garden, cut the grass with a useless rusty handmower, trim the front privet hedge and keep down the weeds. There were some immaculate front lawns in Caird Avenue, but our garden always looked a dump, giving totally the wrong impression, as if we were potters, not a family with a mother who read Dickens.

I picked up my love of going to the public library from my mother. It was in Tullie House, now a smart, prize-winning museum. The building itself is a Jacobean gem, built in 1689, but from 1893 it had housed the City Library. It also had a museum, very old fashioned, with glass cases, stuffed animals, Roman remains, daft collections which had been donated to the city. Children visited it with their school, and were told not to talk or touch things. I found it very dreary at the time, but now I greatly miss such museums. Far too many modern ones have gone madly audio-visual and interactive, strong on display but with very few actual objects.

Moving up from the children's library was a huge stage in life, like going into long pants, transferring from primary to secondary school, or from the cubs to the scouts. I can still smell the polish and wood. I came across the same smell once in Caracas in Venezuela, and immediately thought I was back in Tullie House. In my mind's eye, the librarians had their hair in buns and were fearsome, telling you off if you breathed too loudly or ran around. You were only allowed a limited number of books, so if you came across any Just William or Biggles books, newly returned, which you hadn't read, you hid them in a far corner or on the wrong shelves, hoping they would be there next time, or so your friends could find them. The Buns, of course, over their specs, were usually watching, and smartly put them back.

I don't think I have ever loved books as I loved Just William books. They removed me completely from my world, caused me to choke with laughter, roll around, holding my stomach. Oh, I do hope that children reading Harry Potter today get the same enjoyment I did from Just William.

As we all know, the life of William, in his Home Counties posh house, with maids and tennis courts, was light years away from life in Caird Avenue, but that didn't matter, no more than it worried us that the *Wizard* and *Hotspur* featured public schools, fags and tuck shops, which were equally remote from our own experiences. Did we long to be there, to escape? Was that the attraction? I don't think so. They were exciting stories, so we thought at the time, or funny stories in the case of Just William. We did identify with William himself, if not his social context, with his socks hanging down, being told off all the time, his relationships with adults and of course having his own little gang, their schemes and plots. Our gangs in St Ann's Hill had much the same object, either to defeat or confound our supposed enemies or how to get money to buy sweets.

I played football in the allotments, or lotties, behind our house most days after school, despite my asthma, puffing and panting, coming in red in the face at precisely 6.45 to listen to 'Dick Barton, Special Agent'. The sound of the signature tune coming through an open window was enough to have children stopping at once whatever they were doing and haring home. 'Haring' home, that's a period word. I must have got it from boarding school stories.

I also listened to 'Children's Hour' – on the Scottish Home

Service, which our wireless was always tuned into. In the morning, we got delivered the Scottish edition of the *Daily Express* and the *Sunday Post* on Sunday. Lots of people in Carlisle still get Scottish papers, being a Border town, with so many families having migrated, but I can't remember there being other Scottish families on our estate, so when I was playing in the lotties or the street next day, and I talked about Tammy Troot or Doon at the Mains, or repeated Jimmy Logan's favourite phrase, 'sausages is the boys', no one knew what I was on about.

I loved Norman and Henry Bones, the boy detectives, who were on the mainstream 'Children's Hour', and 'Wandering with Romany' or 'Nomad' which were nature programmes, during and after the war, about two children being taken on a country walk, and having things pointed out and spotted, the sort of thing Miles Kington in the *Independent* ridicules today.

I never knew, in all those years of listening, that the man behind 'Romany' had been living amongst us in Carlisle, the Rev George Bramwell Evens, a Methodist minister, who had been responsible for the building and funding of the Methodist Central Hall in Fisher Street.

Every child of course loved 'Toy Town', 'Uncle Mac' and 'Aunty Kathleen'. I think 'Aunty Kathleen' might have been a Scottish version, who spoke nicely to Scottish children only, while 'Uncle Mac' was national, uncle to us all. One of my proudest moments in childhood was getting a letter from the BBC, Queen Margaret Drive, Glasgow. I'd entered a competition for a poem on 'Scottish Children's Hour', presumably under the encouragement of my mother. I didn't win, but I got a silver pencil. I also had a poem published in a Sunday School magazine for children.

The most nerve-wracking, intense, radio listening took place when England was playing Scotland at football. I longed for Scotland to win, my little heart pounding. In my football album, I mainly had Scottish stars, such as Billy Houliston, a cannon-ball centre forward who played for Queen of the South, the Dumfries club. I cut their photos out of the newspapers, especially any Pink 'uns I could find, and stuck them in with home-made paste, made out of flour. They started off all soggy and gooey, but after a day or so, they stood up stiff on their album pages, as if they had come to life, become three-dimensional.

My dad was interested in football, and had played a lot while in the RAF, but he never took me as a boy to Carlisle United. It wasn't his team, his town, so he had no connection with it and no tradition of going there, and probably didn't know where Brunton Park was. Being passionate about your local club runs in families. Football relies on fathers taking sons along while still quite young, so the baton is handed on.

It was cheap enough in the 1950s to watch Carlisle United, but for a long time I couldn't afford it and rarely went, except on big occasions, which of course were very few. CUFC seemed doomed to be one of nature's Third Division North also-ran clubs.

Reg, my best friend, was not a football fan, which was surprising, considering his father – also called Reg Hill – had been a professional and had actually played for Carlisle United in the 1930s, before ending up at 14 MU. None of my other close friends in my teenage years were football fans either, but that didn't stop me being passionate about the game.

Carlisle also had its own superstar in Ivor Broadis, probably the best-known person in Carlisle in the 1950s, who had once played for England and had two spells with Carlisle, in the late 1940s and again in the late 1950s. He was a household name, even to those who didn't follow football. You could tell jokes about him and everyone would get it. Which footballer needs a big sofa? Ivor Broadis! I've a Broad Arse.

Carlisle's greatest achievement in the 1950s was a goal-less draw in the third round of the FA Cup with the mighty Arsenal at Highbury in January 1951, though our manager, Bill Shankly, thought Arsenal were lucky. 'I'm disappointed, we should have won,' he was reported as saying when the final whistle blew. 'I'll give them what for in the dressing room.'

Several thousand had gone down from Carlisle to London for

the game, taking with them some Cumberland fox hounds, which were paraded on the pitch before kick-off. But the excitement was nothing compared with the return fixture at Brunton Park with the whole of the city desperate for tickets.

The match was to be held on the Thursday afternoon at two o'clock, there being no floodlights in those days. Everything came to a standstill, including the local schools, who were given the afternoon off. Over at the High School, we heard about one of the younger girls who had petitioned against this half-day, maintaining that it was ridiculous schools being closed for a silly football match. But fortunately her protests were ignored.

On the afternoon itself, Thursday, 11 January 1951, Brunton Park was full, with 20,900 inside. As so often happens on such occasions, the better, mightier side doesn't make the same mistake twice and underestimate the opposition. Carlisle got beaten 2–0. I've still got my ticket, priced 1/6d to the ground, but not the programme. Perhaps I was not able to afford one.

I did not go as regularly as I would have liked to Brunton Park in the 1950s, as it cost money, but every weekend I still trudged all the way to attend Warwick Road Presbyterian Church. The elders and regular worshippers were pleasant enough, but the sermons were endless and boring, the whole atmosphere cold and depressing.

My father never went to church, even when he was well, although he banned me from playing football or riding a bike on a Sunday, on religious grounds. I always argued against this, pointing out he was not religious. 'Do what I say, not what I do.' Most respectable working-class parents, especially Scottish ones, were the same, brought up to revere the Sabbath, even if they were not churchgoers.

My mother always went to church and forced me and my sisters and brother to attend Sunday School when we were young and then accompany her as we got older to church services as well. At Sunday School, I was awarded a Lord Wharton Bible, which I still have. To win it, you had to memorise and recite reams of psalms and verses from the Bible. I don't know how I did it, as I am lousy at memorising, can never remember my own children's phone numbers, or why, as it was all so boring.

My mother was not a disciplinarian, never forced us to do things with threats or punishment, but she would nag on, look pathetic or sad, hoping my better self would make me want to go to church. Most Sundays I did, to please her.

Warwick Road Presbyterians didn't have a scout troop, so I joined the 17th Church of Scotland Troop in Chapel Street, along with my friend Reg. I loved the scouts, and never missed, unless I was ill. We played boisterous games of British Bulldog, running up and down on the bare floors of the church hall, did tests and exercises, went on scout parades. I eventually became Patrol Leader of the Owl Patrol, what an honour, and yet I never passed any badges, except my tenderfoot badge. We considered ourselves an intellectual troop, at least Reg and I did, making a deliberate point of not being competitive or pot hunting, compared with those other Carlisle troops we met on scout parades, whose patrol leaders had badges covering every part of their uniform, so much so that they could hardly walk, weighed down with all their honours.

The highlight of the year was the annual proper camp, which lasted at least a week, usually in Scotland, as we were a Church of Scotland troop. One year it was Edinburgh, another time Aberdeen. The food was always awful, burned and tasteless, the tents smelly and uncomfortable and the sleeping bags cold and wet. I was usually wracked with asthma, but still I always enjoyed it. I didn't have a holiday, otherwise.

There was always some older kid in the tent who would show off his erection, or get you to do the same, or tell dirty stories in the dark, but all the scout leaders were above reproach, genuinely loved teaching and instructing the younger boys. It was only later I heard people making sniggery jokes about scout masters and what they got up to, nudge nudge. Our Skip was always a hero to us, admired by all.

I was once on a train, aged about ten, going to visit my

relations in Scotland, on my own, standing in the corridor waiting to go to the lavatory, when I felt this hand going up my short trousers. I didn't understand what was going on at first, but the look in this middle-aged man's eye made me realise something unpleasant might be about to happen, so I ran away, back to my seat, but never told anyone.

In Caird Avenue, there was an older boy, probably aged about twenty, and when I was about ten or eleven, he invited me into his house one day and asked me to hold his cock. It was huge, hot and rather steaming. I was fascinated by it, rather than revolted. I couldn't work out where it had come from, or whether he was unusual in having such a throbbing monster. He didn't make me toss him off, nor did he do it to himself. It just sort of lay there, then he put it away and went upstairs. Again, I didn't tell anyone about this incident, yet the image stayed in my mind for many years, becoming rather unsettling, more horrible and frightening than it had done at the time.

Amongst the healthiest, most approved of and most enjoyable activities for children in the 1950s was the ABC Minors, the cinema show for children held every Saturday morning. In Carlisle, it took place at the Lonsdale cinema in Warwick Road. I can still sing the song we used to shout out at the tops of our voices.

> We are the boys and girls well known as
> Minors of the ABC
> And every Sa-tur-day we line up to see
> The films we joke and shout about with glee.

I think those are the right words. It went to the tune of the march called 'Blaze Away'.

We got cartoons, little films, and then the big picture which was usually an exciting serial, mostly cowboys and Indians, or cops and robbers with lots of chases and escapes, the goodies always winning. Before the show, there were announcements and notices, and kids whose birthday it was were invited on stage and all got a big cheer, plus a present. You'd often spot the same kids coming up every week to get their birthday present. There were row monitors, older kids who were supposed to help keep the unruly from fighting and the bored and restless from climbing over and under the seats. Some monitors, especially ones slightly older and more mature, wouldn't care about the noise, their arms around and up a girl who was equally advanced, taking advantage of being able to sit in the dark, unseen by adults.

From a fairly early age, probably about ten or so, I was sent to violin lessons. I don't know how my mother ever afforded it, when we had so little money to spare. I was the only boy on our estate who did such a thing, and I was a bit ashamed, as it seemed such a girly, pretentious sort of activity. It was as if my mother was trying to be socially and culturally something she was not. Her father had played the fiddle, and probably never went to lessons, just picked it up, so that was doubtless my mother's motivation. She had always loved her father, while being a bit scared of her mother. I think she may have got a special discount from my violin teacher who probably knew about our family circumstances.

I hated the lessons, was useless at it, but I liked the teacher, Alf Adamson. I always put off practising until about half an hour before I was due at my weekly lesson. Mr Adamson had a daughter at the High School. She was called Norma and had big breasts, and when I got older, I used to ogle her, hoping she would come into the room. Even though I was useless, I did develop a liking for classical music, especially Sibelius, which stayed with me for a long time, until I realised I preferred music written for me now, by people like me, not dead music from another age. I must eventually have got reasonable enough on the violin to appear in public – notably at a scout concert. I'm sure it was excruciating, but people clapped politely.

My mother loved the theatre, going most Mondays to Her Majesty's Theatre in Lowther Street to plays, either amateur or professional. The Salisbury Arts were the professional rep company I mostly remember, who seemed forever to be putting on *Black Mischief.* They came to Carlisle every season, alternating several plays at a time. They seemed so slick, so talented, so clever – how did they manage to memorise all the parts one week, then move on to something different the following week? Their lives appeared bohemian, exotic, all of them either handsome or pretty. You would catch glimpses of them at the stage door, a whiff of their French cigarettes, a hint of their London-style clothes and smart lives. Were they all sleeping with each other, so we wondered as we got older, having a marvellous, carefree life? In reality, they were probably in scruffy digs, on very low pay and hating each other, bitter and twisted that they hadn't made the West End. The theatre also staged Carroll Levis and his discoveries and Billy Cotton's Band Show. When there was a play, the programme always said 'Cigarettes by Abdulla, Telephone kindly lent by the GPO'.

Variety shows still came to Carlisle, on probably number five tours of the smaller cities, and I sometimes went to see them with Reg or other friends, if just to laugh and mock. There was a woman who did bird noises who had us convulsed at the stupidity of it all, yet how seriously she was taking herself. Or contortionists, jugglers, ventriloquists. 'That's very difficult,' older members of the audience would mutter, clapping very politely, while we sat bemused and unappreciative.

I was impressed by Her Majesty's, by its size and grandeur, seating 900 people, by the stalls and boxes and the gods where we sat, right up in the sky, but at the time I was not aware of its glorious history, how many of the greatest acts and stars of the nineteenth and twentieth centuries had played at Her Majesty's, if only on their way to even bigger, grander theatres in Glasgow or Newcastle. It opened in 1874 and Charlie Chaplin, Laurel and Hardy, Harry Lauder and Noel Coward all performed there. By the end of the 1950s it was coming to the end of its great days. In 1963 it closed. For a time it became a bingo hall, finally being demolished in 1979 to become, oh, the sadness of it, a car park.

The Public Baths in James Street are still there, in the building which was opened in 1884, though thankfully they have been smartened up and extended in recent years. I went swimming with the Creighton School each week, and often on Saturdays as well, if I had the money. Being small and weedy and asthmatic, I wasn't much good at swimming, and usually stood around the dressing room for a lot of the time, shivering with the cold. I was never in a swimming club. They entailed a membership fee, which I could not raise, and regular attendance and practice, but what put me off was the look of the sadists who seemed to run these clubs, shouting at kids in the water, poking them with long sticks, making them do length after length.

Looking back, I don't know why I went to the baths so often. But it was what one did at a time of relatively few attractions for children. If you were in a little gang, someone would say let's go swimming. In the summer we would go to the River Eden, but mostly it meant the baths. You went along with what the gang did, otherwise you were on your own. No one wanted that. If you did fall out with your gang, and they went off and did exciting things without you, you were distraught, even when you knew that all they were doing was hanging around in the street or mucking around in the new buildings, till a watchman chased them.

The main pleasure of going swimming was what happened afterwards – touring the grocery shops, begging for a penny bag of broken biscuits. Our favourite places were Liptons and the Home and Colonial. There were one or two nice smiley friendly women in each, probably only teenagers, but they seemed grown up to us. If you smiled nicely and looked appealing, they would fill a bag with really good biscuits, hardly any of them broken. If you got one of the mean, nasty ones, you had wasted a penny on a bag of dust.

I loved all sweets, especially anything with sherbet, which fizzed in your mouth. With age and sophistication, say around twelve or thirteen, I got a passion for Palm Toffee. My mother loved bars of Cadbury's milk chocolate, especially when drinking a cup of tea, and she would often spare me a square, which was kind.

I haven't eaten sweets since I was child. I never buy them, not even chocolates, and refuse them when offered. I hate the taste of all of them now. Yet as a child I dreamed about them and my fantasy was to be let loose alone in a sweetshop. I find it bizarre when so called grown-ups stuff their faces with sweets. They say a sweet tooth comes back in old age, especially a longing for ice cream. But then, in the end, everything from your early life is likely to come back in some form.

Chapter Six

Work, Play and Study

I started work in 1950 when I was fourteen. Not down the mines, pulling donkeys, or naked up the chimney swallowing soot, but as a paper boy. It seemed to me just as knackering and exhausting as any of the nineteenth-century sweated labour jobs which children did. I got taken on by Clark's, our local shop. It must have been a pretty thriving business, but Mr Clark always seemed tired and miserable, especially first thing in the morning, glaring at any paper boys who were late. There was great competition to work there, so no one wanted to upset him and lose their precious job.

We had to be there at six o'clock each morning, which meant that most of the year it was still dark, making it even more hellish to get up in time. I moaned and groaned every morning and often my mother had to force me out of bed, knowing how much the job mattered to me. When I was ill with asthma, which often happened, and I couldn't walk, far less carry the huge paper bag, my mother would waken the twins, Marion and Annabelle, and make them get up and take my place, as Mr Clark could not be let down. I'd then have to pay them for doing my round, which always annoyed me.

I delivered papers for at least four years – and also delivered groceries on the shop bike. Afterwards, when I'd eventually given up, my mother used to tell me that I was never as bright and good tempered in the mornings as in those years when I did the papers. That was never my memory, but she later insisted on telling it to my wife, who still trots out this idiotic remark every morning around 8.30 when I'm still unable to open my eyes and face the day.

In the 1950s, my paper-round money was absolutely vital to me as it provided the only earned income coming into the house. Not that I gave any of it to my mother. It all went into my Raleigh Lenton Sports. Oh, the joy of having one's own bike, freedom at last. I got it from T. P. Bells in Abbey Street, paying up 13/11 per week on the never-never. That sum has stayed clearly in my mind, yet I can't remember what I was paid for the paper round. Perhaps ten shillings a week at first, hence I needed tips, but it went up, very slowly, each year on your birthday.

My bike was green and had three-speed Sturmey Archer gears and racing handlebars, the most desirable model on the planet, lusted after by every boy in the 1950s. I was so proud that I'd bought it all by myself. Until I started the paper round, I never had any money. I got no pocket money, and never expected it, as I knew my mother had nothing to spare. All I relied on, till I got the paper job, was a half-crown from visiting relations, or perhaps money from empty pop bottles. If you collected the right ones, took them back to the right shop, you got a penny on each.

My bike also enabled me to play football further afield and I joined Kingstown Rovers in the Carlisle and District Under 15 Christian Welfare League. I wasn't very good, but ever so keen and eager. I had a good football brain, so I liked to think, an inside forward able to spot the killer pass and thread it through. The trouble was I didn't have the strength. A football in those days, with brown leather panels and a rubber bladder inside, weighed about a ton when it got wet, as it retained all the moisture, so it was like trying to kick a lead balloon. My killer passes often travelled only a few yards, very slowly, and were easily cut off.

At home, I played in the street, under the lamp-posts when it was dark. There were so few cars that even an eleven-a-side game, running the length of Caird Avenue, would hardly get interrupted by traffic. I practised against our back wall for hours with a tennis ball, making myself return the ball with either foot. I thought, If I was going to become a professional, I'd need to be two-footed. I even took dead balls, such as corners and free kicks, with my left foot, i.e. my wrong foot. Now that is hard. David Beckham, for all his skills, always takes free kicks with his best foot. When you are running, in full flow, then it is not so hard for a half-decent player to use his so-called weaker foot, if the pass requires it. But with a stationary ball, and time to think and worry, even the best players will decide to use their best foot.

Despite my passion for football, and by the age of fourteen and fifteen playing every week in a proper little team, at school I still got myself excused games on health grounds. My asthma was still there, but when it came to football, I'd learned to force myself through the pain barrier. If I could keep going, somehow, the excitement of the game would help me, if only to forget my wheezing.

In 1952, aged fifteen, I went to France, with the Creighton School. It was an educational trip, mainly aimed at those doing French O-levels. I don't know how my mother afforded it, or whether the school helped in any way, for I certainly didn't pay for it. I realised it was a big sacrifice for my mother, that I was getting special treatment, something Marion, Annabelle and Johnny didn't get. Neither of my parents had ever been abroad, though my father boasted that he had once flown in a plane, when in the RAF, going right across the English Channel and back, without landing in France.

We stayed at the railway hotel in Abbeville. The first smells and tastes and sights of France were startling, so different and exotic in every way. Even the plumbing was different, and the little fat bottles of orange juice, the fat tyres they had on their bikes, the shoes and clothes people wore, the smell of Gauloises and of course the food, which I had never come across before.

None of it had ever appeared in the boxes of groceries I delivered from Clark's, which contained mainly sliced bread, tinned beans, H P Sauce and custard powder.

The trip included a stay in Paris, where we did the Eiffel Tower, Notre Dame and the usual sights. In Paris, I fell ill with asthma and had to stay in bed. One of the teachers stayed behind in the hotel with me, which was very kind, and must have ruined his trip to Paris.

There were about a dozen of us, boys from my year at the Creighton, including three teachers. Although the object was to help our French, I can't remember speaking French to any French people, except asking for drinks in bars. I brought home a model of the Eiffel Tower in a snowstorm for my mother and a miniature bottle of three-star cognac for my father, both of which went straight into our cocktail cabinet, souvenirs of a foreign trip but also to impress any neighbours. 'Go on Hunter, speak some French', so my mother would say to our neighbours. I thought my French was pretty good, compared with most people in my class, but that turned out to be pure fantasy.

I sat my General Certificate of Education O-levels at the Creighton School in 1952. I did nine subjects – English Lang, Eng Lit, French, History, Geography, Maths, General Science, RE and Technical Drawing. I passed seven and failed two. I never expected to get through Tech Drawing, as I was so useless at it, but I was appalled and ashamed to fail French, after that expensive trip to France, after saying how much I liked it. I'm not sure if anyone else in my class got through or not, which would indicate the teaching was at fault, but that's beside the point. I should still have passed.

And then a strange thing happened. I found myself at the Grammar School.

I say strange because I have no idea how it happened. I have no memory of it being discussed beforehand, or even being mentioned as a possibility. I didn't have an interview with anyone at the Grammar, which I'd had to get in to the Creighton, nor did my parents request it. To the best of my knowledge there was no system at the time of Creighton boys going on to the Grammar after O-levels. There should have been, in a fair and ideal world, and perhaps that was one of the original intentions after the 1944 Education Act when the Eleven-Plus came in, to give people a second chance at sixteen, but I'd never heard of it happening. And I'm sure I would have been aware if anyone in the year ahead of me at the Creighton had gone on to the Grammar. After me, it certainly did happen because I can remember old Creightonians who followed a year later.

I can't believe it was activated by the Grammar School. Hard to imagine someone there waking up one day and saying, 'Isn't it about time we gave some of those lesser human beings at that school along the road, now what's its name, another chance in life?' So I have to give thanks to either the Creighton teachers or someone at the education department. And yet, even though it came as a surprise, I can't remember making alternative plans, such as applying to Laings to be an apprentice draughtsman, which I wouldn't have got anyway, or looking for a job at 14 MU. In my mind, which is not of course totally reliable, I just woke up one day and there I was, walking through the ancient front doors of Carlisle Grammar School. An honour in itself, as I quickly discovered. Only Sixth Formers and staff could use that front door. The rest of the school used another entrance.

The fact that I went straight into the Sixth was also remarkable, because the Grammar had a Fifth Form Remove in which people re-sat a year, if they were not thought quite up to the Sixth or did not have enough O-levels. But I went straight into 6B Modern – which stood for Lower Sixth, the modern bit indicating I was taking Arts subjects. There was also a Science Sixth and a Classics Sixth, though by the 1960s the Classics Sixth was small and they came in with us on the Arts side.

Two other boys came from the Creighton with me into the Lower Sixth, and we were to take the same three subjects at A-level, English, History and Geography. We were then informed that in order to have a chance of getting into a decent university we would have to have Latin at O-level. That was the system in the 1950s and it didn't just apply to Oxbridge but to most other universities. I also discovered that I had to re-sit French, as I needed to have passed that at O-level as well.

For my French re-sit, I joined the Remove's French class. That wasn't too daunting. After all, I'd had five years of learning French at the Creighton, in theory. But Latin was going to be a problem. How could we hope to do that from scratch, never having had a Latin lesson in our lives, while still fitting in our Sixth-Form A-level timetable in English, History and Geography?

I wonder if it would have happened now, if any present-day teachers, over-worked and over-stressed as we know they undoubtedly are, would have agreed to do what Mr Hodges did? He was a Latin master, small, mole-like with a moustache, who bustled about with piles of books under his arm. He didn't know us, was unaware of our personal capabilities, but must have realised our grounding in languages, coming from a sec tech school, wouldn't be exactly top class.

Mr Hodges gave up his free periods in order to take the three of us, on our own, at times which fitted in with our other subjects, and started to teach us Latin from scratch. We met in this funny little attic room at the top of the building, all of us hunched round a little desk. At first, I had no idea what the hell was going on; it was all gibberish. Once we'd roughly got the hang of the basic grammar, he decided that we would concentrate on the set text which was Tacitus and formed a large part of the O-level mark. He reckoned if we could memorise enough of it, parrot fashion, as opposed to being able to understand it, word for word, we would be able to translate into English and scrape through the exam.

Mr Hodges – I can't remember his first name, if I ever knew it – was brilliant, but I have to say some of the other Grammar School masters were a bit superior and condescending towards us, at least that was how I felt. It was understandable. We had come from a poorer school but most of all, they didn't know us. They had been teaching all the other boys in our class for five years, seen them growing up, knew their talents and potential, and also had their favourites, the ones they liked. Socially, with the other Sixth Formers, I had no problems at all, because I was already in Reg's gang, having been his chum since we were four.

The main building seemed very public school-ish to me, with its Gothic-style imposing entrance and ancient tiled hall, compared with the brutally modern, brick-built Creighton. All the masters did wear gowns and there was a feeling of intellectual rigour. The headmaster was V. J. Dunstan, a Classics scholar, who seemed not quite of this world. He floated around, in a dream, often followed by his wife, telling him things. She seemed equally weird.

The Deputy Head was Mr Banks who was in charge of discipline. You went to Mr Banks to get whacked. He was big and bald and had one time been a professional goalkeeper, so I was told. He taught Geography, but not very well. All he did was read out stuff at dictation speed from his ancient notes and we had to write it down. No discussions, no enthusiasm, no spark. I couldn't believe it. Even at the Creighton, no teacher had done that.

As Sixth Formers, we considered ourselves intellectuals, a cut above the rest of the school. As well as going to the theatre, we did our own play readings in a hall at Stanwix and were all into classical music. I went to the Edinburgh Festival one summer with Reg. We saw Richard Burton in some Shakespeare play, and Menuhin and Isaac Stern playing the violin. I also went to the Proms while in the Sixth Form, hitch-hiking down to London and queuing up outside the Albert Hall for tickets. Reg was going to go with me, but something happened and he didn't. I went alone, staying in a youth hostel, going to a Prom concert every evening. Looking back, I now can't believe I did it. Doesn't sound like me at all, preferring symphonies and violin concertos to popular music, but that was me aged seventeen to eighteen in the early 1950s. One reason was pretension, trying to be cultured and artistic. The other was that popular music at the time was awful, silly novelty songs or sloppy ballads sung in phoney mid-Atlantic accents, aimed at shop girls, not intellectual Sixth Formers.

There was a school magazine, the *Carliol*, the official mag, run by a master and full of boring poems, twee stories and sports results. There was also the *Sixth Form Debating Society Magazine*, an unofficial, semi-underground publication, mainly written by Reg. It didn't have much to do with the Debating Society at all, but Reg and others had found out that as it was deemed part of it, and therefore respectable, they could use the school's duplicating machine and paper to print it. I thought it was absolutely brilliant, so clever and witty. It was a precursor of *Private Eye*, in that its purpose was satirical, with drawings and stories, poking fun at the school and Carlisle people and institutions. I never wrote a word for it, as far as I can remember. I believed I couldn't possibly compete, ever be as clever and original as Reggie.

Despite doing A-levels, considering myself a full and proper member of the Sixth Form, I still felt slightly second-class, not one of the leaders, not quite knowing how the system worked, still a bit of an interloper.

But at the end of the year, I had begun to catch up. I passed my French re-sit and, more amazingly, all three of us from the Creighton got through our O-level Latin, after only nine months. So thanks a lot, CGS. And especially Mr Hodges.

Chapter Seven

Wine, Women and Song

From the moment I arrived at the Grammar, I decided to play games, which meant of course rugby. I had continued to be excused at the Creighton on account of my asthma, right to the end, despite playing football every weekend. It seemed false while still at the Creighton to suddenly announce I'd had a miracle cure, as they all knew how I used to be when I was younger and forced to play. But at the Grammar, I wasn't known. I was a new person, creating a new life. They were not aware of, and didn't care about, what had gone before.

Being small and not very fast, I decided I had to make myself a good tackler. I realised that if even the titchiest kid caught a giant round the legs, and hung on, the giant couldn't move much, far less run. I also realised that on such an impact, with both the giant and the titch falling, the chances were that the giant would hurt as much, if not more, because of his greater weight. So I turned myself into a demon tackler, throwing myself at players, hanging on for dear life.

By the second-year Sixth, I did get into the First XV. Oh, the glory and the status, seeing my name on the team sheet. I never made it as a prefect, though I think eventually I was created a sub-prefect, for I have a vague memory of being allowed into the sanctum of the prefects' room. Such things mattered so much at the time, but now I'm not even sure.

Being in the First XV, that is very clear in my mind. We went away in a school coach on Saturdays to places like Whitehaven, Workington and Cockermouth to play against their grammar schools – and usually got thumped. We also played St Bees, West Cumbria's local public school, who beat us as well. Our longest trip was to Newcastle to play the Royal Grammar School, but only their Second XV, who also hammered us. It was a bit like being in the scouts with Reg. The ethos was not about cups and glory, but taking part and enjoying it. Singing on the coach on the way home, trying to smuggle on bottles of beer, that was the best part of playing rugby.

The highlight of my rugby career was one New Year's Day, by which time I had become an established member of the school's First XV. I was contacted by Carlisle Rugby Union Club, the city's main rugby club. They were a man short, desperate for anyone they could find, trying to raise a team for a seven-a-side competition at Galashiels. I think they were only sending their second string, but it was still a fairly important event in the local rugby calendar.

There were people in the Border teams we played against who were outstanding, so fast and clever, who left us standing. It was also incredibly cold. I got frozen, just waiting for a pass, or to tackle someone. In schoolboy teams, it was usually pretty clear who was the lump, who might look frightening in the flesh, warming up, but you could soon see he was overweight, unco-ordinated, clumsy and slow, and relatively easily brought down. It didn't work this time as I couldn't catch them.

I became less interested in rugby after that, realising I wasn't any good, could never improve, and that it was more than enough to represent the school. I decided to concentrate more on the other things in life associated with rugby, such as drinking and chasing women.

I started going to pubs about the age of sixteen or seventeen, forcing myself to down half a pint of mild and bitter. I didn't like the taste of State Management beer, though experts boasted about its quality and good value. It was stupid to drink stuff I didn't like, purely for the sake of appearing grown-up and manly, but the theory was that I would acquire a taste for it. I just had to look around at all the blokes in the pubs, pouring it down, pint after pint, no bother. It had worked for them.

All the pubs we went to seemed cheerless, drab and dreary. That of course had been the whole ethos of Carlisle's State Management scheme – to keep control of local drinking, stop it being too much fun. The scheme had begun during the First World War when massive munitions works were created at Gretna. On Saturday evenings, up to 5,000 workers, most of them Irish navvies, came into Carlisle for the sole purpose of getting pissed out of their heads. They would pile off the train at the Citadel Station, straight into the nearest pubs where the landlords would already have lined up 500 glasses of whisky on the counters. Very often they would have only a short drinking time, depending on the trains and their shift work, so they had to get a lot down in the shortest time. The result was bedlam in the pubs, then chaos in the streets as drunks fought each other, wrecking the town. 'Drunkenness amongst munition workers,' said Lloyd George, Minister of Munitions, 'was doing more damage in the War than all the German submarines put together.'

The solution was to nationalise all the pubs and hotels in Carlisle and District, an unusual move for a so-called capitalist country, well ahead of the communists taking charge in Russia. Only a handful of licensed places stayed in private hands, such as the Crown and Mitre, Carlisle's poshest hotel, patronised by the quality, where navvies would not have gone anyway. Grocers lost their licences, no longer able to sell beer and spirits. Half the pubs were closed and drinking hours in the ones retained were severely restricted.

Even in the early 1950s, when I started drinking in Carlisle pubs, I was aware of the limited drinking time, having to hang around on Sundays for pubs to open at seven o'clock in the evening. If you wanted to buy beer or spirits to take away, perhaps drink at home, you could only do so at a pub or a hotel, at its so-called off-licence department, which was a joke. Usually it was just a hole in the wall, with no display or proper counter. You had to bang on a trap door on the wall for service, wait and wait, only to be told it was closed. The State Management's brewery produced its own brand of beers and whiskies. On the occasions I did move on to a half and half, as they call it in Scotland – half a beer with a small Scotch – I realised that State Management whisky, Border Blend, was relatively cheap, as were the beers, compared with prices elsewhere in Cumbria or in England as a whole.

All Carlisle's pubs were state managed until 1971 when the scheme was de-nationalised, but its heritage remains in the architecture and also in various displays in the museum at Tullie House. If only I'd known when I started my drinking life that I was drinking social history.

The first girl I remember fancying was called Jennie Hogg. I was in the scouts and she was in the girl guides. I don't think I ever took her out, though I might have walked behind her, admiring from afar. To get to know girls properly you had to pick them up at dances, ask if you could walk them home, then take it from there, which was usually not very far.

Local dances or hops were held in church halls or village halls, sometimes with three-piece live bands but often with just a wind-up gramophone on the stage. People danced a valeta – whatever that was – dashing white sergeants, perhaps even a dinkie two-step, or am I making that up? The older-fashioned, church-based dance halls still had a lot of Scottish formation dances, where you lined up, did various stupid movements, but never got to get a girl in your arms, one to one. You tried to steer clear of those.

To get close to a girl, physically, you had to learn to do the quickstep which the fast set always preferred. Once you had mastered it, you could, with a bit of cheek, making the most of a twirl, get your leg between a girl's legs. That way you could feel the shape of her body, if not much else. Girls often wore stiff petticoats, which had been soaked in starch or icing sugar, making them stick out, so that it was harder to get close, though if you twirled them hard enough, the skirts often blew out so you could catch a glimpse of white thigh.

The vital dance was the slow waltz at the end of the evening when the lights dimmed and you might manage to get your arms round her, perhaps even feel her breasts against your chest, if you were lucky. Getting an erection was awkward and embarrassing and there were innocent girls who really did think you had a pen in your pocket. There were others, more worldly, who were cock teasers, who knew what they were doing, but you also knew that that was as far as it would ever get, this being the 1950s.

If they agreed to be taken home, you often found they had a friend, usually less pretty, not to say ugly, whom you had to take home as well, so you got nowhere. If the girl was on her own, you might get a quick kiss on the doorstep, and that was that, excitement over, then you had to find your way home from some far-flung housing estate on the other side of Carlisle.

Reg was not much of a dancer so I usually went to dances on my own or with other boys. I often went out into the country, hoping the girls would be easier there, but they weren't. Eventually, I started to go to the Crown and Mitre Hotel, when I got a bit older, and could afford it, at times such as Christmas when I was getting good tips from delivering the papers and the groceries at Clark's. I never had any luck at the Crown and Mitre which was for slightly older people. There were often a few county types there, gentleman farmers, so they thought, who stood on the edge of the dance floor, jangling their keys, show-ing they had access to a car, if only their father's, and they got all the girls. Some of them were at St Bees, and looked more affluent, more mature, more sophisticated with better accents.

I never had much luck with so-called lower-class girls, from backgrounds the same as mine, who perhaps were working in offices or factories. In theory, they were supposed to be easier, but I never got a click. My chat, such as it was, didn't work, my jokes failed, my appearance didn't help, looking much younger than I was. I had better luck with some of the younger middle classes, or what I thought at the time were the middle classes, who lived in Stanwix.

We discovered a sort of youth club which was being held on Saturday evenings in a large wooden hut in the garden of a big house. I think it was meant to be educational, or perhaps religious in intent, some rich woman providing well-brought-up local girls with soft drinks and biscuits and a nice, safe place to meet together and play harmless games. Parents allowed their younger teenage girls to go there, as the woman was well known and it was in her garden, not a public place, safe from any rough youths from council estates. Reg and I used to gatecrash it, then put the lights out. The girls were mainly at potty little fee-paying schools, but with incredibly imposing uniforms, for the sort of girls who hadn't managed to pass the Eleven-Plus and get into the High School. At the time, they seemed rather classy, Carlisle's answer to Roedean or Cheltenham Ladies' College. Once the lights went out, some of these girls were not quite as classy as they might have appeared, more than willing to engage in kiss chases and a bit of fumbling.

Two of them once called for me, in Caird Avenue, to invite me to a proper party. I could see them getting out of a car outside our house, walking down our little front path, about to knock at the front door. I was so shocked by the sight of them that I panicked with embarrassment. How had they found out where I lived? That was my first thought. I hadn't lied, but I certainly hadn't gone around telling Stanwix girls I lived on a council estate. I dashed into the parlour and crouched down beside my dad. He was in his bed, eating peanuts, bits of the shells clinging to the hairs on his chest and the front of his vest. He didn't know what the hell was going on.

I shouted to my mother that I wasn't in, telling her to keep quiet and not answer the door, but before I could stop them, my sisters had got to the front door and were opening it, all smiles and hellos, inviting les gels to step inside. Luckily, my mother shouted that I wasn't at home.

Of course nothing happened at these parties, nor when boys and girls sat cuddling together on a bench in the park, or even if they got into a clinch against a hedge or up an alleyway. I mean nothing of a truly sexual nature. I never personally knew a boy or a girl in Carlisle in the 1950s who was not a virgin up to the age of eighteen, and more likely twenty-one. We heard stories of course, people boasted, and at least once a year there was a rumour about some High School girl who had disappeared, who had fallen, been forced to leave school prematurely, gone away somewhere, reputedly to have, gulp, a baby. But it was very, very rare – and also very shameful.

It was mostly petty fumbling and heavy petting, messing around amongst the low numbers on the rating scales. Number one was a kiss. Number two was feeling her breasts. Number three was getting your hand up her skirt, hoping to feel her fanny, or 'finnin' her, as it was called in Carlisle, or 'finger pie' in Liverpool. Number four was when she tossed you off. Number five, that was going the whole hog, the full treatment. No one I knew got to number four, never mind number five.

There were variations on these numbers, in different parts of Carlisle at different times, as there were throughout the land amongst all teenagers, so I discovered later. Perhaps all cultures have forms of the same thing, with their own slang or euphemisms to denote the stages in the sexual stakes.

Birth control pills did not exist. Condoms did, but we were too scared, too embarrassed to even think of going into a chemist and trying to buy any. All we did was tell jokes about johnnies, rubbers, as if we knew what they really were, pretending we had a packet in our inside pocket, ever handy, in case we struck lucky, which we never did. I would probably have run a mile, if some girl had allowed me to get to number four or five.

When I got into the Upper Sixth, there was a youth club in one of the old lanes in the middle of the town called the Garrett Club. It was frequented by Grammar and High School Fifth and Sixth Formers. I think it might have been sponsored or somehow run by the council's education department, who had made the premises available as a meeting place for the city's Sixth-Form students.

One Saturday evening, at a do in the Garrett Club, I spotted a girl called Margaret Forster. I already knew about her because she was said to be the High School's star pupil, a right blue stocking, who thought only of her studies, so I'd gathered. She looked attractive to me, so I thought I'd chance my arm and I asked her if she fancied a dance.

'Certainly not,' she said. 'In fact there's nothing I would like less. I hate dancing . . .'

And with that, she was off, leaving the Garrett Club.

I don't think I talked to her again, for perhaps two years, though I often saw her from afar, heard about her from other people. She clearly had better, more serious, more worthwhile things to do in her life than mess around or waste time with stupid, silly boys.

Chapter Eight

Durham Days

I sat my A-levels in 1954, aged 18. They didn't give grades in those days, unless you got a distinction, though you could find out later through the school what your marks had been. I passed all three of my subjects – English, History and Geography – nothing startling, but comfortably enough, with a mark in each of 55–60, which today would count as three Bs. Perhaps even a couple of As. So I like to tell myself.

I then found myself going to Durham University. I know I said that about going from the Creighton to the Grammar, as if I was in a dream, and had no hand it, but the same sort of thing occurred. I have no memory of looking at lists, thinking now, which university should I apply to, what are the rules, the conditions, where might I get in, what should I study? I knew so little myself about the system, and neither of course did my parents.

I left it to the school, who said I should apply to Durham. They were sending them there by the charabanc at the time, mostly to the same college, University College. Presumably good contacts must have been made, for about half a dozen boys from the Grammar School were already there, and had not yet been chucked out. The college seemed happy enough with them. So Durham was the first and only place I applied to.

You had to fill in your father's occupation, so I asked him what I should put, which was how I came to know he was a Higher

Executive Officer (retired through ill-health). You had to have references as well, so my mother said put down the minister of our church, Warwick Road Presbyterian. I said not him, he's boring, and he doesn't know me anyway. But I couldn't think of anyone else. Working-class kids did have a problem of describing what their dad did and finding a suitable professional-sounding reference.

During my final term at the Grammar School, I went over to Durham for an interview in the Castle and saw a moral tutor called Dr Thomson who was lounging in his study on a sofa, with music playing in the background, palm-like plants flapping away, lots of Turkish-looking rugs and carpets around. For some reason we got talking about opera, about which I knew bugger all. Perhaps I'd boasted about having been to the Edinburgh Festival. It didn't seem to be a proper interview, just an idle chat, so I didn't know what to make of it, but when my A-levels came through, all the bumf appeared from Durham, and off I went.

Before I departed, the minister of the Warwick Road church asked to see me at his manse, which was a poky semi somewhere in Stanwix. He was the minister I'd always considered to be a drip and his church dreary. I thought it might be a moral talk, telling me to keep off the women and booze. He then presented me with a £10 note, to spend on anything I needed, as a reward from the church for getting into university, from some fund which he controlled. Wasn't that kind, after all the moaning I'd done about his church.

Almost everybody in our Upper Sixth form seemed to be going off to some sort of university. It appeared to be what happened, how it was. I don't think I was really aware that in the 1950s I was in an elite minority with only about 4 per cent of eighteen-year-olds going on to higher education. Now it's getting near 40 per cent. And the aim is eventually to have half the population going to university. All must have prizes, and if not prizes, letters after their names.

Two of my best friends, Reg, and Mike Thornhill, neither of

whom had done as well as they had been expected to do at A-levels, had decided to stay on for a third year and try Oxbridge. (And both eventually got into Oxford – Mike to Balliol and Reg to St Catherine's.) One friend, Dicky Wilson, was already at Oxford, having won a scholarship to Queen's at the age of seventeen, while another had got into Cambridge. So that was four from my exact year, in the Arts Sixth, who went to Oxbridge, plus around another ten who went to other universities. Not bad, for a little provincial grammar school in the 1950s.

University College, Durham, founded 1832, was and is situated in Durham Castle, all suitably ancient with courtyards and towers and galleries. It did have the feeling and appearance of an Oxbridge college, not that I'd ever seen one at the time. Durham prided itself on being totally residential, on the collegiate system. There were quite a lot of ex-public school boys, though nowhere near as many as today, who had tried and failed to get into Oxbridge. Many of them arrived with a bit of a chip on their shoulder, feeling they were having to make do with second best. I couldn't understand this mentality, not having tried anywhere else.

I loved it right from the beginning, but the best feeling of all was starting from scratch, on equal terms with everyone else. I had never felt that at the Grammar School, that I belonged, knew how things worked. And at the Creighton, I had recently arrived back from Scotland and felt lost for a long time. At Durham, coming from different schools all over England, none of us knew what to expect, and no one knew us. We were all beginning together, at square one. If anything, coming from Carlisle, we did have a slight advantage, as there were several Old Carliols already at Castle.

Durham seemed enormous, with so much to learn, colleges and departments and buildings to explore, yet there were only 1,500 students at Durham in 1954 – compared with the present number of 12,000. We were technically the Durham Colleges in the University of Durham – six men's colleges and three for women. King's College in Newcastle, which was much bigger than us, was also part of Durham University, till it broke away and became a separate university.

You had to wear a gown for all lectures, and for dinner in Hall, and to see your tutor. I bought a college blazer and scarf, as everyone did. I eventually bought a suit as well, the first in my life, from Burton's while home in Carlisle. It was in grey charcoal, the height of cool, and I wore it for years till the seat was so polished it shone. I could never afford what all students wore in the 1950s, the absolute must, proof that you were a varsity chap – a duffel coat. How I longed for one. Instead, when taking a girl out and wanting to impress, I borrowed one from Edmund Vardy-Binks who lived below me in the Keep. Sometimes, I have to admit, without telling him first, which pissed him off as he had to stay in.

My subject was History, and I was in the Honours school, which people seemed to think was an honour in itself, but I found it totally utterly boring. When it wasn't boring, it was incomprehensible. We did no modern history, or even modernish history, such as nineteenth-century social history which I had enjoyed so much at school. Instead we did ancient Roman history, under Eric Birley, said to be the country's leading expert on Hadrian's Wall, which I later discovered to be true, though he just seemed an eccentric old buffer to me. He was clearly an enthusiast, but he failed to enthuse me.

There were lectures on Anglo-Saxon England which were even more dreary. Prof. Birley did clearly enjoy his subject but the main Anglo-Saxon lecturer, called Offler, seemed to be dead, or at least half asleep, even while talking, only waking up to light his pipe.

We had a series of lectures on the history of economics which to me made no sense at all. They seemed to be delivered in a foreign language. I did try at first to get to grips, and came to the conclusion that basically it was all common sense. All they were doing was wrapping it up in fancy words and silly notions.

Lectures were not compulsory, so I soon started missing the really boring ones. Tutorials were compulsory, as were essays, which I left to the last moment, staying up all night long when one had to be handed in.

They often say that university, from the academic point of view, is wasted on the young. For many people, it comes at the wrong stage of life. They might have a facile, superficial aptitude for learning, or at least an ability to cover the ground with the minimum of effort, but they have no real love of learning for its own sake.

I didn't discuss my feeling of boredom with anyone, or confess I didn't know what was going on. There seemed no choice. No one changed courses, dropped things. You just had to stick at it. I quite envy students today who have such a huge choice of subjects, and are able to mix and match, even if some of their courses get ridiculed for not being serious. I think all subjects, all disciplines, are equally worthy of study. No one subject is in itself better or more useful or more important than another. The History of Football is to me just as worth studying as the History of the Roman Empire.

Not that I was interested in any sort of studying. Drinking, talking, playing sports, rushing around, chasing girls, were much more fun. I played a bit of football and rugby at first in college teams, but soon realised there were a lot of people so much better than me, unlike at school, so I gave that up. Instead I took up rowing. The college boat club was mainly dominated by public school types, yet for some reason, this didn't put me off. They were keen for any absolute beginners to take part. I was a cox at first, in a four, and took part in one regatta, then took up sculling, just for fun. I liked the individuality of it, that you could go out on the river when you liked, on your own, no one shouting at you. You could just glide along at your own speed, yet come back feeling ever so healthy. I left a pair of beat-up old shoes permanently down at our college boat house, and put them on and staggered along in them till I got into my little boat. It amused me, having this special pair of old shoes. It would have suited my mother. She only wore beat-up old shoes, all her life, often second-hand, often odd pairs, and always ill-fitting.

Most of all, I enjoyed the boat club dinners. Each term, they were the biggest piss-ups in college. At one of them, I threw an orange which hit one of the medieval stained-glass windows in the Great Hall of the Castle. I don't recall seeing the window break. I was under the table by then, hiding, or collapsed.

I shared two rooms – a big, wood-panelled, stone-walled study and a small bedroom – on the top floor of the Keep with a very studious, serious boy called Hugh who came from Peterborough. He had been to a very good school and was doing Geography Honours. He loved trains and would sit for hours with his stopwatch on a chain looking out of our window, high up in the Keep, spotting trains on the main line, steaming in and out of Durham station, making notes on their names and which were running late. I would scoff and mock him for this soppy, pathetic hobby.

He must have hated being lumbered with me as a room-mate. In the first year, you had no choice, being told who you had to share with. I would come back drunk and be sick out of the window, or on the floor, if I couldn't reach the window in time.

On Sundays after lunch, I would chuck him out of our rooms, saying he couldn't use either of them till I said so, because I would be entertaining some girl I had picked up at the Saturday night hop. We'd have a walk along the river, me in my blazer and white shirt and Edmund Vardy-Binks's duffel coat, then I'd bring her back to my rooms for tea and crumpets. I'd try to talk her into our bedroom for, well, not very much really. Heavy petting, that was the most you could expect, if you were lucky.

I usually did have a girl on the go, for a week or so, usually from one of the training colleges, but it was never serious and rarely lasted long. It was a status thing as much as possible, to show the chaps you would do it, you were a hell of a feller.

At public dances and hops, such as in town at the Town Hall or the County Hotel, as opposed to college or university hops, the biggest rivals for any students hoping to pick up a girl were the local young miners. They were blokes about my age, but seemed older and more mature and definitely bigger and stronger. They had been working in the local collieries since the age of fifteen and seemed to have quite a bit of money in their pockets, compared with students. They could buy girls drinks, treat them to meals, which I could never do. Often they had their own car. They were confident, cocky, as of course they had a well-paid job for life. Or so they thought. So we all thought, back in the 1950s.

I had better luck with girls from one of the many training colleges in and around Durham. Doing a proper degree, in a college such as Castle, which was seen as Durham's best college, was a help in picking up training college girls. On Saturday evenings, there were often coaches laid on specially for us from Palace Green, taking us out to the remoter colleges such as Wynyard Hall, which was then a girls' training college. We'd all rush into their college hall, eye up the talent, try to get off with someone as quickly as possible. If it went well, you might fit in a walk round the college grounds and later a quick goodnight snog, then make a date for her to come for tea on Sunday afternoon.

Most students were pretty serious and hard working, but there was a small group in each college who did spend all afternoon in one of the local pubs playing shove ha'penny and drinking stout. Pete Ellis from Carlisle was one of these. He was always coming to my room after lunch and tempting me away from the essay I was supposed to be doing, the books I should have been reading. It did seem gloriously wicked. Drinking in the afternoon, wasting away the day, one's life, wilfully not making the most of all the privileges we had been given. A bedder did our rooms for us, cleared up after I'd been sick. She was usually a middle-aged local woman whose accent I could never quite follow. We had maids in uniform to serve us at meals and a butler called Eddie in charge. Only afternoon tea was self-service. Tutors gave us sherry parties. College servants took messages, addressed us as Mr, referred to us as gentlemen, yet we'd been scruffy schoolboys just months previously.

Life revolved round the college and everyone lived in, either in the Castle itself or in nearby large houses on Palace Green or the

Bailey. No one was more than a few minutes' walk away and everyone came into the Great Hall for all meals, including breakfast.

Our college had been going for well over 100 years and had developed traditions of its own. You 'sported an oak' if you didn't want to be disturbed in your room. Most rooms had double doors and if the outer was closed, this meant your oak was up. There was a college bar and a pantry where you bought basic things like milk, tea, bread, sherry, wine, if perhaps you were entertaining in your room. The college wine and college sherry came with the college's coat of arms on the bottle which I thought was awfully posh.

It was all so different from life on our council estate. Being able to bring people back to your rooms, not just girls, was something I had never experienced before. Drinking wine with meals, going to sherry parties, it was all new to me. And it was all free, more or less, at least I personally was not paying. I had no money anyway, nor did my parents. And yet I don't remember feeling all that grateful at the time.

I had received a generous award from Carlisle Education Committee, thank you very much, as did all Carlisle students who had got into a university. Everything was paid for, maintenence as well as tuition fees. A large cheque arrived at the beginning of each term, a Midland Bank cheque which I presumed when it first came had to be put into the Midland Bank in order to be used, not realising it could be paid in anywhere. My parents had never had a cheque book or used a bank. Why should they, when they had no savings?

During term time, it covered all my expenses, including drinking. I don't remember ever being in debt, or having to borrow from home. I did send my washing home every week to my mother in Carlisle, being too mean to use a proper laundry – launderettes had not of course been invented – and she returned the clean clothes, along with a large piece of home-made gingerbread.

I sent my best white shirt and Van Heusen collars to the real laundry, to get them stiff, as my mother always mucked them up. For college hops or dances, one always wore a pristine white shirt. The collars were detachable, kept on by studs. I found that I could re-use them by turning them inside out. My collar studs were my father's. He had no use for them any more, being an invalid.

Until I got to Durham, I had not been aware of having a Carlisle accent. Nor had I heard any accents which had not been either Scottish or Carlisle. Now I was surrounded by Geordies, Scousers, people from Yorkshire and Lancashire. Most people were from the North, from grammar schools similar to the one I had gone to, but there was a sprinkling of middle-class boys from the South who had been to public schools.

What I envied about them was their confidence and fluency. In JCR meetings, they would stand up and just keep speaking, beautifully, making sense, perfect grammar, not stuttering, getting lost, mumbling, which was how I spoke. Was it a trick? Had they been taught it? Did all public school boys have these skills? And yet most of them, when I got to know them, seemed pretty stupid, certainly no cleverer than me.

That first year went so quickly, almost in a haze, it felt unreal, a fantasy world. No one appeared to be aware that I was missing so many lectures. There was no one to worry about, no invalid in the back room casting any shadows. I had absolutely no idea what I was going to do in life, or where it was leading, but I didn't really care.

At the end of the year, I got a terrible shock. I found I had failed my first-year examinations. I couldn't believe it: surely I had managed the minimum requirements? One or two of my friends had fared even worse than me. They were not being allowed back. That was it, their university career was over.

I was being demoted, from the Honours History school to General Arts, a course of study which was looked upon as decidedly inferior.

It was made clear this would be my last chance. If I failed my General Arts exams, at the end of my second year, that would be it. I would be out.

Chapter Nine

Jobs and Teenagers

Coming back to Carlisle for that first Christmas, in my college scarf and blazer, I got a job at the Post Office. The sorting office in Junction Road was a riot of university scarves with everyone, boys and girls, flaunting their varsity colours, boasting about all the drinking they'd been doing, the essay crises they'd had. I think it took me about two years to realise how naff it was to wear a college scarf.

I worked at the Post Office every Christmas during my Durham years, as most students did. The only awful part was one Christmas, when I was working away sorting, I turned to find I was beside my mother. She had also applied to be a Christmas casual and got taken on, without telling me, much to my embarrassment. She insisted on asking me things, what names meant, where streets were. Despite all her years in Carlisle, she still didn't know her way around.

Getting Christmas work at the Post Office was easy. Acquiring some sort of job for the long summer vac was much harder. I wrote endless letters, hoping to be fixed up the minute I arrived back in Carlisle in June. Otherwise, what could you do till October? With no money, there would be no holiday, no fun, nowhere to go, nothing to do.

I so envied my Stanwix friends in their posh semis who through family contacts managed to get an easy vac job, such as helping out at the golf course or Carlisle Airport. Carlisle did have an airport in the 1950s, struggling along as ever, announcing wonderful new services which never happened. One of my Sixth Form friends, Ian Johnstone, once got a job there unloading luggage, thanks to a family contact. It was dead cushty for him, as there was only ever one plane a day, if that. I was surprised, many years later, hearing the word 'cushty' on 'Only Fools and Horses'. I'd always imagined it was a purely Carlisle term.

In one long vac, I got a labouring job with Carlisle Corporation, who were building their own council houses. I was a hod carrier. Not one of those brawny ones who could fly up ladders with about a dozen bricks on his hod, held high on his shoulder. I needed about a dozen trips, taking one brick at a time. I was assigned to a team, serving two or three bricklayers, mostly middle-aged and very friendly, interested in who I was and the fact that I was at university. I always tried to keep this quiet when doing vac jobs, not wanting to be seen as someone just passing through who might be thought to consider himself superior. I can remember one called Pineapple Balls, or Chunky Balls, who for years afterwards would shout from roofs as I happened to pass by, ask me how I was getting on. Several showed off about their sex life, telling me what they did to the wife last night. 'I put my hand across on her minge, like, dead hairy and that . . .' I would quickly try to change the subject. Another gave me some advice for when I was married, saying the best time for sex with your wife was when she is five months pregnant, as she would then relax.

I got to know several of the other labourers, some not much older than me, full-time labourers, not students, who were in it for life. One of them, a fading Teddy Boy, still with his quiff in place, took me back to where he lived in a little terrace house, all damp and threadbare, one of the slum terraces knocked down when they created Carlisle's ring road. In it, crouching almost in a corner, were his wife and a kid, which I never realised he had. I wondered how he was going to get through life, provide for them, on his miserable wage. Most of all I thought about the dreariness of doing the same manual job, year after year, yet he seemed an intelligent enough bloke, not stupid or half-witted. Many of the bricklayers struck me as decidedly clever.

It all seemed so unfair, unequal, that they were not going to do as well as they could have done in life. It made me realise how lucky I had been, managing to get on a conveyor belt which was transporting me, so I presumed, so I hoped, to a better, more satisfying job in life. I still, however, had no idea what I would do. If asked, I would have said I'm hoping to become a teacher, saying it because I knew it would please my mum.

The best-paid vac job, if not the one which turned out the most useful, was the following year when at last I got taken on by the Ribble buses. There was a long waiting list to be a bus conductor, and you had to be a certain age, but it was the one most desired by all Carlisle students in the 1950s.

The Ribble company had a proper training scheme, including a residential weekend at Preston, at their HQ. We were put in digs for the weekend, somewhere near Deepdale, Preston North End's football ground, for I remember walking round it, thinking how much bigger and grander it was than Brunton Park. We had tests at the end, which they took terribly seriously, lining us all up in a passing-out parade.

Working as a bus conductor on the Ribble in Carlisle, you had to wear uniform, which quickly got very shiny, and to carry a huge leather money bag and an equally heavy ticket machine which had to be altered all the time, according to the fare stage. I remember the first week or so thinking I'll never cope, there was so much to think about, plus the bell to ring, passengers to chase to stop them getting off without paying, and of course keeping an eye out for an inspector who might appear at any moment from behind a hedge, jump out and stop the bus. As a passenger, not having paid, you think you will be the only one to get it in the neck, but the bus conductor got most of the blame.

On one of my shifts, I happened to notice, sitting upstairs, all on her own, Margaret Forster, the girl from the High School I had previously tried to chat up at the Garrett Club. Showing off, being Big Mick, trying to impress, I said, 'Don't worry, pet, you don't have to pay, I'll let you off.' I then went downstairs again, keeping a good eye out in case an inspector called.

She followed me, almost at once, and insisted on paying, despite my protests. She certainly wasn't going to be let off, cheating the system. She handed over her fare and got off at her stop, without ever a glance back. I stood on the bus platform as it pulled away, trying to look cool, a man of the world, who didn't care, wasn't bothered.

One of the significant developments in the 1950s in Carlisle, in fact in the whole of England, Europe, the world of Western Civilisation as we know it, was the arrival of teenagers. I later told my own children about this, when they became teenagers, and of course they didn't believe it. How could teenagers 'arrive' when surely they were always there, i.e. people aged between thir-teen and nine-teen? Technically true, but teenagery as a culture, with its own separate styles, fashions, music, marketplace, was unknown to previous generations, until the mid-1950s.

I expected, as I was growing up, that I would eventually emerge pretty much like my father, not him in particular, because of his condition, but like almost all fathers who had gone before. I would gradually change from being a child into adulthood, the traditional signals including starting to wear his overcoat, putting on his collar studs, as I was already doing, plastering his Brylcreem on my hair, getting it cut at the same place, the Co-op barber, as he had done, and in the same style, looking and behaving and acting very much like him, till one day I would realise I'd done it, the metamorphosis was complete, I'd become an adult. I would hardly be aware of any separate intermediary stage, because there wasn't one.

The Teddy Boys were an early sign of the changes taking place, when youths affected a special style of dress not shared by adults, but the real catalyst was pop music. We had enjoyed singing along to Pat Boone and Guy Mitchell and other American singers with their soppy or silly early 1950s songs, even while mocking them. There were British versions of these American singers, like Dickie Valentine and David Whitfield, who had been popular as well, though they tended to sing in mid-Atlantic accents, wear shiny suits on stage, tell us we were a lovely audience.

The first of the three defining dates for the arrival of what became known as rock 'n' roll was April 1954 when Bill Haley and his Comets produced 'Rock Around the Clock'. It took about a year for it to have any effect but when it was used as the theme tune for the film *The Blackboard Jungle,* young audiences across the USA and then the UK started dancing in the aisles and tearing up the seats. When it came to Carlisle, there were equally exuberant audiences of young persons, jiving away. Jiving took over from the quickstep as the fast dance, the one to show off with, get to grips with a girl and twirl her round. I was quite good at it, so I liked to think at the time, though when I have demonstrated the steps later, at family parties, everyone cowers in embarrassment. Places like the Crown and Mitre, which considered themselves a superior dance venue, would not at first allow jiving, no more than they had allowed Teddy Boys in. For a while, there was a strange intermediary stage in some dance halls where at one end there would be couples jiving, with people crowding in a circle to watch them doing it, while at the far end of the dance hall, old-fashioned quicksteps and waltzes would still be taking place, two cultures, two generations, enjoying themselves in the same room at the same time, but in a different way.

Bill Haley was fleshy, flabby, with a stupid quiff, not exactly a young sex symbol, but then came the second big event – the arrival of Elvis Presley. By May 1956, his 'Heartbreak Hotel' was top of the charts in fourteen countries.

The third and perhaps most influential development was skiffle, which came in just before rock 'n' roll. In Britain, the important date was January 1956 when Lonnie Donegan's single 'Rock Island Line' became a surprise number one hit. He had recorded it back in 1954 on an LP record (long player – don't say you've forgotten) with Chris Barber, but it took a year for it to appear as a single, and then it shot up the charts.

In Carlisle, as in all parts of the country, skiffle groups emerged almost overnight, like mushrooms, sprouting up in schools and youth clubs. The big attraction of skiffle was that you could join in, take part, without being able to read music, play an instrument, or even have a proper instrument. I found myself on a washboard one evening where an impromptu skiffle concert was taking place. At Durham, along with another friend, Mike Bateman, I organised skiffle parties, hiring local skiffle groups to perform in rooms we had booked in pubs.

Like all other teenagers of the time, I was desperate to have tight trousers, which of course my father had never worn, so there was no point in asking to borrow his. Many parents would not allow it, so that boys would often have their trousers narrowed secretly; then hide them at a friend's house, changing into them when going to a dance or a party. Girls did much the same, hiding their more extravagant teenage styles from their parents. There was a woman in Caird Avenue, just along from us, who would tighten your trousers for a few shillings.

At the end of my second year at Durham, I got through my exams OK, so I was therefore set for a third year, and a degree, so I assumed, unless I did anything really stupid, though I still had not the slightest idea what I'd do with a degree, or even what I'd like to do, in a fantasy world.

But in that last term I had stumbled upon something quite amusing, which I had never ever thought about before. My room-mate, John Davies, was giving up a little job he had as advertising manager of *Palatinate*, the student newspaper. I offered to take it on, purely in order to have something to put on my CV, to indicate I had done something at Durham, other than drink, play sport and go out with girls. By going to the

Palatinate office, which was then run by a group from Hatfield College, as these things often are, passing jobs around amongst themselves, they all struck me as very ordinary, not to say pretty stupid, certainly no cleverer or more gifted than me. I had never thought of writing anything, either journalism or creative stuff, partly due to the fact that at the Grammar School Sixth, my friend Reg Hill had written such brilliant pieces that I thought I could never hope to do as well.

Palatinate had a hole in the pages one day, when I went in with some ads I had secured, so I said I would fill it. I wrote a first-person column about a day in the life of a boat club hearty, basing it on various half-witted boat club, public school types at Castle, complete with bad spelling and lots of vomiting. It went down well, so I did another for the next edition, about a theology student, then I did one as if written by a science student. I called this little series 'A Life in the Day of'.

I then found myself writing bits all the time, putting down on paper every little thing that happened to me, however trivial, trying to turn it into an article for publication, or just for my own sake, to see if I could do it.

Before the next long vacation, I wrote to the editor of the *Cumberland News*, John Burgess, later Sir John, head of the family which still controls the group, asking for a holiday job, doing anything. He agreed to see me, which was kind, and fixed a time for me to come to his office when I returned to Carlisle. I thought our little chat went quite well, but at the end, he said I gabbled too much. He hadn't been able to understand half of what I said, due to the way I spoke. Because of that, so he said, I would never make it as a journalist. Very sorry, he had nothing for me.

So I went across the road to the *Carlisle Journal*. Lucky for me that there existed a rival paper. Today, in Carlisle, it would have been impossible. I saw the editor and, amazingly, he took me on for the summer hols. I wouldn't get a wage, as such, but he would pay me lineage for every story I got in the paper. I worked out that I would never earn as much as I had got on the Ribble buses, and therefore I was going to be very hard-up all summer, unable to go off anywhere on hols, but I thought it would be worth it, just to work on a real paper, and have some real cuttings to prove it. And it might help me get a real job, out in the real world.

Chapter Ten

Enter Margaret

I was walking through town, going past the City Picture House, on the way to catch the bus home. It was June, or perhaps July, 1956. I know it was the long vacation of '56, after my second year at Durham. The fact that I'm not sure whether it was June or July might suggest the date cannot have been all that vital, but it was, it was.

There was a big queue for the cinema, as there always was in those days, right along the pavement. At the top of the queue were a couple of my old school friends, Ian Johnstone, who was then at Durham with me, and Mike Thornhill, who was at Balliol. They were with two girls, Margaret Crosthwaite and her best friend Margaret Forster, both of whom had just sat their A-levels at the High School. They were in a little quartet, but I felt for some reason they were not in couples, had not paired off, were not items, not that I was aware of. And if they were, I decided to ignore it.

On the spur of the moment, even though I was on the way home, I decided to barge in, joining them at the top of the queue. People behind started muttering and complaining, but I thanked my friends, loudly, for having kept my place. I went in with them, sat down with them, or at least as near them as I could. The cinema was already pretty full, with not many empty seats, but I ended up in the row behind as the four of them had managed to sit together. This didn't put me off and during the film I kept up an inane conversation over their shoulders, trying to be smart and amusing.

When we all came out, I stood around talking to them on the pavement. They had made it pretty clear that I was a bit of an interloper, not having been invited on this particular outing, but I continued to ignore all this, and kept on nattering away. Eventually, it was obvious they were now about to disperse, going to their various homes or catching their respective buses. And they expected me to do the same, perhaps the sooner the better.

Instead, I found myself asking Margaret Forster if I could walk her home. Amazingly, considering that twice at least in the last couple of years she had repulsed my advances, she said yes. And that was it. I walked her home. It turned out to be a very long walk . . .

I didn't know where Margaret lived, nor did she know where I lived, but she had remembered our encounters, and also watching me play hockey for the Grammar against the High School. She had heard I was back from Durham, having a rest from a dissolute life, which of course I denied.

On the way home with her, I mentioned going to the Edinburgh Festival and the Proms, trying to give myself an artistic, intellectual image, and in passing said how much I loved Sibelius. 'What's he written?' asked Margaret, assuming he was a novelist. That was a relief. She wasn't quite the all-round brain box I had been led to believe.

Having finished her A-levels, she was marking time, waiting for the results. That was probably why she had weakened and accepted my advances, feeling demob happy, wanting a break after all that heavy-duty studying. I was lucky, catching her at the right time. If I hadn't gone past the City Picture House that particular evening, if I hadn't pushed my way into the queue, who knows if we would have ever met.

Is life all about luck and chance and happenstance? I don't actually think so. Accidents, disease, that's almost wholly bad luck, over which you have little control. But good luck, I think you can help to make that happen. The more you try, the more chances you have of getting lucky. But back to 1950s Carlisle.

Margaret lived in Longsowerby, at 180 Richardson Street, at the top end, opposite the cemetery, a very neat, immaculate house, especially the garden. The hedges and lawns had been sculpted to within half an inch of their lives by her father, Arthur. He was working at Metal Box, setting off each morning on his bike in his boiler suit, never late, never a day off, oh, since Pauline was born. This was a family joke. Margaret's mother Lily always used to say she had not been to the pictures since Pauline – Margaret's younger sister – had been born, which was about sixteen years previously. So anything that had not happened for a long time, was not since Pauline was born.

I said goodnight, on her doorstep, not being so bold as to attempt a kiss, but arranged to meet again. I walked all the way back to St Ann's Hill, in a daze, walking in space, seeing poetry in the litter fluttering around the old Town Hall, going over all the things I'd said, and should have said, and what she said, or appeared to say.

Apparently, I gave the impression that I was from a relatively pukka family, what with letting it slip out that I played the violin, my sisters played the piano, and we once lived in a big house in Dumfries where I rode a bike down the corridors. I don't remember ever saying the latter, but it was enough to make it a slight surprise for her when she discovered I lived in Caird Avenue, in a council house, just like hers, though not quite as neat and kempt.

Margaret had only been in Richardson Street for about three years. Before that, until she was fourteen, her family had lived at 44 Orton Road, Raffles, the house in which she had been born. She always looked upon their Raffles house as her real home, not Richardson Street.

Raffles in the 1950s was not quite the ideal garden estate that it had been when created in the 1930s, which was why they had moved. They now had an inside lavatory, which they hadn't had before. But Raffles was nothing like as rough and depressed as it later became. Last time I passed Margaret's birthplace, a wrecked car had gone through the front hedge, leaving a massive hole; the garden which her father had kept immaculate was completely overrun; the downstairs windows were boarded up and the area appeared to be full of drug dens.

It was through Margaret in the long hot summers of 1956 and 1957 – which will always be hot to me, whatever the temperatures really were – that I got to know Cumbria. Forster is one of those true Cumbrian and Border surnames and her family, on all sides, had been there for centuries, unlike my family. I can't believe now that I had never been to Silloth, out on the Solway coast, till I met Margaret. I'd heard about it, of course, from so many Carlisle people, who made it sound like a cross between Blackpool, El Dorado and what could now be Disneyland. Margaret reminisced about her childhood outings to Silloth, how passengers had been jam-packed into each carriage as the train left its own platform at Citadel Station, then the excitement of counting all the little stations, till at last they arrived at Silloth and the sea.

When we couldn't afford the train to Silloth, we would go on our bikes out to Glasson Point, then on to Port Carlisle and Bowness, strange little isolated, left-over Solway villages I didn't know existed. If it was pouring, we would take a Ribble bus, back and forwards across town, from terminus to terminus, sitting at the front upstairs, hoping there would be no one else there by the time we reached the terminus, talking all the time. That's all we did that first long hot summer, talk non-stop. One of the problems about courting in the 1950s was having somewhere to go, preferably dry, preferably inside or under cover, and free or very cheap. No one we knew had a car to drive us anywhere and in families like ours, no one had their own bedroom. Not of course that any parents would have allowed one's boyfriend or girlfriend into a bedroom.

I eventually got invited into her house, on the evenings I walked home with her, and her mum would make me a cup of Camp coffee, made with milk, and a Carr's sport biscuit, yum

yum, before I set off on the long walk back to St Ann's Hill. I didn't see much of her dad; in fact I did my best to keep out of his way, apart from trying to ingratiate myself by talking about Carlisle United, which failed totally.

Apparently, he thought I looked foreign, Spanish or Italian, with my very dark hair which did get really greasy, as I hardly ever washed it. I was unaware at the time of stuff called shampoo, thinking it was just for women. He also didn't approve of the fact that I had got out of National Service, so far, by being a student. Several of my friends from the Grammar, such as Reg, had gone off and were serving the Queen, getting their Nat Service done first, before university. It was already known that my age group would be one of the last batches to be called up, and I certainly didn't want to be amongst them. On 4 August that first summer – I know that date because we celebrate it every year since – Margaret's parents were away, visiting relatives in Scotland, and we went off for the whole day to Keswick. It was the most incredible weather, blue skies, cloudless, the sort that makes you realise Lakeland is the best place on the planet. We lay at Friar's Crag, letting the sun go down, and down, till we realised we had missed the last bus. So we set off, about eleven o'clock, to walk back to Carlisle.

After about five miles, I began to feel very tired. After ten miles, I was knackered. After another ten miles, I was on my knees with Margaret helping me along. The final ten miles I walked in a trance, semi-conscious, except for breaking into a cold sweat and an attempt at a quick dash when we were staggering through Thursby. A lumbering figure had appeared in the dark behind us, shouting something awful which scared me to death, thinking we were about to be murdered. It was only a tramp, whom we had disturbed while he was sleeping in a hedge. We got back to Margaret's house about five in the morning. I think I fell asleep, shattered, in her front room, passing out for a few hours, before dragging myself on to the first bus to St Ann's. Margaret always was stronger, fitter than me. When we went youth hostelling, she usually carried the rucksack, except when we passed through villages or habitation, then I would take it for half a mile or so, pretending to be a real man.

We had two nights once at Grasmere Youth Hostel, which had been excellent, doing lots of long walks. Margaret counted up our monies and reckoned we had just enough for one more night at a youth hostel, or we could have a proper meal, and go home this evening. It was up to me – I could decide for both of us. I opted for the meal. I was never forgiven. What it meant, so she said, was that I preferred some horrible pie and chips to another night in her company. It is true that when we were sitting somewhere really fantastic, like the top of Place Fell looking down on Ullswater, she would ask me what I was thinking and before I could stop myself, I did often find myself saying, 'A pint and a pie, that's what I really fancy.'

People did wonder what she saw in me, why such a blue stocking, clever, original, talented, forthright, strong-willed girl should get mixed up with me, her first-ever boyfriend. I wondered that myself, especially when her A-level results came through – distinctions in English and History, plus a pass in Latin. The High School headmistress, Miss Cotterell, sent her actual marks in English and History, which were 95 per cent in each, unheard of for those sort of arts subjects.

For the glory and greatness of the school, and to get her name up in lights for ever, or at least in letters on the wooden honours board in the school hall, she really did have to try for Oxbridge, so all her teachers said. I thought if she does that, and gets in, mixing with the cream of the nation's youth, brilliant golden boys from the top public schools, many of them with flaxen hair, probably even their own shampoo, I wouldn't stand a chance and would never see her again.

To celebrate her A-level results, her dad Arthur came home from work one day, got off his bike, put his hand in his boiler suit and presented her with a ten-shilling note. 'Here y'are, lass.' We were all amazed, especially as he was from the generation that believed girls did not need to be educated and would be just as well off as a cracker packer at Carr's.

I immediately worked out a good way of spending it. I said let's go out on the bus to Wetheral, a village about five miles away, and have a slap-up meal at the Fantails. This had not long opened and was the most fashionable, smartest local restaurant – not that there was much competition at that time. I put on my best charcoal grey suit and borrowed Arthur's best umbrella.

I was horrified to see the expense of even the humblest dish on the menu. I had imagined that her dad's ten-bob note would have been more than enough to cover a proper tuck-in. It was all the money I had, so I steered her towards the cheapest item, which was a cheese omelette. She has always liked omelettes so that was OK, but I hate them: ugh, so boring.

When the bill came it had somehow jumped to twelve shillings. I hid it from Margaret and ushered her to the front door of the Fantails which is at the top of a flight of stone steps, while I went off to see the owner manager. He was a very posh, fleshy man, with thick grey hair, all smily and charming, at least up to that moment. Confronted by a customer unable to pay the bill, his smile immediately faded. I had visions of having to wash up. I apologised profusely, explained the reasons for the celebration, but he wasn't impressed. He wanted me to leave some security, and come back and pay the difference tomorrow, but I didn't have anything. I emptied all my pockets, giving him everything, the ten-bob note, plus some coppers for the bus home.

I was eventually allowed out. I rejoined Margaret at the top of the steps, holding Arthur's umbrella, twirling it to show how debonair I was, what a man of the world – I know how to treat a girl – when the umbrella came to pieces, bits flying down the steps. That would be more expense and Arthur would be furious.

Opposite, hanging around the Wetheral bus stop, were some uncouth local rural youths, who had been watching me with the brolly and smart suit, thinking what a prick. How they roared.

We had to walk the five miles home to Carlisle during which time I admitted what had happened. Next day, having borrowed two bob, I had to trail out to Wetheral again. I remember thinking one day, when I'm rich, I'll buy the Fantails and sack that bastard.

A lot of the arguments Margaret and I had were about my lack of punctuality. Her idea of catching a train on time means being on the platform, all ready, half an hour before the train is due. My idea of good timing is to arrive and jump on the train, just as it's leaving. We used to meet at Burton's corner, still there, which was handy for both our buses, coming into town. I was very often late, or I got the rendezvous wrong, thinking we were meeting outside the City Picture House, so she would stand at Burton's for hours, and be absolutely furious when I eventually turned up, maintaining I'd been standing at the City, which was usually a lie.

Margaret, like me, had a problem finding any sort of summer holiday job to earn herself some money. The worst she'd had was at the Steam Laundry, sorting dirty clothes. The whole place was filthy, noisy, unbearably hot and the women who worked there foul mouthed.

In the summer of 1956 she got a part-time summer job at Marks and Spencer which was an eye opener – but in a different way. She was astounded by how clean and well organised it was behind the scenes, with an excellent canteen and a hair salon provided for the staff. The only boring part was the actual work, serving on the knicker counter. In those days, Marks, like all big shops, had a sales assistant behind every counter, who took the money, there and then, rather than customers having to trail to a pay desk in another part of the store.

Paying in shops in the 1950s was a very complicated business. I used to love as a child going into Liptons and seeing the overhead cables which conveyed the cash canisters, sending them whizzing and clattering all round the shop. I longed to pull the handles, and start the mechanism. In Binns and the Co-op there were chutes, little tunnels running between the floors, which seemed to blow or suck the metal capsules which carried the cash. What was the point of it all?

During that first long summer going out with Margaret, exploring Cumbria, finding out that girls had the same sorts of problems getting holiday work as boys, I discovered it was she who had petitioned the headmistress of the High School not to give a half-day holiday for that visit of Arsenal to Brunton Park in 1951. Spoilsport.

I also discovered that we had nearly met, many years earlier in Motherwell, of all places. It turned out that we had relations in exactly the same road there, Bellshill Road, where my Grandma Brechin lived and also her Aunty Jean. I had actually played with her cousins, the Wallaces, whom she often used to visit. The chances are that we had been there, at the same time, without realising.

Well, what a coincidence. It seemed a good omen. Fate had been conspiring to bring us together for longer than we had realised. Ahhhh . . .

Chapter Eleven

Oxford in Drag

The offices of the *Carlisle Journal*, where I started my holiday job in the summer I met Margaret, were in English Street, near the City Picture House. They had a dusty, old-fashioned front window display which had nothing to do with the newspaper itself but contained envelopes, writing pads and lavatory paper, which was apparently a sideline run by one of the directors.

You entered by a side door, in a side passage, and then went upstairs and reached a series of ancient rooms with wooden floors and bare walls. That's how I remember them. The printing works were on the ground floor.

The paper had had a long and distinguished history, far older than the *Cumberland News*, having been founded in 1798, which makes it one of England's, not just Cumbria's, oldest newspapers. In the nineteenth century, it had the largest circulation of any journal in Cumberland, Westmorland and Dumfriesshire, covering all the towns from Annan down to Penrith. By the time I joined it in the mid 1950s it was a shadow of its former self, with a small staff, small circulation, overshadowed by the bigger, more successful, more professional *Cumberland News*.

The editor of the *Journal* was Mr Fred Humphrey, OBE, an award he had received for work in the Ministry of Information during the war. The paper came out twice a week, on a Tuesday and a Friday. Friday was the main paper and it would often run late as the head printer liked to go for a drink at the Sportsman Inn on Thursday evenings, then come back and stand in the print room shouting 'Fuck the Duke of Edinburgh'.

I sat in one of the little rooms and had access to a rackety old typewriter, which I could only use with one finger – now I have advanced to two – and mainly re-wrote press hand-outs and announcements, or lifted stuff from other publications. When I was allowed out, which wasn't often, it was mainly to flower shows and prize givings where my main job was to write down the list of names and winners correctly, as many of them as possible, the theory being they would all buy copies in order to see their name in the paper.

The biggest event I can remember covering was the Penton Sports on the Scottish border. I went there on the bus with Margaret. I dutifully copied down all the winners. In passing, I had noticed during one of the racing events that a horse pulling a trap had reared its head a bit and refused to start. I remember thinking that could have been nasty, if it had got free.

My report, in the *Journal*, said it had been a successful show, grand weather, and then listed all the winners. The *Cumberland News* report had a big headline saying, 'Horse runs amok at Penton'. I hadn't even realised the *Cumberland News* had been there. I got a bollocking for that, for missing the big story. I denied it had been a big story, just a trivial little incident, with no danger to anyone, but of course that was not the point. I learned two things. First, to make the most of anything, even if it means flamming it up, in order to get a good intro, and second, to find out who else is covering the same story, then agree with them if possible what actually happened.

Back at Durham, I continued to write for *Palatinate*. I seemed to be able to work so hard when I was doing stuff for the paper, totally concentrating, getting carried away with what I was doing, loving every minute of it, compared with writing boring old essays or attending lectures.

I eventually became editor and put even more energy into

student journalism. The paper didn't have much money and couldn't afford many photographs, so I would often split a block in two – the wooden block from which photographs were made, back in the days of steam printing. One week we would use half a photo of the President of the Union. Next week, his other half. Third week, for all you girls out there, we would print the whole of the president. Well, it amused us and saved money.

On a student rag, you do everything, not just the writing, pasting up the pages, laying out pictures, the headlines, but also writing the posters to pin up in each college on publication day and even going round the shops trying to sell advertisements. By the end of the year I had got the sales of *Palatinate* up to 1,500 – which was amazing, considering that was the total student population at the time.

I found some excellent writers, or at least they had come out of the woodwork or the bar when they saw the paper was doing so well. They included Dan Van Der Vat, who went on to work for the *Guardian* and write many books, and Colin McDowell who did our film reviews, later turning himself into one of the country's leading fashion experts and writers. There was also a hard core of really keen women from St Aidan's who did all the donkey work and didn't worry about the size of their by-lines. We seemed to spend most of our time doubled up at our own wit and wheezes.

I learned so much, working on *Palatinate*, about journalism and about myself, yet it had happened purely by accident. If John Davies hadn't asked if I wanted to be the advertising manager, I would never have got into it. Student rags tend to be run by cliques, who pass on the jobs to each other, so if you are not in that gang, or that college or that group at the right time, you are unaware of all the possibilities.

Palatinate was doing so well that I decided to enter us in the student newspaper of the year competition which was being run by *The Sunday Times*. We got on to the short list for one of the categories and I went to London for the awards ceremony.

Bayles, the Durham printers, who had printed *Palatinate* for years, ran me off six special copies of the paper, on glossier and thicker paper than usual, and these were the ones I had entered, trying to appear as impressive as possible. We didn't win anything. In fact, one of the judges criticised us, saying a student newspaper should not be printed on such high-class paper.

I found out how to sell stuff to the nationals, after I realised that various local freelances were lifting stories from our pages and making money. I sold one story, which was a page lead, to the *Daily Express*, complete with photo, about an all-girl crew in the rowing regatta which included a man, disguised as a girl. Apparently, at the last minute a girl had taken ill, and the crew were being forced to withdraw, when their male coach decided to take her place.

I also sent a so-called funny article to *Punch*. They accepted it and I got a cheque for six guineas, but it never actually appeared. Bastards.

As editor of *Palatinate*, I got to see the various student newspapers from most of the other universities, as we all sent copies to each other, and did a little round-up of what was happening elsewhere. I remember reading *Varsity* and for the first time chancing on a column which was being written by someone called Michael Frayn. It was so totally brilliant, clever, witty, original it rather depressed me. How could a mere student, of my age presumably, write so well? It made me realise that Durham was not just an ivory tower, but a small, isolated, very amateurish one, cut off from the real world, and from all the real talent.

Meanwhile, Margaret took the Oxbridge entrance exams – and was awarded a scholarship to Somerville College, Oxford. In those days, a lot of the big, famous Northern grammar schools were able to enter for what were known as closed scholarships, limited to certain schools, but Margaret had won an open scholarship, meaning it was open to any school, anywhere. She had also won an award at Girton College, Cambridge. She chose the Oxford one because Girton had seemed gloomy, Gothic, and she didn't like the food.

She left school at Christmas and then went off to France as an au pair in Bordeaux. Oxford had told her she must improve her French, if she wanted to read History. She started at Oxford in the autumn of 1957, while I was still at Durham. We wrote all the time, but I was more than convinced someone would come along and whisk her away.

I hitchhiked down to Oxford from Durham as often as I could. Everyone hitchhiked in those days. In a previous long vac, I had hitchhiked round France and Germany with my room-mate from Durham, John Davies. We were aiming for Tübingen where a German student we had become friendly with at Durham was now studying. We got to Tübingen, found the address we were given. He wasn't there, so we turned round, and hitchhiked straight back to England. Moving was the thing, experiencing new places, rather than the arrival.

When I hitchhiked down to see Margaret in Oxford, I slept on the floor of Mike Thornhill's room in Balliol. In those days, women could not entertain male friends after a certain time. One evening, I overstayed by an hour or two, forgetting the time, while visiting Margaret at her room in Somerville. I realised I would be seen leaving through the college main entrance, which at that time of night was the only way in or out. I could try and climb a wall, but that would be dangerous. I could stay the whole night, and leave the next morning during normal visiting hours, but that could also be risky. We decided the best way to leave and not be noticed or apprehended was through the front lodge – disguised as a woman.

I rolled up my trousers, put on Margaret's coat, wrapped her college scarf round my neck and walked boldly through the lodge gateway. I went up Woodstock Road and then turned into an alleyway and rolled down my trousers, took off Margaret's Somerville scarf. There was a couple in the alleyway, in a heavy clinch, and I could see the man had been watching me. What I didn't know was that the bloke kissing the girl goodnight was the editor of *Cherwell*, the Oxford student newspaper. He'd noticed my hairy legs and realised what I must have been doing, so ran a story about a man escaping from Somerville, disguised as a woman. He didn't know Margaret's name, but later in the week, some kind person at Somerville must have told him or let it slip. This time he flogged the story to the *Daily Sketch*, a popular tabloid, later bought out by the *Daily Mail*. When this story appeared, Margaret was hauled up before the Principal of Somerville, Dame Janet Vaughan, for bringing the good name of the college into disrepute. Margaret got gated for the rest of the term. It was near the end of term, so that wasn't too worrying.

On my visits to Oxford, when I met her with her chums, especially male chums, I got all chippy and twisted. She became for a while an actress at Oxford, starring in *The Caucasian Chalk Circle* with Dennis Potter. I became convinced I was being looked down upon by some of these bright, clever Oxford types because I was only at a provincial university. It was all in my head; they didn't actually care, if they were even aware of me, but that was how I felt for a while. Very silly.

I decided to stay on for a fourth year at Durham, for various reasons, none of them very logical. I wanted to avoid National Service, that was one reason. When my call-up papers did come, I got my Carlisle doctor to send proof of the awful asthma I had always suffered from. I did have a medical test – and failed it. So I didn't need a fourth year after all.

What I decided to do in that year was a postgraduate Diploma of Education, the thinking being that it would give me some sort of qualification. I still had nothing fixed up in the way of a job or training, so at least I could be a teacher, if nothing else turned up. And it would please my mum.

I also thought that as Margaret was still at Oxford, having another year as a student would somehow fit in with her life better, our holidays would coincide, it would be easier to be together.

But probably the main reason was that I wanted to continue as editor of *Palatinate* – which I thought would give me a better chance of finding out if I wanted to be a real journalist. And also perhaps discover how you went about it.

The Appointments Board at Durham seemed pretty dopey, as most university appointments boards were and probably still are, full of jobsworths, who don't know how to get a proper job themselves. The person I saw had had no experience of anyone from Durham going on to be a journalist and didn't seem able to help me. I did find out, though, that an ex-student from my own college, so one of the Castle dons told me, had been an editor of *Palatinate* about six years previously and had gone on to get a job in journalism. This was a bloke called Harry Evans, but no one knew where he was now working.

Through a friend on the local newspaper, the *Durham Advertiser*, an Oxford graduate called Michael Bateman with whom I had organised skiffle parties, I discovered that two national newspaper groups had graduate trainee schemes. One was the Westminster Press, which he had joined, and the other was Kemsley Newspapers, which was the better one, owners of *The Sunday Times* in London and lots of big provincial dailies and evening papers. I decided to send off applications for both, with my cuttings from *Palatinate* and the *Carlisle Journal.*

I didn't know whether either would come off, so through the Appointments Board I also applied for the usual milk-round type jobs, mostly management training schemes, one of which resulted in an interview with a firm called Benzole. I had always thought the name was made up purely for the sake of a schoolboy joke. 'She was only a garage man's daughter, but she loved the smell of Benzole.' Benzole was a big oil firm, with plush offices in Newcastle. I went for the interview – and was turned down flat.

During my last year at Durham, I was elected Senior Man. It meant I was President of the Junior Common Room of my college, a position I was very proud of, and still am, though Margaret mocked the title all the time. And still does. It meant I got better rooms, a set on the Norman Gallery, and a sherry allowance, for entertaining visitors.

In Carlisle, during the summer of 1958, there was great excitement for the arrival of the Queen to celebrate Carlisle's octocentenary. Its first Royal Charter had been granted by Henry II in 1158 and there had been scores of special events going on all year. For the celebrations, I had a small but very enjoyable role. I was asked to edit *Octopie*, a student magazine, a bit like a rag mag, with all proceeds going to charity, which was to be produced by Carlisle students as their contribution to the octocentenary celebrations.

I amused myself by doing a parody of the *Cumberland News*, calling it the *Cumberland Spews*. I did a mock-up of its front page, making up silly news stories, getting my own back on them for not offering me a job. I included joke classified adverts, on the lines of many you saw in Cumbrian papers at the time. The *Cumberland News* always had lots of vacancies for 'Strong Lad Wanted' or 'Experienced Lad', so naturally I turned it into 'Strong Lad Wanted For Strong Lass' or 'Experienced Lad Wanted For Experienced Lass'. Another one said 'Cowman wanted at Candlemas – bring own cow and candle'. Well, it amused us at the time.

The Queen's visit, the culmination of the octo celebrations, and the focal point of six months of preparations, was timed for 11 July 1958. That morning, the Duke of Edinburgh, who had already arrived, announced from the Town Hall that the Queen had been taken ill and had gone straight on to London. You could hear the groans from the thousands of people who had already gathered in the streets of Carlisle. The Queen did return, some time later, but it wasn't quite the same. I didn't see her, as I wasn't in Carlisle by then. I had been accepted by both the newspaper training schemes I had applied for and had chosen the Kemsley one.

I still treasure the letter sent to me by the news editor of the paper I was going to in August 1958, confirming my appointment and saying I would be on a salary of £14 a week. It seemed an enormous amount. When I showed the letter to my father, he said it was more than he'd ever got in the whole of his working life at 14 MU. My mother was pleased, but apprehensive, thinking journalism was not a proper job, it had no security, but at least I would have teaching to fall back on. And so in the autumn of 1958 I cleared out my few things from my half of our bedroom in Caird Avenue and left Carlisle for ever.

Chapter Twelve

Manchester, Cyprus and Carlisle

I started work on the *Manchester Evening Chronicle* on 1 September 1958. Its offices were in Withy Grove and the building was the biggest newspaper printing plant in Europe, perhaps the world. Over 10 million copies a week of up to twelve different papers were produced there. They included all the Northern editions of the national papers owned by Kemsley which a year later, in 1959, became Thomson Newspapers – such as *The Sunday Times, Empire News, Sunday Graphic, Daily Sketch, Sporting Chronicle*. They also produced the Northern editions of the *Daily Telegraph, Daily Mirror, Sunday Mirror*. Over 4,000 people worked in the building. Night and day, it never slept. The *Evening Chronicle* itself, so it said on the paper's masthead, had 1 million readers every evening.

I was overwhelmed by the building and by Manchester itself, compared with Carlisle, which wasn't surprising, as, at the age of twenty-two, I had not been further south than Penrith. A slight exaggeration, of course, and one I frequently came out with. But in essence it was true.

One of the minor things I had to get used to in Manchester was their use of the words 'North West'. When I first saw it as a headline in the Chron, on the lines of 'Family from North West

Lost in Spain' or 'North West Couple Wins Pools', I thought, Oh, that's interesting, they've got a story about someone from Cumberland, perhaps from Carlisle, but of course it never was. We in Cumbria consider the North West to mean Cumbria, where we live, which is clear enough to any fool looking at the map of England, but to media folks based in Manchester, the North West stretched from about Stoke to Scotland.

I had never been to Manchester before, didn't know one district from another, so from a map of the city I picked a flat as near as I could to the office, in order to get to work quickly. It was in Cheetham Hill which turned out a real dump, full of run-down raincoat factories. I called it a flat, but it was just a room on the ground floor at the front of an old terrace house with a kitchen in an alcove. I shared a bathroom with the other people in the house.

Margaret stayed with me there, when she came to visit, but of course I had to keep this secret from the landlord. I had taken it as a single man. If I had said it was for two, I would have had to prove I was married. Even in a run-down area, landlords wouldn't let places to unmarried people in the 1950s.

One day, when we were in bed together, we thought we heard the landlord arriving for his rent. I jumped out while Margaret hid in the wardrobe. I stood in front of the bed, hoping to hide any signs of her presence, and handed over the rent to the landlord. As I did so, the bed, which was just a battered let-you-down couch, decided to put itself up, jack-knifing together, giving Margaret, still hiding in the wardrobe, a terrible fright.

The *Evening Chron* was in deadly rivalry with the *Evening News* which was owned by the *Guardian*. I used to meet some of their reporters on jobs and one day, covering some story at Manchester University, I met Harry Evans, the journalist I'd been told about, who had been at the same Durham college as me, a few years earlier. He was now personal assistant to the editor of the *Evening News*.

He came for supper one evening in my so-called flat, with his wife Enid, also from Durham. Margaret was staying with me at the time, otherwise I would never have attempted any sort of entertaining. She made the room as attractive as possible, with candles and soft lights. She cooked fresh herring coated in oatmeal, very 1950s. Harry took one look at the fish and became worried about getting bones in his mouth. Suddenly he jumped up and switched on all the lights, and revealed the full horrors of the room.

I was officially a graduate trainee, but there was no training, as such, not like today with one- and two-year full-time postgraduate media courses. I was supposed to learn shorthand and paid half-a-crown a week to go to lessons in the front room of an elderly woman's house in Cheetham, along with six schoolgirls of about fifteen who were miles better than me. I gave up, after about six weeks, but no one at the office seemed to notice. I had acquired a few gramalogues by then, and made up my own, or pretended to. I found I could get down most things that mattered, writing very quickly, with my own abbreviations, as long as I typed them up as soon as possible. The shape of the words or squiggles on the page brought back the sound of the person speaking. But if I let a day go by, my notes became meaningless.

For the first few weeks, I wasn't allowed out on my own. Instead, I shadowed a senior reporter, Barry Cockcroft. He had gone to Manchester Grammar School, which I'd never heard of, but he was very proud of it and wore their tie all the time. It did seem to help him on stories.

I was in awe of Barry's skills. We would go on a fire or a road accident or perhaps even a murder and Barry would speak to the chief policeman, the fire boss, a couple of witnesses, languidly writing down a few of their quotes in his reporter's notebook – then he would go straight into a telephone booth and dictate a 600-word story that made total sense, all out of his head, without having written anything down. How on earth did he do it? He must be a genius, or have gifts I'm never going to acquire.

Even when I was eventually allowed out on minor stories on

my own, I couldn't do them as well as Barry. I would crouch behind the telephone box, trying to think of a good intro, laboriously writing out my story. Eventually, after an hour or so, I'd ring the office and get a bollocking for having missed the Eccles and the Wigan slips.

In due course, I realised Barry's trick. He actually had only five intros, standard forms of beginnings which he could fit to suit almost any accident or crime story. Having got the story running, on formulaic lines, he just read out his best quotes from his notes.

The first story I got in the paper, written by me, though without my by-line, as they were a very rare occurrence, was headlined CRUMPSALL VANDALS STRIKE AGAIN. It was about two broken panes in a greenhouse on an allotment. It only made the first edition, in Crumpsall, but I carefully cut it out for my cuttings book which I had bought on my first day. I told myself I'd need it when Fleet Street editors started ringing.

One day I wrote what I thought was an amusing intro to a flower show report and miraculously, my clever intro had not been cut, which it usually was. When the first edition came out, and I was beaming with pride, I was taken to task by Mac, a very senior, grizzled reporter who sat next to me. He said I should stop trying to be a smart arse. He then gave me a lecture on news journalism, saying that with things like flower shows, all the reader wanted was the list of winners.

All the reporters sat at a long, wooden table, each with our own sit-up-and-beg manual typewriter. That did impress me. On *Palatinate*, we had one typewriter between the whole office. On my other side sat Beryl who was the fastest typist I had ever known. She hardly left the office and tended to be stuck knocking supplements into shape. I couldn't understand why anyone so clearly talented and quick was content to do the same old stuff. I was also surprised when it turned out she was a Cambridge graduate. Where had her ambition gone?

The Chron reporters had in fact a surprisingly good opinion of themselves. They considered they were on a par with Fleet

Street, or at least the Northern editions of the Fleet Street papers. Some of them had actually worked in London, but had returned to Manchester. Most of them, unlike me, had worked their way up from purely local, weekly papers, in different parts of the country. Reaching the Chron was a sign of their success.

On stories, we were competing with the national papers, as well as the *Evening News*. Now and again I could meet, or at least admire from afar in press conferences various *Guardian* reporters, such as Terry Coleman. I longed to have their freedom, be able to write offbeat intros and not worry about lists of names and correct ages. Our news desk would send you back if you had missed out someone's age. And if you said they were called John Smith, you had to check the spelling of John and also Smith. You must never assume the conventional spelling. It could be Jon Smythe.

The news editor, Bob Walker, was a kindly, grey-haired gent who addressed all reporters as Mr. But his deputy was an absolute bastard, Harold Mellor. He used to scare the shit out of me, bawling out my name, throwing my copy in the air, shouting abuse. It was clear he hated graduates, especially any trying to be clever and, worst of all, one who couldn't spell. He did love that, being able to ridicule my spelling in the office, pouring scorn on graduates. It's not that I can't spell, OK I can't, but I am in such a hurry, trying to get down my thoughts as quickly as possible, that I don't worry about boring things like spelling. If I concentrate, I can usually get someone's name right the first time. Next time, it's likely to come out different because I can't be bothered to go back and see how I spelled it first time.

During the day, the Chron had about five or six slip editions, with special pages and stories for readers in Warrington or Wigan or wherever. They came out roughly on the hour and if you had copy for one of them, and missed it, you were for it.

On big stories, like a murder, on which you might be stuck all day, following progress, looking for angles, you would go round witnesses saying, 'Anyone here from Wigan?' You'd then hope to be able to work in a local quote for the Wigan slip. An hour later, you wouldn't care a toss about anyone from Wigan. You were now looking for an Eccles angle.

In the office, on big news stories, there would be a line-up of copy boys, who were hardly boys, more like elderly men, who would rush off with your story, par by par, sometimes sentence by sentence, and run with it to the linotype room.

It did feel exciting, and I told myself I was a real journalist, but at the same time, there wasn't the fun of *Palatinate*, being involved in all aspects of the paper. I didn't really know what was going on outside the newsroom. I knew we had feature pages, and feature writers, but didn't know who they were or where they sat.

I used to catch sight of our two football reporters, one who covered Manchester United, Keith Dewhurst, and Ray Wergan who covered Man City, putting on their white raincoats with the collars turned up, on their way to games. I envied them so much. How I longed to be a football reporter, and to have a white raincoat.

One day, Harold Mellor called me in and said he was sending me to Old Trafford, for the big derby, City versus Man Utd. My little heart gave a flutter. At last, I was going to be taken off dreary news stories and endless hours doing the Calls – which meant each morning ringing round the local hospitals, police and fire stations, to check up on running stories and to find out if anything had happened in the night.

I was even allowed to be driven to Old Trafford in an office car, as opposed to going on the bus, which you took for minor stories. That proved I was on a big story. But I never got inside Old Trafford, or saw the game. My job was to do a colour piece, interviewing the crowds *outside*, before and after the game.

After about two months which seemed to have lasted two years, in November 1958, I was told I had to see the editor, John Goulden. I had never talked to him or seen him since my first day, when he'd given me a brief welcoming chat. I was sure he had no idea how I was getting on, or even knew of my existence. The training scheme was of course a nonsense. All it did was give you a start, then you were on your own.

He told me I was being sent to Cyprus, on an RAF plane. I thought at first I had mis-heard. It must be a suburb of Manchester I didn't know about, perhaps near Crumpsall, so why would I go there on a plane?

Cyprus had been in the news for months, not that I had followed it closely. It was the time of the EOKA terrorists, trying to chuck out the British and get independence. Most days there was some new atrocity with snipers, gun battles, bombs left on army premises, trying to kill our brave lads. The latest had been seven airmen killed when a bomb had gone off in the Naafi in Nicosia.

One of the regiments out there, trying to keep the peace, was the Lancashire Fusiliers, the local Manchester regiment. The RAF was offering to send an *Evening Chronicle* reporter, and one from the *Evening News*, to live with the Fusiliers, report on what life was like out there, what a good job they were doing.

I was thrilled to be picked, seeing it as a huge honour. The editor must have been monitoring my progress after all. I had never been on a plane before, or travelled anywhere as far away as Cyprus. What a change from broken window panes.

One of the senior reporters rather brought me down to earth by pointing out that I had been chosen because I was young and single with no commitments. They wouldn't want to send a married man with children, would they? When I told Margaret the news, and also what the old reporter had said, she said it was probably true. So why did I want to go if it was dangerous? It had never for one moment occurred to me to turn it down. Overnight, I could already see myself as an ace foreign correspondent.

For several weeks before I went, we ran a feature in the Chron – with my photograph, the first time ever on a story, oh rapture – saying I was going out to Cyprus, to stay with the Fusiliers, and I would personally take out letters, by hand, and give them to loved ones. It was a smart move, which the *Evening News* hadn't thought of, and we were inundated with letters.

The reporter from the *Evening News* was Brian Hitchen, about the same age as me, also single. He wasn't a graduate and had worked his way up from being a copy boy, but he was very smart and smooth, much better dressed than me, wearing hound's-tooth suits and a jaunty trilby. He also beat me to the first story. The plane out to Cyprus, which was an RAF transport plane, taking out troops, ran into a thunderstorm. It had basic fittings, no soft furnishings or padded seats, in order to carry troops and gear, so the noise on the bare metal was frightening as we got lashed by the storm and objects were thrown around. Brian filed his first story the minute we arrived – about our brave troops escaping death in a freak, nightmare thunderstorm. I copied him, although I hadn't even seen it as a story.

In Cyprus, outside Nicosia, we lived under canvas with the troops, amongst the officers, with our own tent and batman, eating our meals in the officers' mess. We were offered our own revolver each, in case we needed it, but we both refused. There were several serious pissheads amongst the officers, knocking back the whisky sours all evening, which made the dinners very entertaining, a bit like being back at Durham.

I went on several early morning 'soft-shoe patrols', through the back streets of Nicosia, all the soldiers heavily armed, but keeping very quiet. They did wear soft shoes, not normal army boots, in order to spot any snipers or bomb makers. It was similar to the scenes we later all got used to seeing in the streets of Belfast, British soldiers guarding each other at street corners, ducking into doorways and behind walls. I didn't like getting up so early, but it made good copy. During the time we were there, more British servicemen were attacked and killed, but I don't remember ever feeling scared.

For years I used to boast that I had been a war correspondent, seen service at the front, oh yes, which was technically true. I tried to give the impression I'd had a long spell of duty, but now I look back at my cuttings, and my diaries, I see we were actually out there for only two weeks. It seemed so much longer.

On my return, I got called to London, to the Gray's Inn Road headquarters of the Kemsley empire, where I saw Jimmy Fraser, who had interviewed me the previous year, when I became a graduate trainee. He congratulated me on the Cyprus stories and said *The Sunday Times* was thinking of sending a staff man to Johannesburg. Everyone expected there was going to be a bloodbath in South Africa, so it would be useful to have someone permanently out there. They were looking for a single man, no commitments, with a bit of experience of foreign reporting.

I came back very excited and rang Margaret in Oxford. She wasn't at all impressed. She certainly wouldn't want to live in South Africa. Then there was silence. No word at all from London, or from Mr Goulden. I badgered his secretary, saying I was expecting an urgent message from the London office, which might come when I was out in Crumpsall on a job.

I soon began to forget all about it, till one day I got called in by Bob Walker, the news editor. I was being moved, to a new position, in a new office. Could this be Jo'burg, as I'd already learned to call it? Not quite. I was being sent to Wigan, to work in the Chron's branch office, writing full time for the Wigan slip edition.

I felt this was a terrible demotion. I might mock the reporters on the news desk for thinking they were big-time Fleet Streeters, but in Withy Grove, you did feel at the heart of things, handling big stories, shouting 'Hold the front page', whereas out in the sticks you only did piddling church fetes and swimming awards.

One of the things I had to do, when I moved to Wigan, was cover Wigan magistrates' courts where suddenly my lack of real shorthand proved a definite handicap. The old sweats, local freelances who had sat in the court for decades, were very unhelpful.

After a few weeks, I was beginning to wonder if I would be stuck in Wigan for ever. Should I perhaps move there, find a flat or a room which would be handier for the office and save me travelling each day from Manchester on the local train?

I had moved, after about three months in Manchester, from my horrible flat in Cheetham Hill, which Margaret had hated so much, into a much superior one in Daisy Bank Road, not far from the University and the Grammar School.

When Margaret came from Oxford to stay with me for weekends, she worked hard, painting and decorating the flat, making it very presentable. When she stayed for longer periods, such as the long vacation, she couldn't of course tell her parents where she was and what she was doing, even though she was by then aged twenty and we had been going out together for about three years.

Some of her well-off girlfriends from Oxford were spending their hols in exotic places in Europe, like Venice, Florence and Rome. She told her parents she had been invited to go along with one of them, staying at their family holiday home in Italy. She wrote a series of letters to her parents from each of these places, with different dates, describing the different places. Her girlfriends duly posted them to Carlisle on the correct dates. Margaret meanwhile was in a sunny Daisy Bank Road with me.

Sounds daft now, and very complicated, but it worked and kept her mother happy. It has always made me wonder, when you read biographies of famous people, if letters supposedly written at a certain time from a certain place were in fact true or perhaps a cover for something we will never know about.

At Christmas times, we both usually went home to Carlisle for a short spell, to stay with our respective parents. I slept with my brother Johnny in our shared bed, as I had always done when I lived at home. On one occasion, on returning home unexpectedly, while I was still at Durham, I found someone else in my bed. My mother had let out my half of the bed to a boy from a local children's home.

My mother also had a long sequence of French assistants, male and female, who had secured teaching jobs at the Grammar School and came to live with my mother for up to a year at a time. They all seemed to be called either Michel or Michelle.

What was strange about these French teachers, at least to me at the time, is that they absolutely adored Carlisle, finding it exciting and exotic, even living in our council house in Caird Avenue. Years later, they often returned to Carlisle for their holidays, with their own families. We are still in touch with two of them, even now. One is a well-known French academic author.

During my stay in Carlisle in the Christmas of 1958, I had noticed that my father was very ill. He was still in the front parlour, bedridden through his multiple sclerosis, but he had now developed a very bad cold. On the night of 27 December, just after all the Christmas festivities, I could hear my mother coming quietly into my bedroom. She said 'Shush, don't move, don't get up', and she went to a chest of drawers and got out a clean white sheet.

I turned over and went to sleep, but subconsciously I knew what that must mean. When I got up in the morning, my father had died. On his death certificate, the official cause of death was pneumonia.

As the oldest child, and fortunately being at home at the time, I did all the official business, going to register his death and the assorted paperwork. We had the funeral tea at our house, in Caird Avenue, and all his Scottish relations came, as well as Margaret who helped my sisters make the sandwiches. It was miserable weather, and a miserable occasion, right in the middle of that dead time between Christmas and the New Year.

He was buried in Carlisle cemetery, up at the top end, past all the graves of the wartime servicemen. He was aged only fifty-two. On his gravestone, his age is given as fifty-three, but this is a mistake, my mother never being reliable on dates.

It seemed quite old to me at the time, but now I realise how young he was, cut off by illness, well before his prime. Since I turned fifty-two, I have been counting every year as a bonus. Which I still do.

Chapter Thirteen

Hello London

I moved to London in the summer of 1959. It just seemed to happen, like going to the Grammar School, going to Durham. I can't remember applying, or having any interviews, waiting and wondering, thinking had I got in, had I been taken on? One day, instead of going to the *Manchester Evening Chronicle*'s office in Wigan I turned up for work on the *Sunday Graphic* at 200 Gray's Inn Road, London.

Manchester still looms large in my mind, memories of people and places often flood back after all these years, and yet I was there only nine months. There are much longer periods of my life from which I can recall almost nothing. Biographers always find this, especially if they are biographising a living person. The past seems to be bigger, closer, the further they get from it. While last year is à blur, the person's early years remain totally vivid.

Technically, I was in Fleet Street, working on a national newspaper, but the *Sunday Graphic* is not one that anyone has heard of today. At the time, I knew of its existence, just, but had never read it.

The *Sunday Graphic* was one of Kemsley Newspapers' three Sundays – the others being *The Sunday Times* and the *Empire News*, all of them with their London HQ in Gray's Inn Road. The *Graphic* was a tabloid, while the other two were broadsheets, but not of the sensational, scandal-mongering type. It didn't do sex

stories, unfrocked vicars or naughty boy scout leaders, but it did
do its fair share of sentimental stories about a little girl weeping
for her dead mother, her lost aunty, even just her missing pet
dog, if the child was attractive enough and the picture suitably
heart-breaking. It was safe and homely, a bit like the *Sunday Post*,
still going strong in Scotland, which has always managed to exist
without getting the boot in or the tits out.

I was aged only twenty-three, so there was some trouble from
the union, the NUJ, still incredibly strong in those days, as you
were supposed to be twenty-four to be on the staff of a Fleet
Street paper, but that was sorted out.

My main concern in the first few weeks was finding somewhere
to live. I had arrived so suddenly that I had nowhere to stay. At
Euston, when I got off the train, all I had was a scrap of paper and
an address in Archway. The day before I had rung Squire
Barraclough who worked at Kemsley House on the London desk
for the regional papers and had earlier been in Manchester on
the Chron. I hadn't been able to think of a single other person I
knew in London. Squire had kindly said that if I was stuck, I could
sleep on his sofa for the night. I didn't really know Squire
Barraclough, and I'm not sure I'd even met him before in
Manchester, but I knew his name, how could I not? When I'd first
heard it, I immediately thought what a brilliant by-line.

My previous visits to London had always been day trips, in and
out, so it was a totally foreign city to me. In every way. It smelled
different from Manchester, so much hotter, richer, more exotic.
The cockney accents, for they all seemed to speak cockney to my
ears, were like stage accents, the sort I had only ever heard on
the radio. Everyone seemed so confident, cocky, smart,
knowledgeable, whereas I felt Northern and lumpen.

Squire had a ground-floor flat in a long street of Victorian
terrace houses behind Archway Road. He shared it with another
journalist. I slept on their sofa, in their only living room, folding
up the sofa each morning as neatly as possible, putting my things
behind it, out of sight, trying not to be a bother or interrupt
their normal life too much.

I stayed there for at least two weeks, feeling guilty, as I'd only been offered the sofa for one night. I don't remember eating with them, as each evening after work I went trailing round the whole of London, looking for a place to rent. One Sunday lunch time, they took me for a drink to a very smart pub in Highgate village where they went every Sunday. The barmen knew them. They seemed to know how London worked, to be in touch, to know where places were, what Tube lines to get. I wondered if I would ever cope, far less find a place of my own.

I learned that you had to get the first edition of the *Evening Standard* and then ring every likely-sounding flat at once, or it had gone. I didn't know one district of London from another. Even with the famous places whose names I was aware of from the Monopoly board, such as Mayfair or Pentonville, I didn't know where they were in relation to the rest of London.

On arriving in Manchester, I had wanted anything, anywhere, as near to the office as possible, not realising I had picked a dump in a crummy area. In London, I decided I wanted a self-contained flat, with my own front door, so that when Margaret was visiting me, we'd have a bit of privacy. I wanted to be roughly in North London, for no logical reason, except that people from the North of England tend traditionally to settle in North London, landing at Euston or King's Cross.

I had picked up that Hampstead was nice and desirable but all the flats there were out of my range. So I began looking at adjacent areas. I was thrilled when I did finally find something suitable – at 6a Kingscroft Road, NW2, just off Shoot-up Hill, near Kilburn High Road, but in quite a suburban street. The flat was half of a semi which had been converted. I had the upper flat, and my own front door, with a bedroom, living room, k and b. It was nicely furnished, with a light cream fitted carpet, quite smart, so it seemed to me. It was the cream carpet, fitted throughout, that did it. I had never seen a house like that before. I would be able to walk around with bare feet all the time. Something you could never do with linoleum.

The landlord was a Polish gentleman who lived somewhere

else across London and he was very strict about taking up my references and making me sign forms. On 19 June 1959, for I still have the signed receipt, I paid him a £25 deposit, to cover furniture and fittings. The money would be returned at the end of the tenancy, if I had not damaged anything.

I was thrilled to have found such a nice flat and couldn't wait for Margaret's first visit, to show it off. Now I look at that receipt again, I see it is addressed to Mr and Mrs Davies. I must have lied and said we were married. I didn't want to get into all the complications I'd had in Manchester.

Margaret hated the flat the moment she saw it. She said it was poky, suburban, the sort of nasty little semi we'd come from Carlisle to escape. What on earth was I thinking of? Ugh. Horrible. I was so upset. She does tend to give her opinions very strongly, whether asked for them or not. I told her about the agonies and hours I had put in, trailing round London after work, when I was already exhausted. She should have seen the dumps I didn't take. This was by far the best I had seen. Easy for her to criticise, oh yes, she should have gone through all I'd gone through, she should be grateful, very pleased, not having a go at me. Then I slammed the door and went into the bedroom to sulk.

The rent was £6 a week, normal for the time, for such a flat, and I could quite easily afford it on my £20 a week wages. Out of my very first week's money, I sent £2, in cash, to my mother. I have to admit that it was Margaret who insisted. In Manchester, I hadn't had much spare money, on my £14 a week, but now I was so much better off, so Margaret maintained. I should help my mother, who had no income, after all she had done for me. At first I'd said yeah, good idea, but er let's wait a year, see how it goes, London is more expensive than Manchester. Margaret said no. Do it now, or I never would. And so I sent my mother £2 a week from then on. I sent it in cash, with my weekly letter to her, and never once did the letter or the money get lost.

I was even better off than I had expected because I discovered I could claim generous expenses. That was the first thing that was explained to me on my very first day, not by the management but by the other reporters. I had never had regular expenses before. On the *Evening Chron*, we had got none, apart from bus fares. The notion of 'entertaining contacts' or 'social expenses' when reporting a street accident or a broken window pane in Crumpsall would have had Harold Mellor hitting the roof.

Staff spent the whole of Tuesday morning each week, the first day of a Sunday paper's week, filling out their exes, then they would go for lunch, exhausted, for some the hardest part of their week over. I was told what I should aim for, given my lowly status on the paper, which was around £5 a week. All I had to do was submit bills for lunch or dinner, with anyone, anywhere, it didn't matter, as long as I had a piece of paper and could name someone who might or not be a contact. Just make sure the total came to around £5 each week. It did seem a bit immoral. I was told the management knew, it was an accepted part of Fleet Street life. Everyone did it. If you didn't, you would muck up the system. And of course be very, very stupid, turning away free money, in cash, non taxed.

If of course you did a big story, travelled somewhere, stayed overnight, ran up genuine bills and, best of all, got a story in the paper, then you could charge almost anything. If of course I ever got to do any big stories.

For the first few weeks, all I did was follow up stories. The news editor, John Relph, would hand me a clipping from a national or more often a local paper and ask me to find a new angle. Most of his ideas, so I thought, were pretty pointless. I spent one whole day in an office car, with an office driver, going up and down a busy main road in South London, near Kingston, because new road markings had come in, double red lines, to indicate you could never park. I prided myself on being able to flam up trivia, get 500 words out of a brick if I had to, but I could see absolutely no story in these new road markings – certainly not a story written on a flat Tuesday which could possibly last and make the paper on Sunday.

The atmosphere in the office was very laid back and relaxed. No one shouted at you or bollocked you for a mistake. In fact it was positively soporific for most of the week, till Friday and Saturday when gangs of freelance subs appeared and there would be a bit more noise and excitement.

There were two other male reporters, a couple of years older than me, who had worked their way through the provincial papers, who did hard news, and three women reporters who did more feature, colour stuff. The oldest of them was Dorothy Harrison, probably aged about fifty at the time, who took me under her wing and was very kind, encouraging and helpful. I often had lunch with her, in the pub, but I never found out much about her personal life, whether she had been married, where she lived, or who with. She wore a lot of make-up, strong perfume and rather flowing, colourful clothes. I imagined she must have been very attractive and voluptuous in her day, and probably still was. At twenty-three, I didn't see her that way but as a motherly, elderly figure.

Almost from the moment I arrived on the *Graphic* I heard rumours about its impending closure. Dorothy was full of doom, it would be the end for her, she'd never get another job, not at her age, but it would be all right for me, so she always insisted. I'd survive, I would be looked after, I would do well, she could see it. She didn't say this bitterly or in a resentful way. It was as if she knew something I didn't know.

Although the office was friendly and relaxed, I slowly discovered a subtle men-and-officer division. We reporters, men and women, were the lower ranks, and somehow we looked it, in our clothes and social status. Then there were a group of officer types, such as Robert Robinson who did the films, Peter Wilsher who did the serious stories and Terence Feeley who was features editor. He wore immaculate clothes, cut-away white collars with a blue shirt and a rose in his buttonhole. He later became a successful playwright. All of them seemed superior beings, cleverer, more polished, more artistic, as if they were doing the *Graphic* a favour, just by being there. On the *Evening Chron*, there had been none of this division. Everyone seemed much the same, socially, intellectually, and everyone dressed and talked with the same sort of accent.

I was pretty useless at any sort of news stories, never quite taking seriously the things others got excited about, such as finding a new piddling fact and beating the opposition. I wanted to write, not report. There is a famous C. P. Scott saying, which all young reporters were taught, and probably still are, stating that 'comment is free but facts are sacred'. I never went along with this. Personally I think facts are cheap. Hire enough reporters and you'll get loads of facts. Getting a good, interesting, well-argued opinion, or an offbeat feature, or a good interview with someone interesting, that's what takes real skill and talent. Good features are what I most want to read in any newspaper, not news. Fortunately, the way the media has developed, news has taken second place unless there's a mega, national dramatic news shock-horror event. Mostly, so-called news pages are filled with disguised cod surveys for some product or company, or a minor celebrity-PR-created non-story. Consider the enormous salaries that star columnists, from Richard Littlejohn to Simon Jenkins, can now command. They show that opinons are certainly not cheap today.

I wrote one news story which did make the front page – and of course enormous expenses for me. Sometime in April 1960, we got a tip that Princess Margaret and Tony Armstrong-Jones were going to spend part of their honeymoon on HMS *Britannia*. No announcement had yet been made. Buckingham Palace would not confirm it. Despite this, I was sent down to Portsmouth to poke around for a few days, see if I could pick up any local rumours. I managed to track down some of the crew, and it became clear from the way they talked, and certain hush-hush arrangements being made, that it was more than likely. I got some good quotes, which appeared to stand up the story, and lots of colour about life on the *Britannia*, and we led the paper on it. Luckily, it all turned out to be true.

After about six months on the paper, I found myself given my own by-lined column. It wasn't quite as glamorous or prestigious as it sounds. For a start, the by-line wasn't mine. I had become Peter Raymond, a hard-hitting interviewer, friend of the stars, so the strap-line asserted, who would pull no punches in asking questions of the famous in a major new series – NOTHING BUT THE TRUTH – by Peter Raymond.

The format was a simple question and answer. Easy enough to do, no writing required. It's been used since journalism began and still gets trundled out, in its various forms. Papers with few staff and small budgets love it. They usually make it even cheaper by getting readers to ask the questions.

The only celebs I could ever get to cooperate were faded or pathetic or unknown. Few big stars of the day could be bothered spending time talking to the *Sunday Graphic* and the questions I had to ask, mostly thought up by Terence, were equally pathetic and soft, such as 'What's your favourite meal, favourite film, happiest moment?' I was pretty ashamed of the whole format. I didn't normally even meet the stars, but either spoke to them on the phone or their press assistants filled in the replies.

But I was in Fleet Street. I was still only twenty-four. I had even been to El Vino's and ogled the quality. And I had my own flat, which I thought, even if a certain person didn't, wasn't bad really, in fact it was quite nice, considering.

Chapter Fourteen

Marriage

We always had rows, ever since we met, violent arguments over really silly things, who said what, who was to blame, who started it. It very often ended in screams and shouts, from her, not me, as I never lose my temper, well, that's my image of myself, and she would storm off, accusing me of being stupid or crass, or never listening or being insensitive. Or it would end with me, not shouting, but sulking, going off and into my shell.

I had never met anyone before who got so worked up over what I thought were purely mundane problems and decisions – or anyone with such a clear, logical mind, who analysed everything, who could work out motives, what other people were thinking, what was most likely to happen, and usually coming to the worst possible, pessimistic, awful conclusions. It all made sense, the way she saw things. Intellectually she could always persuade me her dire predictions were possible.

Yet I tended not to look ahead, to life in general, or even next week. And if I did, because Margaret forced it upon me, I was always sure things would work out, no need to worry, pet, don't fuss yourself. As personalities, we appeared so different, which was why our friends were sure it would never last.

But without making any conscious agreements or discussing it aloud, while courting in Carlisle we always tried to finish the evening as friends again. So we'd part with a few brief words, even if I still felt limp and exhausted, having been put through an emotional wringer. Next day, we started again, with a clean sheet, not bringing up the old arguments, though the new ones turned out to be surprisingly like the old ones.

One of her predictions was that she was bad for me, she brought me down, upset me, made me unhappy. Therefore, so she argued, it would never work, so we might as well part now rather than carrying on like this. It was very hard to argue against this, or deny it, when we'd just had a row. I'd either pooh-pooh it, saying she was getting it out of proportion. Or lie and say I quite liked arguments, really. I'd maintain I wasn't worried, not really, anyway it won't be like this in the future when we can properly live together and have a proper living life, i.e. sex and all that stuff.

A lot of the tensions in our early years did have a sexual element. Because, of course, we were not sleeping together, not in 1956, when we first started going out.

She had always said she didn't want to get married anyway, right from being a little girl, nor did she desire to have children. She didn't want to be responsible for bringing another human being into the world, which was such a terrible place anyway. She wanted to be free and independent, able to pursue her own career, whatever that turned out to be, not as her mother had done, devoting her life to her family.

As a little girl, she'd wanted to be a missionary. Later she wanted to be an MP. In the Sixth Form, there was a teacher who thought she should go to art college and be an artist, as she had such artistic gifts. Another suggested she should try for RADA, as she was always so good in the school plays. But mostly they had encouraged her towards Oxbridge. This was for the sake of the school as much as anything, to have an open scholarship up on the honours board in the hall for all to see.

At Oxford, she found she didn't have the academic bent which most others had presumed she had. She could do it, produce the flashing ideas and theories in tutorials, write brilliant essays, but her heart wasn't in it. She didn't really care.

And she also felt the constraints of writing essays in an ordained way – on the one hand, on the other, all very measured and dry – was running contrary to her natural flow and enthusiasm. With her contemporaries, she felt older, more mature, which was strange, as she had been nowhere, done nothing, compared with so many of them who had already travelled the world.

What was also interesting was her total classlessness. She had no chips on her shoulder, either way, as so many working-class Northern students had at the time. Me, for example. At Oxford, people like Dennis Potter were forever parading their leftie, working-class credentials, but Margaret didn't join in that game. She was equally at ease with the middle- and upper-class girls at Somerville, many of whom were from the best families and top schools.

So many of these well-bred girls from the very best schools were keen to be her friend, have her to tea, wanted to hear her opinion. There were also some, as there had been at school, who were a bit wary of her, not to say scared, knowing that her views and opinions and honesty could be devastating.

She kept on saying she didn't want to get married and I'd say, 'Yes, dear, who's asking you?' But as the years went on, it wasn't that we drifted into it, it just seemed to become inevitable, without us ever properly discussing it. Things like flats, in Manchester and London, and booking into seaside guesthouses, were made so much easier if you really were married.

At Durham, sex had not arrived, in fact it appeared non-existent. Philip Larkin said it didn't exist anywhere till after the Beatles' first LP, but at Oxford there were quite a lot of girls in the late 1950s sleeping with their boyfriends. The higher up the social and professional scale, the more enlightened their mothers would often be, dragging their darling daughters off to Harley Street to get fitted with a cap the moment they started at Oxford. They had all the contacts, and the knowledge and the money, unlike our parents in Carlisle.

I had no idea what a cap was, till one day Margaret told me that her best friend was using one. A Dutch cap, it was sometimes called, or more correctly a diaphragm. Sounded horrible. As for having to fit it in beforehand, coldly and calculatingly, ugh, how could a woman bear to do it?

Some time during her last year, Margaret decided to get fitted. Through the mother of a friend, she got an appointment with a woman called Helena Wright, one of the leading experts on female contraception. She went off to London for the day and got fitted. She hated the experience, didn't like the woman, finding her unpleasant, but at last she had done the deed.

Margaret was mortified next day, when Helena Wright herself rang up and said that Margaret owed her ten shillings. Margaret had not made the booking herself – it was done by the mother – and had not quite realised that the whole consultation was private, not part of the National Health.

Why hadn't I organised our contraceptive arrangements, taken the matter in hand, investigated and acquired some condoms? Behaved like a real man, in other words? Good questions.

Scared, I suppose. I still haven't used one in my whole life. Perhaps it was because I didn't trust myself not to make a mess of it, nor did Margaret. Anyway, that method did very often go wrong. The point about the diaphragm, so we were led to believe, was that it was foolproof, if you used it properly.

We got married on 11 June 1960, at Oxford Register Office. Margaret had finished her final exams but technically was still a student, until the end of term in a few days' time, so had to get permission from the college.

There were just two witnesses – Margaret's friend Theodora Parfitt and Mike Thornhill, our friend from Carlisle, who was still at Balliol. And that was all. No other persons were present, either at the register office or later. The four of us went to the Bear at Woodstock for lunch, then returned to Oxford, to Theo's family home in Northmoor Road, where we took some photos in the back garden amidst the roses. Just snaps, on a cheap camera.

I wore a suit, but not a new one, Italian-style with a squared-off jacket. Probably came from Cecil Gee in Oxford Street. It was thought very smart in 1960, for about half an hour. It was my only suit, which I wore to work, so it was becoming a bit shiny. But I did buy a new stiff Van Heusen white collar which killed my neck, it was so tight. My tie was also new. It was in blue silk and Margaret had chosen it for me.

Margaret wore, well, clothes. Looking now at the snaps taken in the back garden, I can remember that her going-away outfit of light jacket and skirt was in lilac. For the ceremony, she had worn a white cotton sleeveless frock, straight at the neck. That's my memory, but I'm useless on clothes.

Our parents and nearest relations, especially old aunts and uncles, would have liked a proper do. I suppose it was unfair, but at the time, we thought, It's our day, our marriage, this is how we want it, no fuss, no palaver.

Our plan, for the first stage of our honeymoon, was to drive to London and spend the first night in our new flat, which we had just acquired. I now had a car, a 2½-litre 1947 Riley which had cost me £100. I had wanted to buy something more expensive and more modern, but when I went to the Midland Bank at King's Cross, the rotters wouldn't lend me a penny.

It was Mike Thornhill who had talked me into the Riley. He knew about cars and I didn't. It did look beautiful, long and sleek and racy, with a hard-soft top. I was proud of it, the look and the feel, but it was hellish to drive and a load of trouble right from the beginning. The roof always let in, it wouldn't start and it cost me a fortune in repairs. I suppose today it would count as a classic car and be worth a great deal more than I paid for it.

Although I had a car, which no one in my family had ever had before, I failed my driving test the week before our wedding. For the second time. Oh, the shame. It meant Mike had to come with us on the first leg of our honeymoon. I drove the Riley, with the L-plates on, very symbolic, while Mike sat beside me and Margaret cowered in the back.

Our honeymoon was in Sardinia. It was our first foreign trip together and Margaret's first time on a plane. (My second, as I'd flown to Cyprus, as a fearless war correspondent.) The mother of one of Margaret's Oxford male friends, John Bassett (who went on to bring the *Beyond the Fringe* foursome together), had recommended Sardinia and suggested a very nice little hotel for us in Alghero. I booked it through a package holiday company, Horizon, which had recently started and was doing very well. I had in fact interviewed the boss of Horizon, for a story. I even managed to get some sort of minor discount, which I have never been allowed to forget. How typical, even getting a discount on his honeymoon, how mean and mercenary is that?

About a week into the honeymoon, I developed a boil on my bottom. It grew bigger and bigger and I was soon in agony. We managed to call an emergency doctor who came to our hotel bedroom. She threw me on the bed and proceeded to pummel my boil with her bare hands, trying to bring it to a head. I was being very brave, as I am with most such things. I suddenly heard a crash and realised Margaret had fainted and was lying flat out on the bedroom floor. The doctor continued with my boil, till she had managed to lance it, totally ignoring Margaret's body on the floor. When she had finally succeeded, she picked Margaret up and brought her round. '*Un peu de courage, madame,*' she said.

This is still one of our family phrases, which of course I use to mock her. Yet thinking about it now, why did the doctor speak French when we were in an Italian-speaking country? Was she French? Now I remember, she didn't speak English, and we didn't speak Italian, but we had told her we could speak French, after a fashion.

We came back to London to our first home as a married couple. We had printed its full address and phone number on our wedding card in big bold letters because we were so proud of it – 9 Heath Villas, Vale of Health, Hampstead, London NW3, tel HAMpstead 3847. I realised by then, having become a Londoner of a sort, how smart it was to have an NW3 postcode and best of all, a HAM telephone number.

Christmas cards. For years we got Frank Herrmann to photograph us for our annual family snap. He took this one of us (right) in period clothes just after Flora's birth in 1972

And in more modern mode in 1990: Jake and me at the back; Flora, Margaret and Caitlin

FRANK HERRMANN

FRANK HERRMANN

January 1986, on my fiftieth birthday. I insisted on a hol in the Caribbean to make up for all those freezing-cold birthday mornings in Carlisle. And persuaded Margaret to come with me

For my seventieth birthday, 2006, we all went to Crete. *Left to right*: Richard (Flora's husband), Flo? Margaret, Ruby (Caitlin's daughter), Jake, Amelia (Jake and Rosa's daughter), Rosa (Jake's wife), Caitlin, Grandpa Humper

My mother Marion, née Brechin, and father John Hunter Davies, pay clerk in the RAF – both true born Scots – in their early married years in the 1930s. They met while she was working in the NAAFI in Perth

Studio snap, which can't have been cheap, with me aged four, and my twin sisters, Marion and Annabelle

Me, rather hunched with asthma and wearing an itchy suit, with Marion, Annabelle and Johnny in Dumfries, 1944

Outside our Carlisle council house, 1954. *Standing, left to right*: Annabelle, mother, me, Marion. Johnny is at the front. My father is in a wheelchair, in the early stages of MS

Carlisle Grammar School hockey team, 1954. I'm in the front row, second right. Reginald Hill, now a famous writer, is at the very back

Durham days. At last I felt I was starting from square one with everyone else. Ever so smart in a college blazer at University College, Durham, 1954; and, in 1957, I did manage to graduate – and got photographed with a flawless complexion

Marriage

The Vale of Health is a little, exclusive rural enclave inside Hampstead Heath, at least inside the edge of it, off East Heath Road. It was so pretty, so artistic, so wonderful. I couldn't believe our luck and couldn't imagine there was another place as attractive, anywhere in the whole of London.

D. H. Lawrence had lived there at one time, and Leigh Hunt, whose cottage was still there, and several other famous people. When we moved in, there was still an old Victorian pub in the Vale of Health, later knocked down and replaced by luxury flats. The barman was Scottish and on sunny summer afternoons, when people were still drinking up, refusing to leave, we could hear him shouting, 'Have yous nae hames to go to?'

Behind the pub was a huddle of caravans and fairground stalls, many of them still there. At Easter time, it blossomed into the Hampstead Heath Fair. Several of the fairground people lived there permanently. It was strange to have this scruffy, untidy gypsy-looking settlement right in the middle of such a totally middle-class and expensive enclave. At Hampstead Fair time, most residents moved out, to avoid the noise and all the vulgar cockney persons enjoying themselves.

Our little flat was arranged in an odd way. The owner, Leonard Elton, who lived on the top floor, had never got round to converting the house in the normal way by making it into three separate units. Our bedroom was on one floor, next to the sitting room of an elderly and very refined lady called Mrs Woodcock, who lived in the basement. We shared the bathroom and lavatory with Mr Elton himself. He was a bachelor who had retired from the Civil Service and lived on sardines on toast and half bottles of wine. He was very shy and reclusive and avoided speaking to us, sliding past in the corridor or on the landing as if he had not seen us. Instead, we communicated by notes, left on the hall shelf. Often he would pass us on the way to leave us a note, but still wouldn't speak.

The rent was only six guineas a week, very reasonable for such a choice and desirable location. I loved stepping out of the front door, walking through the trees and greenery and little hills, up and across the main road, through the back lanes and cobbled streets of Hampstead village, best part, past the Georgian and Queen Anne houses, till I got to Hampstead Tube station where I caught the Northern line direct to King's Cross.

I felt so proud to be living there, with that address, that phone number, and also to be married to Margaret. How fortunate we had been, to have met each other, to have persevered.

The only small blot on the landscape was our bedroom. It was at the back of the house, overlooking the Vale of Health pond. The view of course was stunning, with the ducks and birds, but I slowly discovered it was making me ill. A mist which often hung over the pond, in the early mornings and evenings, had begun to bring on my asthma, something I had forgotten about for eight years, pretending to myself it no longer existed. So much for the name, Vale of Health. We were told it came from the fact that during the plague of London, this little enclave had remained plague free. I had one attack which was so severe that Margaret called our new GP, Dr Josie Day. She came to the flat and gave me an injection which knocked me out.

Apart from that minor blemish, we counted our blessings, unable to believe that any young couple could be luckier or happier.

Chapter Fifteen

Sunday Times

It was quite an interesting year, 1960. Mr Macmillan gave his 'winds of change' speech about South Africa. Prince Andrew was born. British rule ended in Cyprus and it became a republic. Hugh Gaitskell became leader of the Labour Party and John Kennedy became US President. The farthing ceased to be legal tender. In June, I'd got married. And then in December, I learned that I'd got a new job.

All summer there had been rumours of closure, ever since Kemsley Newspapers had sold out to Roy Thomson. Overnight, Kemsley House became Thomson House, not just in London but in all the other major cities, such as Manchester and Newcastle, where the Kemsley empire had newspapers. All the signs, letterheads and addresses had to be changed.

In Gray's Inn Road, Roy Thomson began to create a penthouse suite on the top floor, for his own use, and a private lift, for him only, so he wouldn't have to mingle with the workers. Not long after his acquisition, he appeared for a few brief moments in the *Sunday Graphic*'s editorial offices, to inspect his new possessions. We expected some young whiz-kid, finger-clicking North American but he turned out to be a rather doddery old-looking Canadian with pebbly specs who appeared half-blind.

One day, a photographer from another paper played a neat

trick on him. Roy Thomson was known for being careful with his money, as of course most rich people are, that's one way they get rich. The photographer had noted what time each day Roy arrived in his chauffeur-driven car at the front entrance to Thomson House. He decided to place a sixpence on the pavement, just where Roy would alight from his car. Sure enough, Roy got out, spotted the coin, and immediately bent down to pick it up. It made a great photo, demonstrating two things. He could see perfectly well and, yes, he was canny with money.

It was obvious that cuts and rationalisations were going to be made throughout the group. Some regional papers were sold, or swapped for others. In London, it was expected that both the *Empire News* and the *Sunday Graphic* would be closed as they were not making much money. A few weeks before the end of the year, three of the *Graphic* staff, Robert Robinson and Peter Wilsher and the sports editor, were moved to *The Sunday Times*. No one said a word to me. I thought that's it. The *ST* has taken its complement. The rest of us will be sent back to the provinces, or offered redundancy. All the old sweats were desperate to be made redundant, as many had been there for years. As last in, having been on the paper for only eighteen months, I would get very little.

The death of the paper was officially announced the week before Christmas 1960. Managements do manage good timing. The *Sunday Graphic's* office Xmas card was already at the printers, showing the front pages of another glorious year in the *Sunday Graphic's* long history, but they managed to add the headline 'Swan Song 1960. Something to remember us by. A Merry Christmas to you anyway . . .'

I'd gone, before the final wakes in the local pubs, so I never did find out what happened to those I worked with so happily over the previous eighteen months. I gathered later that most of them did find work in London, mainly on magazines, or went freelance. I'd been told, just a week before the end, that I would after all be joining *The Sunday Times*.

Since arriving in London, I had been in awe of *The Sunday*

Times. Their journalists seemed so superior, their offices were said to be wood panelled and posh, and of course the paper's very name impressed people. Ringing up, saying you were from the *Sunday Graphic* rarely got a rapturous response. And when people had stories to tell you or sell you, they didn't immediately think of the *Sunday Graphic.*

I had been called for a brief interview with the *Sunday Times* editor, Henry Hodson. He seemed totally uninterested in me, and the paper, and in fact journalism, his mind still floating somewhere in the Oxford clouds above All Souls. I couldn't believe that this person was a journalist, or had ever been out on a story. He knew nothing about me, or indeed about the *Sunday Graphic,* which he appeared not to have read. He chanced to ask if I was interested in archaeology. Which was lucky, as I was able to boast about my deep knowledge of Roman Britain and Hadrian's Wall, suspecting he would know less than me.

I then got a note from him, on 23 December 1960, to say that as a member of the *Sunday Times* staff my salary would be £1,350 a year. He welcomed me to the team. 'And I hope that you will work happily with us for a long time to come.'

Hodson didn't last long as editor under the new thrusting Thomson regime and in 1961 he was retired to become Provost of Ditchley, whatever that was. He was replaced by Denis Hamilton, who was equally strange in a different way, special-ising in silences. He just sat there, waiting for you to speak, which meant you usually blurted out something stupid to fill the vacuum. He wasn't a public school, Oxbridge academic type like Hodson, in fact he hadn't been to university at all, which was unusual for *The Sunday Times.* He'd had a brilliant war career, becoming a Lt. Col., commanding a battalion of the Durham Light Infantry at a very young age and becoming a member of Montgomery's staff. He was clearly highly professional, clever and calculating. Before the war, he'd been a sub on his local paper in Middlesbrough. Afterwards, dripping with medals, he'd become editorial assistant to Lord Kemsley.

For the first week or so on *The Sunday Times* I was placed in the news room, given odd stories to follow up by the news editor Michael Cudlipp. The two star reporters, who got their names in the paper, were Susan Cooper and Gavin Lyall. There was a handful of younger male reporters of around my age, such as Lew Chester and Mike Hamlyn, who like me had mostly been Kemsley or Thomson graduate trainees and had spent some time in the provinces, but all of them seemed to have been at Oxbridge.

In the background were old Etonians like Cyril Connolly and Ian Fleming floating around. Fleming had not long before given up writing the Atticus column and was something to do with the foreign desk. He tended to disappear on a Friday afternoon to play golf at Sandwich. Many of the old guard did the same, yet this was a Sunday paper, whose most important working days are Friday and Saturday.

There was indeed a lot of oak panelling and old-fashioned desks like a gentleman's club. John Pearson (later Fleming's biographer), one of my friends on the paper, used to say that if he ever got into *Who's Who*, he'd put down Thomson House as his club. There was no shouting, no bollocking, and if a person was thought no longer quite up to their job, or it was decided someone else should have a go, they were just left there, on full salary, with their desk, their office, their secretary and status, doing nothing in particular, apart from filling in their exes and pink forms.

The overmanning, throughout the whole of Fleet Street at this time, was ridiculous, on the broadsheets as well as the tabloids. Editorial management men used to complain about the power of the print unions, and all their mickey mouse tricks, charging for non-existent work, or non-existent printers, downing tools for piddling reasons just when the first edition was rolling in order to get even more money or perks. But both sides were as bad, milking the system for their own good and greed.

Journalists fiddled their expenses and enjoyed three- or four-hour lunch breaks. The drinking culture, especially on the tabloids, was incredible. I once went to the *Daily Mirror's* local pub and saw ordinary reporters shoving down the oysters and champagne, yet it was only 12 o'clock. I later got to know several people on the *Daily Express* and *Daily Mail* features pages, all on salaries twice mine, and massive expenses, yet they hardly got a thing in the paper. They just sat around, playing silly games in the office, then went out for drunken lunches that lasted for hours.

I knew when I joined *The Sunday Times* what my actual job was going to be, as it had been announced on the staff notice board. I presume it was because of the Christmas and New Year holiday period, and thin papers, that I had to spend the first week or so hanging around the news desk.

I was to be the boy on the Atticus column. The column itself was being run by Robert Robinson, who had also come from the *Sunday Graphic*. Atticus was the paper's column about people. We didn't use the word gossip, nothing as vulgar as that. We were much higher class, concerning ourselves with nicely written paragraphs about the next Master of Balliol, the retiring Ambassador to Washington, or who might be in the running to be the next Bishop of Durham. Atticus, over the years, had been edited by many well-known journalists and writers, such as Sacheverell Sitwell and Ian Fleming.

I hadn't really known Bob Robinson very well on the *Graphic*. He was older, more senior than me, and appeared terribly clever and witty, fluent and erudite, like a modern Dr Johnson, even speaking in a slightly archaic, precise way. It was strange that someone so obviously gifted should have been stuck for so long on the *Graphic*, interviewing filmstars. He had at the same time been doing some TV and radio work, about films and filmstars, and yet he appeared rather to despise or mock most of the filmstars he was interviewing and the films he was reviewing.

Bob tried to make Atticus less establishment and upper class and introduced an occasional piece by someone called Mayhew – harking back to Henry Mayhew, the nineteenth-century social writer. Our Mayhew would go and interview an ordinary, working person, perhaps a taxi driver or dustman. They would just speak, verbatim, one long quote. The object was to get the flavour of the person, his speech patterns and peculiarities, as well as facts about how he did his job. I did most of them, and loved it. There was a temptation of course to improve on what the ordinary person had said, to make him or her more Pinteresque, but I found if you talked to anyone long enough, about themselves and their work, everyone could be made to sound interesting and offbeat.

But mainly we still had to cover the traditional people, those of interest to gentlemen's clubs, Oxbridge common rooms. Bob tried to break the pattern but there were people like the managing editor, Pat Murphy, who had been on the paper for ages and didn't want it changed. Even worse, he expected us to have a lead item every week, some piece of news, however boring, as long as it was about a bishop, or similar.

There were only two Sunday papers that everyone read, *The Sunday Times* and *Observer*. By 'everyone' I mean people of education and taste, those who wanted to see what the star reviewers like Harold Hobson and Dilys Powell, or Ken Tynan and Penelope Gilliatt, were thinking that week. When Jimmy Porter in *Look Back in Anger* goes on about the Sunday papers, those are the two he means. Readers tended to take both, as neither paper was very thick, and there were no separate sections. For a journalist working on either, if you had anything of interest or amusement in that Sunday, everyone you met or talked to on Monday had read it. That no longer happens. There are just so many papers, so many sections, so many columnists, that it's impossible to read them all, or even be aware of their existence.

While people might mention something in Atticus they had read, they didn't know I had done it. My name didn't appear, nor did Bob's, though of course our friends and contacts knew. That's probably the reason I never kept my cuttings from those early years on Atticus. The other reason is that Bob usually re-wrote much of my copy, putting his own flavour on it. I didn't object. I thought he was better, more gifted, more literary than me. I was the labourer, the water carrier.

Bob didn't actually like ringing people up and interviewing them, so I did most of that, providing the raw copy. In the early days, I did worry when I had to ring someone who was known to be pompous or terribly distinguished, especially if it was to ask some dopey or trivial or awkward question, based on a stupid tip-off. I would read their cuttings for hours, so I would be able to ask about other, harmless topics, before getting to the story we were chasing.

In the flesh, when I went out to see people, I often felt handicapped by looking so young. I was aged twenty-four, but looked even younger. People sometimes were disbelieving, that I really was from *The Sunday Times,* whereas on the phone they don't know how young and inexperienced you might be. I remember reading how Harold Wilson, as a young MP, deliberately grew a moustache because no one took him seriously.

The oldest *Sunday Times* cutting I have kept was the first time I got my name in the paper. This was in May 1963, when I interviewed John Masefield, the Poet Laureate. I'd had a correspondence with him for months, before I eventually persuaded him. All his notes were handwritten, on small pieces of blue notepaper, which I've kept to this day. He'd been born in 1878, and so was 85 when I saw him at his house in Berkshire. Ramsay MacDonald had made him Poet Laureate in 1930. In our chat, he reminisced about Thomas Hardy. It was like meeting a creature from another age and naturally I was rather reverential, compared with how I later wrote interviews with silly remarks and cheeky comments.

The very first famous person I had ever interviewed was back on *Palatinate* when I met Flora Robson, the actress, who had been appearing in a play in Newcastle. I knew she was famous because I had to look her up in *Who's Who.* She was pretty boring, or at least I failed to get anything of interest out of her.

The John Masefield piece ran to 2,500 words and appeared on

the main features pages of the paper, not in Atticus. It was a huge struggle, coping with so many words, when I'd been more used to knocking out 250-word stories.

Bob Robinson ran Atticus for only a couple of years until he was moved sideways to write a personal column. I didn't expect to get the job, as I was still so young, and my non-Oxbridge background, so I believed, still counted against me.

Nicholas Tomalin arrived to be in charge. He had been President of the Cambridge Union, seemed to know everyone in the world of the arts and literature and the media. His social life was very impressive, holding large dinner parties almost every night, which must have been hard for his wife Claire, struggling at that time with three young children. Nick had the habit of inviting people at the last moment, usually famous people, whom he had just met, or perhaps had not even met, but wanted to meet. He felt it was vital for a successful journalist to live this sort of life. One day, when he was at our house, sitting in our back garden, he informed Margaret that she was holding back my career by not having an active social life.

But I liked working with Nick – partly because it was thanks to him I began to get my name in the paper. When he arrived, from working on *Town* magazine, he'd got it agreed that at long last Atticus should not be anonymous, so his name went at the end in bold letters. He probably realised this was a bit unfair, when I was still doing most of the donkey work, so he started a system whereby on one story, and one story only, the words 'so he told Hunter Davies' would appear.

I was pleased at first by this recognition, but then after about a year I began to find that some weeks I was writing the whole column, doing every story, subbing it, writing the headlines, cross heads, captions, laying out the page, seeing it through the stone – and yet I was still putting Nick's name in bold at the end, when he had not done a bleeding thing.

It was all to do with women. I didn't realise at first where he had gone, what he was doing. I assumed he was seeing contacts, yet he never seemed to come back with a story. He'd ring up, during the week, ask what I was working on and say, 'Sounds good, go ahead.'

There was a sequence of very attractive and clever young women, several on the fringes of the media, who were most impressed by Nick's status. He was attractive, intelligent, in touch, in the swim. He was particularly close to the very pretty mini-skirted daughter of a well-known MP.

I used to get myself in a terrible state, wondering what to do. I was becoming bitter and twisted that I was doing all the work and getting none of the credit, yet I couldn't shop Nick. He was my boss. I let my friends in the office know the true position, hoping it would get around, but nothing was ever said officially.

Our relationship began to grow strained. I never complained to his face how pissed off I was, but it must have showed. He once sent me, late on a Friday, to Le Mans to cover the twenty-four-hour motor race. Le Mans was a nightmare, absolutely packed and chaotic. I spent hours queueing for accreditation and then finding somewhere to stay. By that time, it was too late to send any story. By chance I'd managed to meet Graham Hill, who took me for a spin in a new car he was trying out, and also Jackie Stewart. In the end, I got so much good material that I wrote a huge piece later on for a colour magazine special on British racing. It came out later as a book, edited by Derek Jewell.

When Nick was eventually moved on, there was an interregnum for a while, with nobody really in charge of the column. I decided I had to leave, move to another paper where I would have a proper job and get proper recognition. I discussed this one day with Jack Lambert, who for years had been deputy literary editor, waiting for Leonard Russell, the literary editor, to pack up. He said the thing to do was find something outside the paper, write a book or play, do some radio as he was doing, contributing to 'The Critics', anything that would make them inside realise you had some worth outside.

I got an interview with the editor of the *Daily Express*, Bob Edwards, who offered me a job as a general features writer, but on reflection, I decided they already had so many I said no. I also saw John Junor, editor of the *Sunday Express*, who wrote and offered me a staff position at £28 a week. I still have this letter and now see it is dated 13 October 1960. I must have been feeling unsettled far earlier than I remembered. In the 1960s, the *Daily Express* was still thought of as the leading, most professional popular paper. If you had worked on it, so most journalists believed, you would always be able to get a job elsewhere.

I also saw David Astor, editor and owner of the *Observer*. We discussed the Pendennis column, which was the rival to Atticus, run brilliantly for many years by Anthony Sampson. Astor wanted me to join the paper, but wouldn't specify in what role.

I huffed and puffed, havered and wavered, thinking I must get away, join another paper, I'm going nowhere here. I was waiting and hoping for a change in my own little working life or, even better, some sort of social change in British life, generally.

Chapter Sixteen

House and Home Work

There was no furniture in our Vale of Health flat when we took it over in 1960. So we sat down and made a list of all the objects we would need for married life – cooker, fridge, table, desk, curtains, sofa. At the end of each month, when my salary came in, we bought one of the items on the list and ticked it off.

Our kitchen table was scrubbed pine, newly built but from old wood, which we got from Ron Weldon in Primrose Hill, later the husband of Fay Weldon. Our mothers were appalled at the idea of a young married couple in our situation buying anything old. At the same time, having bought the next domestic object on the list, if there was any money left we also acquired the odd genuinely antique item, such as an inlaid desk, a Victorian button-back chair, a Sheraton-style tray, all of them highly polished but not practical for everyday use. These were pieces of furniture our parents had never had but we had seen them in the homes of the parents of our middle-class friends. It seemed to be what you did, if you were persons of taste and education, aspiring to be middle class.

After about a year, the basic domestic list was almost completed and we compiled a new list, a wish list, which we knew could not be done like the domestic items, purchased month by month. It would take years and years. This started with a new car and ended, top of the bill – did we dare even write it down? – a house of our own.

My old Riley had turned out a total dead loss, with endless problems and repairs. I decided this time to get a new car. For £500, I bought one of the new and exciting cars which had recently appeared – a Mini. It was in a pale blue. Or was it green? We had the most terrible row about its colour one evening, not long after I'd bought it. Margaret said it was green and I said it was blue. This was when I discovered I was colour blind. I'd gone through life so far not aware that I couldn't see the difference between blue, green and grey.

A house, however, seemed way beyond our means. Buying a flat, about the same size as the one we were renting, would have been more sensible and taken less time, but we had set our hearts on a house and garden.

We wanted to stay near the Heath, which we had grown to love, and walked round it for at least an hour every day, but houses near us, in places like Flask Walk in Hampstead village, cost £7,500. That was way beyond our pocket. We looked at houses in poor condition, which needed lots of work, or had sitting tenants, in streets like Christ Church Hill and Willoughby Road, but even then they were around the £7,500–£10,000 mark.

We realised Hampstead, best part, was impossible, so we drew a line round the whole of the Heath, taking in all those areas within a mile of the Heath itself. We tramped round streets we had never visited before, to see if we could bear to live in them, and came to the conclusion that the Kentish Town side of the Heath was our only chance of ever getting a house in the area and within our budget. Even then, it would take another four years of hard saving and belt tightening to raise enough for a deposit.

It was thanks to Margaret that we did it when we did. On leaving Oxford, she had settled down to write a novel, the moment we had returned from our honeymooon. Thoughts of becoming an MP had long since faded. She decided that writing novels was what she'd always wanted to do, though she had never tried before. For three months, she stayed at home all day long, writing away.

It was called 'Green Dust for Dreams' which I told her at the time was a poncy title. It was set in France, another mistake. It's usually easier for beginners to stick to something they know. She had been an au pair in Bordeaux for several months in the year before going up to Oxford. The novel, sub Balzac, was based on the family she had stayed with.

Neither of us personally knew any publishers or agents, but someone at work gave me the name of Michael Sissons, saying he was a good young agent. Margaret sent it off to him. He replied fairly quickly, saying her novel didn't quite work. He didn't think it could be published as it was, but she should come in and see him and discuss it.

Margaret immediately said, 'That's it, I'm binning the novel, it's useless. Why did I ever think I could write one?' She refused to consider going to see him. Instead, she decided to get a job.

Many years later I did meet Michael Sissons who remembered Margaret's first novel, and recalled wondering why she had never come to see him. It was in fact one of his more encouraging letters, so he thought at the time. He tried not to allow aspiring novelists to come to his office, unless he believed they had a chance. After that incident, he made his encouraging letters more positive and clearer. But it was too late for Margaret. She had given up.

There wasn't much else she could do, with no skills, no training, except teach. In those days, you could teach without having had any teacher training, as long as you had a degree. I of course did have a proper teacher's certificate, which I had done for the wrong reasons, and hoped I would never have to use.

Margaret supply-taught for a few months in some appalling schools in Paddington before being sent to a girls' secondary school in Islington called Barnsbury. She quite enjoyed it, the staff and the girls, and taught there full-time for around the next two years.

So that's how we managed to save money much more quickly than we had ever expected, having two salaries coming in. All her wage went into the bank and by the end of 1962 we had amassed the huge sum of £1,500, enough to put down as a deposit on a house in the £5,000 region.

We had by then fixed our sights on Parliament Hill Fields. The streets were mainly fairly ordinary-looking mid-Victorian terraces, not of much architectural interest, compared with the Georgian gems and little cobbled squares of Hampstead, but they were within a short walk of the Heath and we thought one of them will do for us fine, till we have saved more money and can return to Hampstead proper, our spiritual home.

We got a list from Jennings and Samson, estate agents in Fortess Road. A house in Onslow Gardens was on sale at £5,600 while one in Tufnell Park Road was £5,759 – both of them fully vacant. In Arlington Road, Camden Town, there was one at £5,000 which had a sitting tenant on one floor.

The one which caught our eye was in Parliament Hill Fields in a street 'within a few minutes from the Heath . . . ideally suited for the discriminating buyer who is desirous of carrying out repairs and re-decoration to his own requirements'. This indicated it was a dump. And there was also a sitting tenant on the top floor on a controlled rent of 32/6d per week – about £1.60 in today's money. The asking price, freehold, was £5,250.

It was December 1962, and the street and the back garden were full of snow when we arrived to look at the house. Inside it was freezing cold and damp. It had not been lived in for some time, nor any money spent on it for what looked like decades.

We asked about the sitting tenant, but there was no sign of her. The agent told us she was an elderly woman who had been staying for some months with her daughter in the USA. They had been informed she was unlikely ever to return, so we would be getting the whole house empty.

The house appeared at first sight to be in a terrace of similar houses, but in fact was semi-detached, with a side entrance, which seemed an advantage. It was three storeys, flat fronted, with a rather nice iron balcony on the first floor. Inside, there were some original Victorian fireplaces and ceiling roses and mouldings. We estimated there would be a great deal of work to be done, so we made an offer of £5,000, which was £250 below the asking price. It was immediately accepted.

We got estimates for building work and hired an Irishman called J. P. Brown who lived in Fortess Road, not far away. I went round to his house one evening to pay him some money and found rows of Irish labourers in his basement, sleeping on what appeared to be wooden planks. He was a stage Irishman, in his accent and bluster and blarney, totally scruffy and filthy, but always cheerful. He was unaware of personal danger and walked up dodgy roofs without a ladder, pulled himself up on broken gutters. His estimate for all the work we wanted done was £884. This included repairing the dodgy roof and walls, fixing the windows, knocking down and rebuilding a collapsed outhouse, taking out the old fireplaces. We later regretted it, but central heating was all the rage. Therefore fireplaces were redundant and had to be ripped out.

The sitting tenant did return, Mrs Hall. She was Irish, but denied it, for some reason, telling us various bits of information about herself and her past, not all of which I believed. She was probably in her late sixties, but looked worn and older, always moaning and groaning about her ailments, but she was mentally sharp and quick and clever. And physically stronger than she let on. If she thought we were not in, she could be heard bustling through the front door and running up the stairs to her top-floor flat. Otherwise she went up very, very slowly, huffing and puffing all the way.

She had her own kitchen and two other rooms but shared our lavatory on the middle floor, which was really annoying. She always insisted on spraying it with the most awful cheap sweet-scented spray after she had used it, a pong which then seeped through the whole house. She was very bossy with all her friends, most of them single Irishwomen of a certain age.

Her worst habit was storming into our part of the house,

regardless of what we were doing, and insisting I come upstairs at once to look at her kitchen tap which was dripping. Margaret was much tougher with her. If she burst in when we were eating, Margaret would get up and ask her to leave, saying I would attend to her problems later, when I had time.

'Children' had been the final fantasy item on our mythical list of long-term things to do, but I wrote down the word in pencil, as we didn't want to tempt fate. When we'd bought the house, and finally settled in, it seemed to be the right time to try.

Margaret became pregnant in the autumn of 1963 and immediately I started writing down another list – of possible names. I still have it, kept in the family Bible, the one I was awarded as a boy for memorising all those verses.

Margaret was due to give birth at Queen Mary's, a maternity home at the top of Hampstead, near the White Stone Pond, then part of the Royal Free Hospital. They were offering classes for fathers-to-be, a new concept at the time. My immediate thought was, Oh good, that must be one thousand words. Which I got, writing a story about the classes for *The Sunday Times.*

Margaret gave birth to our first child on 6 March 1964. I was there, with her, for a lot of the time, but it seemed to go on for ever. I was growing more and more hungry so I decided to pop out and get a bite to eat. I walked down Heath Street to the shops, but couldn't find any selling food, so I had to go all the way to the Tube where there was a newsagent's – where Benham and Reeves are today – and I managed to buy a pie.

When I got back, I found Margaret had given birth – and I'd missed it. I could not have witnessed the actual birth, but I could have been loitering in the next room, able to rush in immediately afterwards and hold her hand. As it was, I arrived later, with bits of pie on my chin, and smelling of beer, as I'd fitted in half a pint as well. For years and years, I was never able to live this down.

It was a girl, Caitlin, and she weighed in at 8 pounds 3½ ounces with a mass of jet-black hair, just like me. Her name had been at the top of our girls' list. We thought it was good with Davies, making it sound suitably Welsh, thinking of Caitlin Thomas, without realising that the name Caitlin is in fact Irish. And of course I am Scottish and Margaret English. Anyway, we liked the Celtic feel to it.

On the first day of spring like spring we put Caitlin outside the front door in her pram with the sun-shade up to protect her head. We kept a close eye on her of course, but later that day, when we brought her in, we discovered that in her little hand she was clutching a filthy £1 note. Where had she got it from? Dropped from the sky by a bird? A present from the Good Fairy?

It turned out to be J. P. Brown. He had come unexpectedly to look at the roof. He'd clambered down, in all his filthy clothes, to find a new baby at the front door. He'd leaned over and thrust the £1 note into her hand, his little christening gift, without ever bothering to knock at the door and tell us.

Chapter Seventeen

Writing Life

Margaret didn't quite give up writing, after what she took to be the put-down and disappointment of her first attempt at being a novelist. Despite doing a full-time and exhausting job as a teacher, after a few months she slowly began to write again, in the evenings and at weekends. This time she decided to write about what she knew, from roughly her own experience.

She started a more lighthearted novel, very different from the pretensions and heaviness of her first. It was based on her experiences of Oxford, about a working-class girl who goes there, expecting dreaming spires, brilliant minds, exciting people, and finds it all pretty boring, really. Quite a neat reversal on the normal Oxbridge novel. She called it *Dames' Delight* after that patch of the river, near Parsons' Pleasure, where female dons, allegedly, were supposed to bathe naked.

Not long afterwards, obviously inspired by Margaret's progress with her novel, I also decided to start writing in the evenings and at weekends. I was still feeling frustrated at *The Sunday Times*, believing that I would never be Atticus, never get a proper chance, always be overlooked, which of course was a bit self-important, as I'd only been there about a year and was still only twenty-five. But nothing happening when you are young seems to be nothing happening for ever.

At Durham, I had written one or two more so-called literary

pieces which had appeared in a mag called *New Durham,* as opposed to the jokey stuff in *Palatinate.* I was often beginning scraps of short stories, little observational essays or atmosphere pieces, usually based on some incident I'd observed, but I had never completed them or submitted them anywhere, knowing they were just scraps, going nowhere. In Manchester, I wrote a rather pretentious piece, angled on some lines of poetry, which came out of an event in Cyprus, and I sent it to the *Guardian.* It was printed, with my name on. Nobody I knew or met ever saw it or mentioned it, but I was so proud of it.

I considered I wasn't up to writing a novel, not being imaginative or talented enough, which I could see Margaret clearly was, even if she hadn't got anywhere as yet. I thought I could never cope with a plot, or characters, keep up my interest and most of all, manage to knock out 300 pages of fiction.

Instead, I started writing plays. No one asked me, or suggested it, nor had I ever been much interested in the theatre. I had gone in Carlisle, in the Sixth Form, but had hated all the drawing-room stuff by Terence Rattigan and Noel Coward. In London, I had been transfixed by *Look Back in Anger,* as most people were – it was so different from what had gone before. I also loved *The Ginger Man* and *Billy Liar.*

I tried first of all to do a TV script, about life in a school, called 'Silver Street'. I did one episode and sketched out some plots. At the time, there were no series set in schools, just in police stations, such as 'Dixon of Dock Green' and then 'Z Cars'. I sent it off to the BBC, but I never had a producer's name, or the appropriate department. I couldn't seem to find the code, the entrée, how you got in. After several months, it came back, rejected.

The theatre did seem to have new life in it, and possibilities. Despite getting nowhere with the TV script, I considered I was quite good at dialogue, capturing realistic speech. I also thought that with dialogue, you can fill up the pages ever so quickly, compared with a novel.

I based my play on an incident which had happened to us

not long after we had got married. One of my friends from Durham asked if she could stay a night on our sofa with her boyfriend. I remembered how Squire Barraclough had helped me, so I couldn't very well refuse. One night turned into several weeks until we were at screaming point with them, wishing they would go. We came home one day to find the boyfriend trying to throttle the girl, the blood trickling out of her throat.

In the play, I gave him two wives, at least two women by whom he has children. He moves between them, though he mainly stays with the wealthier woman, whose father has bought her a little flat. He does nothing all day long but play with his children, at home or in a local playground, while the two women go out to work to keep him in drinks and cigarettes and money for books. It was called 'The Herring Gulls', a silly title really, but it was a line from the play.

I sent it off to Curtis Brown, having been told they were the leading literary agency in London, though I didn't know anyone there. To my amazement, John Barber, who looked after their theatrical side, agreed to handle it. And even more amazingly, he sold it to a West End director called Allan Davis. He said he loved it and immediately offered a contract which I signed on 21 November 1961. I got paid £50 on signature, which seemed a handsome amount, and he got a six months' option to stage it in the West End. There would be a further £200 when it opened there, plus 5 per cent of the box office receipts. The contract even included the terms and conditions that would apply if and when it was produced on Broadway.

I couldn't believe it. First attempt, and there I was, a playwright. The £50 was returnable only 'if the Lord Chamberlain refuses to license the play'. The Lord Chamberlain's office was a real force, and a real menace, back in the 1960s, able to censor plays for bad language, sex, sedition and suchlike.

I went to meet and talk to Allan Davis several times. He lived in a very smart set of rooms in Cork Street, Mayfair.

He had a play on in the West End which was proving a great

success and he took Margaret and me to see it. It starred Evelyn Laye, whom we'd never heard of, but she was clearly terribly famous. When she appeared, entering through a French window, the whole audience stood up and clapped – before she'd even said a word.

Allan Davis had directed many West End plays, of a traditional, old-fashioned nature, and knew all the star actors and actresses, but felt he was being left behind by changing tastes. He needed to find his own angry young playwright, with a new gritty realistic play. Presumably nothing better had come his way, so he alighted upon me. He didn't say any of this, of course. I only imagined it.

We worked on the play, changed a few bits, altered some scenes, till he was happy, by which time he was talking to likely actors and actresses. He was planning to open in Brighton, to start the provincial tour, then come to the West End.

At the same time, he was meeting production companies, trying to get them involved. I heard one day that H. M. Tennent were terribly interested in backing the play – then the next day they were not. Michael Codron was said to be keen, so were Oscar Lewenstein and Harold Fielding, but nothing seemed to be definite.

One of the producers Allan Davis approached to back the play was Binkie Beaumont, a legend in the postwar West End lunch hours. In January 1962, he sent back a detailed letter to Allan, which did at least show he had read the play properly. 'I do think that the author obviously has potential talent, but I think he needs to get a much better story in which to put his original characters. I am sorry not to share your enthusiasm, but I think he needs a little more experience.' So it was another turn down, if polite and vaguely encouraging.

I was so encouraged by all the excitement of my first attempt at a play that I started a second one. This was called 'The Murder of Daft Jimmy', a much better title. It was based on our family life in Carlisle, with an invalid father stuck in the back parlour, unseen, but dominating everyone's life. The title was a phrase of my mother's, which she used when we were making a lot of noise. In the play, one of the sisters does murder the father.

After months of waiting, but still convinced that 'The Herring Gulls' would soon open, I learned that Allan Davis was giving up. Every possible production company had now turned it down. He couldn't proceed without their financial backing, so he was not going to take up his option. That was it.

I didn't blame Allan. He had clearly tried his best. Perhaps his own track record, of doing old-fashioned drawing-room comedies for decades, had counted against him. Or my play just wasn't good enough.

I had by now finished my second play. As I had been so near with the first one, this was bound to be better and do better. It was turned down, flat. John Barber didn't even think it was worth bothering to send it round to any directors.

I was very upset. On 24 July 1962, he sent me a letter saying he was 'disappointed after all the time and energy he had spent with me on the first play'. I had learned nothing, so he said. I had been 'wilful, hadn't worked enough on the characters or the narrative . . .'

I'm surprised I kept this letter, as it was so shattering, and did not just tear it up, as Margaret would have done. At the top of this letter, Margaret has written a few words in pencil: 'OOZEEFINKEEIS? How very unnecessarily unpleasantly put.'

So that was it, my short career as a playwright was over. There now seemed no point at all in continuing.

When Margaret had finished her novel, *Dames' Delight,* she too sent it off to Curtis Brown. Their main literary agent, Graham Watson, replied quickly and was very enthusiastic. He then sold it, almost at once, to Jonathan Cape, one of London's leading literary publishers. So that was exciting.

She had to do a bit of work on it, and there were various delays before it was published, one of which concerned a libel problem. At the proof stage, someone in Cape, who presumably had recently been at Oxford, said she thought she recognised some of the people in the novel.

Tom Maschler, the boss of Cape, was furious with Margaret for not telling them what bits in her novel were based on real people and real life. He hadn't actually edited the book. It had been handled by another editor who had not asked Margaret about the background. I thought it should have been that editor's responsibility, not Margaret's. She was young, just twenty-four, totally inexperienced in the ways of publishing and the laws of libel.

Tom called her into his office and Margaret remembers they then walked round Bedford Square, with Tom saying it was all her fault. She was almost in tears. He then took her to see the eminent libel lawyer Michael Rubinstein who was very kind and pleasant. He said what a shame, he had enjoyed the book and found it funny, but yes, it was libellous. He suggested Margaret wrote to three people, including the Principal of Somerville, saying, This is not you, in the book, but if anyone thinks it's you, you won't sue, will you? Two stiff letters were written back, saying how disappointed they were by a scholar, but they would not sue, but one person did want changes. It meant the book was put back and had to be corrected and re-set. It also, so Margaret thought, ruined some of the stories in the book so they didn't quite make sense. She had to pay for all the corrections, and the lawyer's work, which came to more than the £250 advance she had received for the book.

What should have been an event of great pleasure and excitement, having one's very first book published, did rather have the edge taken off it. All the same, it did well, got good reviews, some publicity, but Margaret herself was not very happy. It hadn't been the sort of novel she really wanted to write anyway, even before things had gone wrong. But it had got her started.

After the disappointment of writing two full-length stage plays and getting nowhere, I'd rather given up writing anything for a while. It had been a struggle anyway, doing it in the evenings or at weekends, after my normal work, not that I would ever use that as an excuse. If people want to write, they write. It can always be fitted in, whatever anyone says.

Margaret's novel had used her own student life. I decided to do the same, but go further back and base my novel on my teenage life, the time when I was a delivery boy, on my bike taking round groceries, fantasising about the housewives, living in a council house but trying to pick up girls from a semi. I set it in Carlisle, to keep it as real as possible, though I didn't name the town or the streets.

It took a while to get it going, faced with all those blank pages. I had worked for so long on journalistic stories, which were rarely more than 500 words. I didn't know how I could ever manage to produce 80,000 words. It was as if I'd trained all my life for the 100 yards but now found myself running a marathon instead.

Unlike Margaret, who is self-contained and self-possessed, I needed instant and immediate reaction to everything, which of course you get as a journalist, even if it's just someone saying 'Rubbish, do it again'. On *Palatinate*, the girls on the paper had been a dutiful audience, smiling at my pieces. On the *Evening Chronicle*, Harold Mellor might have shouted at me, but at least it was a reaction. On Atticus, I had the weekly satisfaction of seeing my pieces being read by millions, even if they didn't always know I'd written them.

For the first few weeks, I kept on asking Margaret to read this page, 'Please, I've just finished it, it's really good, don't you think?' Ideally, I would have liked her to read it line by line, but I didn't think she would agree to that. She said that if I was determined to write a novel, though God knows why, I had to do it by myself. The most she would promise was that she would read it all, at the end.

So I struggled on for a few more weeks, then I begged her again. 'I'll be your best friend, help me, help me.' In the end, to get me properly started, she finally agreed to read each chapter, when it was finished. I handed each one to her, as if to a tutor. She then gave me her views, not always flattering, but she did help. Although I was enjoying it, knocking out so many pages a week, laughing at my own jokes, and was able to keep up a good progress, I don't think I would have persevered with that first attempt at a full-length book, or got to the end, without her help.

I sent it off to Curtis Brown. I suppose I half hoped that Graham Watson, her agent, would look nicely upon it, but he was by now the head of the firm. He handed it over to a new and junior literary agent in the office, Richard Simon. On 20 August 1964, I got a letter back from him, a model of how to react and encourage, without letting the aspiring author get too carried away.

'I want to say straight away and with great emphasis that an awful lot of it is immensely enjoyable and truly funny . . .'

Then, carefully, he pointed out there were problems, especially a main one. 'It hasn't got a chance of being published, as it stands.'

But he finished by making some creative suggestions, showing that he had properly read and appreciated what it was I thought I'd been trying to do. He said I should have more girls, keeping it fast and hectic, before finally meeting Mary, who was my love heart in the novel. He said which characters should be cut and gave examples of where I had hammered a joke. All in all, I was thrilled by his tone, his reactions and his ideas. I immediately started working on it, following the lines he had suggested.

As soon as I had completed the revised version, he sent it off to a publisher he thought might be interested. This was Heinemann – who almost immediately accepted it.

Today, when asked, I usually tell would-be writers not to bother trying to interest an agent, they are either snotty and superior or inefficient and useless; better to approach a publisher by yourself. On the whole, that's roughly true now, if you are a total unknown, but in my case, starting from scratch, I have to be thankful to Richard Simon and admit his advice and help and wisdom as an agent were so vital.

Charles Pick, the main director at Heinemann, took me out to lunch and raved about how funny my novel was. They loved it so much they were going to do a really good job on publishing and promoting it. They had, for example, already thought up a novel idea for the dust jacket, something which had not been done before. On the front they were going to stick a pair of three-dimensional lips, in plastic, which would appear to follow you, kiss you, as you moved around. Everyone at Heinemann loved the idea, thinking 'How amusing, how original'. So did *Smiths Trade News*, which was then the bible of the publishing trade.

Even before the book had been published, there was talk of film rights being sold. It all seemed terribly exciting. But then I had been equally excited when I sold that play, thinking I was about to begin a wonderful career as a playwright.

Nonetheless, 1964 was turning out as eventful as 1960 had been. We had had our first child. Margaret's first novel had appeared. Mine was about to be published. Who would have thought it?

Chapter Eighteen

The Sixties

The Sixties arrived about 1964, at least for me and probably a few thousand others, that's when we told ourselves something was in the air, something was not quite as it had been. For millions and millions, the vast majority of the population, things appeared just as they'd always been. Only much later, when it was all over, did people say to some of these millions, 'Wow, you lived through the Sixties, it must have been amazing, tell us about it.'

We are now in an era of rubbishing the Sixties. Clever, well-educated writers, mostly born in 1970, are producing books saying it's all a myth, nothing much changed. They can prove it with statistics and contemporary cuttings indicating that people didn't actually sleep around, take drugs, live a wild life.

All true, all true, certainly in my case. I didn't do any of those things. And yet there were changes, which I felt and witnessed with my own eyes, many of them abstract changes, about attitudes and perceptions, which of course are always hard to prove or pin down. Here's what happened to me, in the little world I happened to be inhabiting.

I'd been trundling on for almost four years on the Atticus column, feeling I was getting nowhere. Despite some minor changes, we still had to appear more interested in the next Master of Balliol than in who was appearing on 'Six Five Special' or had written the latest gritty Northern novel. Those were the people and subjects I personally wanted to interview and write about. Not all the time. Just to give a balance of what life appeared to be really like.

Nick Tomalin was suddenly relieved of Atticus, moved sideways to do more foreign reporting and features. And I got the job. Straight away, I dumped all interviews and stuff about bishops and establishment figures and over the next two years I concentrated instead on the new confident cockney photographers, cocky Northern actors, young fashion designers, new TV playwrights, working-class novelists and young football stars.

In 1965 I went up to Manchester and did an interview with a nineteen-year-old George Best who had just got into the Man Utd first team. He assured me he didn't drink or smoke and in any spare time the wildest thing he did was play a bit of snooker. He was still in digs, sharing with another young player, but he hoped one day to have his own flat.

In 1966, I interviewed Dennis Potter, who'd had a row with the BBC over a play called *Vote Vote Vote for Nigel Barton*. The angle with him was that he was doing a job which had not existed till then – working as a full-time TV playwright. I also did Bill Naughton who was living in the same one-room flat in Pimlico he'd had for seventeen years. He'd done a radio play called *Alfie Elkins and his Little Life* which had become a stage play and now a film called simply *Alfie*.

Another person I interviewed was Alan Aldridge, who happened to be a friend of mine. He lived two streets away and with him I later played Sunday-morning football on the Heath. He was an artist and designer, producing what became known as psychedelic illustrations for *The Sunday Times*'s new colour magazine and also book covers and advertising. What interested me was that he had just been made art director of Penguin Books. This was one of the most prestigious jobs you could get in the design field – and yet Alan had never been to art school, had little education and still talked about 'drawing' as if it had an r in the middle.

I saw Alan as a good example of old traditional barriers being broken down. It didn't matter any more about your accent, your school or university or your formal qualifications. If it was thought you could do the job, you were given your chance. Fashion photographers, for example, had normally been from the upper classes, like Cecil Beaton, or at least they assumed the airs and accents of the quality and tried hard to disguise their roots. New young fashion photographers like David Bailey did not bother to hide their working-class accents and manners.

It is true that these social changes tended to happen in the worlds of fashion, art, design, media, television, novels, not the traditional fields like the Civil Service or the church. And they were mainly restricted to London. The rest of the country was probably unaware of, or had little interest in, what I thought I could see happening. But the results of these changes soon became apparent to all – when women all over the country, of all ages and sizes, started wearing mini-skirts and men grew their hair long, aping Beatles haircuts.

I tried of course to strike a balance on the Atticus column. In 1964, I talked to James Baldwin, the black American writer, walking round Bloomsbury Square with him. He was wearing what looked like a Beatles suit, which naturally I commented on. He said that when he bought it, he hadn't actually heard of them. He didn't admit to being gay, which anyway could have got him into legal trouble. 'I suppose I am exotic. A dancing doll. A Negro who is a writer.'

I interviewed Aldous Huxley, over from his home in the USA, in some hotel in Knightsbridge. When I discovered his next appointment was back in the West End, I offered to drive him there in my Mini. He was delighted as he had never been in one before. Driving down Piccadilly, we drew level with a double-decker bus. Huxley gave a great moan, closed his eyes, and then started to open the car door. He had suddenly seen the wheels of the bus looming above us, dwarfing my little car, as if we were going to be crushed. He was so frightened he wanted to get out and walk. Luckily, being so tall, well over six feet, he wasn't agile enough in such a confined space to get himself out. I managed to drive off, leaving the bus behind.

Another 1966 interview I did was with David Hockney. Unlike Alan Aldridge, he'd had a proper art training, but his accent was still pure Yorkshire. In the lavatory at his Bayswater flat I noticed a cut-out newspaper photograph of Denis Law, scoring a goal. I asked if he was a football fan. He said no. He just loved Law's thighs. I didn't include this remark in the interview, not in 1966. The lawyers would have cut it out, to save him from himself. But I did use a good quote about his newly acquired blond hair. 'My hair is really dark. I came home slightly drunk one night in America and was watching TV at two o'clock in the morning with a friend when this advert came on – "Blondes have more fun." So both of us went out immediately and bought some stuff to do our hair.'

Now and again, I did do people with the sort of background I was trying to get away from, if only to get in some gentle mockery. In 1965 I interviewed Auberon Waugh who had just published a novel which had received some very nasty reviews. He had filed them all away, so he said, to get his own back one day. 'I'm incredibly vindictive. I have none of the humble acceptance of the civilised man.'

As I was leaving, he asked me to give his book a good plug, which I did, in the last paragraph of the interview, quoting him. 'Can't you just slip in somewhere that my new book is brilliant? That's all you have to say. Oh, and if there's room, say, furthermore, that it's selling very well . . .'

I also did a little story about an Oxford student called Jonathan Aitken, nephew of Lord Beaverbrook, son of a Tory MP, whom I'd heard was being accused of some fast practice in the voting for the Oxford Union elections. I didn't actually accuse him of anything awful, just a gentle tease, so I thought, but on Monday morning I got a furious phone call from someone who said she was his sister. I was a pig, a horrible person, and had ruined Jonathan's chances of being elected and probably his chances of becoming an MP as well.

I did have one nasty experience when working on Atticus, as the assistant, which got me into some trouble. It was the time of the Labour Party leadership elections in 1963 when the three people standing were Harold Wilson, George Brown and James Callaghan. Over three weeks, I went to see each of them and did a little harmless boring piece. While waiting for Wilson, his secretary Marcia Falkender was remarkably indiscreet, telling me about George Brown's drinking habits.

The last one I did was Jim Callaghan. After we'd had our chat, I walked with him out of the House of Commons, along with our photographer. My rule, even when I was doing a piece which I knew would be only 500 words max, was always to stay with the person as long as possible, till I was chucked out, or told to leave, as you never knew what might turn up. We got to Westminster Bridge where he said he was now going to catch a bus.

I did my 500 words, all fairly anodyne, but in the caption to the photograph, which showed Callaghan about to get on the bus, I couldn't resist the words, 'Callaghan misses the bus'.

The following week, I was called in by the editor, Denis Hamilton, and given a bollocking. He'd had a furious telegram from Callaghan saying he thought the interview with Atticus was off the record, that it was on a lobby correspondent basis, thus nothing would appear. This of course was complete rubbish and I'm sure he knew it. I had made it absolutely clear to him that Atticus was not part of the lobby, had nothing to do with politics, and I would just be doing a personal piece about who he was, and of course quoting him, as was our style. The real reason for his fury, so I believed, was my 'missing the bus' remark. It came true, as Wilson was elected leader.

I started to tell all this to Denis Hamilton – but he didn't want to hear it, refusing to accept my explanation, saying it was irrelevant. 'You have somehow managed to upset the man who could be Chancellor of the Exchequer one day – and that is bad for the newspaper.'

I was then dismissed from his office. I felt very hurt and

unfairly treated, and of course even more convinced that I would never be allowed to be in charge of the Atticus column.

It didn't count against me, in the end, but after that Callaghan incident, I always tried to ring people after I had interviewed them and read back to them any direct quotes I was going to use. I like to think I have never made up a quote, but if people don't like something, they will deny they said it and the world at large believes them. You can of course give the wrong impression, by taking something out of context, and you can always misunderstand what someone was trying to say. So it covered me for any mistakes – and made sure there were no repercussions. But it was a dreadful bore, having to do this self-imposed task. I always read the quotes back very quickly, and of course never told them what was in the rest of the story.

Professional journalists, then and now, disapprove of such behaviour, thinking it is letting down the side, giving people a chance to influence what you are writing, so I had to keep it very quiet, especially from the heavies on the paper, such as the Insight team.

It's often forgotten that it was in the Sixties, under Denis Hamilton, that *The Sunday Times* really established its present-day reputation and shot ahead of the opposition. It was during his editorship that the colour supplement was begun in 1961, creating a new form of Sunday journalism.

It was Clive Irving from *Town* magazine who was hired by Hamilton to create a new department called Insight. He in turn brought in two assistants, Jeremy Wallington and Ron Hall. I shared a space with them at one stage, with my desk quite near them, and the first time I was aware of their arrival was the smell of boot polish. Ron Hall, who was never the best-dressed hack in the pack, had decided to clean his shoes in the office.

I couldn't quite see the point of what they were meant to add to the paper. Their early pieces just seemed to be aping American magazines like *Time*, with short, impersonal, very serious factual stories which I thought were pretty boringly written, although the topics were often interesting. Clive himself said that what he was looking for was content which had a 'high fascination count' but it had to be done in a serious, non-showy way. They in turn thought the content of the sort of stuff I was doing on Atticus was totally fluffy, frivolous and un-fascinating.

While there had been no polarisation on the paper till the Insight gang arrived, except the one in my head, it did lead to an Insight-against-the-rest mentality, as they struggled to capture the soul of the paper. Which they did, once they had found their feet and moved away from short stories and began a series of enormous and extensive investigations, on topics such as racketeering landlords. They were at their best, I thought, when piecing together some big story which had just happened, such as the Profumo–Christine Keeler drama, giving us all the details, shaping the material into a narrative. They were about the first journalists I had known to turn their big newspaper stories into instant books, which they did very successfully.

They worked incredibly hard, which was one reason why some of the old public school, shooting and golfing hacks did not approve of them, maintaining they were ruining the atmosphere of the paper as a gentleman's club. On a big story, the Insight team would often not go home at all, staying in their office all night, perhaps managing a couple of hours' sleep at their desks. I liked to think I worked hard, but I did consider this was overdoing it.

Eventually, so I thought, they did get carried away by their own importance, especially under Bruce Page, convinced they were cleverer and smarter than the people they were investigating, that what they were working on was going to bring down governments, expose corrupt multi-national firms, put baddies in gaol, which of course often did happen, whereas doing piddling interviews with footballers or pop groups from Liverpool was really of no serious importance.

The Sixties was an exciting, innovative time on *The Sunday Times*, and a reflection of what was happening outside. Insight was one of its best new arrivals, creating a high-powered team of very skilled, clever, investigative journalists who could afford and were allowed to spend weeks, if not months, on one single story, with no time or expenses being spared.

When I took over Atticus in 1964, I was allowed to hire my own assistant. I wanted someone who could do all the boring interviews I didn't fancy, to stand on the stone and see the page to bed, allowing me to get home to Margaret and our baby.

I gave the job to Tim Heald, who was already doing a bit of freelance work. He appeared very personable, bright and amusing. His speed was amazing, for someone so young. I'd ask him to ring someone, to ask them a tricky question, and he'd do it right away, totally confident, without bothering to mug up all the cuttings first, as I always did. He was so fluent and plausible and convincing that he was usually able to get away with it. He was even quicker than me in knocking out a story, once he'd done the interview. He looked incredibly young, with his fresh face, blond hair, white suit with usually a rose in his buttonhole. He had been to public school, Sherborne, and had just left Balliol. Just the sort of upper-class background I had always despised. No one can say I was prejudiced.

Chapter Nineteen

Film Fun

Here we Go, Round the Mulberry Bush, my first book, whose punctuation I could never decide on – should it have a comma in the middle or not? – was published in 1965. The same year as Margaret's second novel, *Georgy Girl.*

The film rights of *Georgy Girl* were sold quite quickly, but to a small, independent outfit, who in turn, after lots of dealing and wheeling, got the backing of Paramount. Margaret was commissioned to write the film script, while pregnant with our second child, Jake. They seemed happy with it, but towards the end, Peter Nichols the playwright was brought in, to do the final draft, which he did very well. We got to know him and his wife, and he was very amusing, when he wasn't moaning bitterly about the new young playwrights like Tom Stoppard who seemed to be getting all the critical attention.

Charlotte Rampling, who played the part of Meredith in the film of *Georgy Girl,* came to our house for tea one day in order for her and Margaret to talk babies. Charlotte herself had never had one, though in the film she has. She was very striking-looking but rather austere, nervous and uncomfortable. I think the film producers had sent her along to meet Margaret and play with baby Caitlin. It hadn't been her idea.

Margaret got invited on to the set at Shepperton despite being heavily pregnant. Naturally I went along with her, to ogle the stars. James Mason, who had been Margaret's mother's favourite filmstar, was charming. Lynn Redgrave was lovely, so natural and friendly. 'Charming' and 'lovely', what am I saying, how corny, but writing about luvvies is very hard, unless you are getting the boot in. Vanessa Redgrave had been offered the title part first, but it clashed with something else, so her young sister had got it. It was a huge chance for Lynn, her first film, and she was brilliant, not to say lovely.

The film came out in 1966 and was an enormous success, all round the world. It won a prize at Cannes, which not many British films have done since, and its theme tune, as sung by the Seekers, became an international hit. I read somewhere that Jim Dale, who wrote the words – not the tune – to the song 'Georgy Girl' made £20,000. Margaret, who had written the novel and worked on the screenplay, made only £3,000. Which did seem unfair. But of course £3,000 was a fortune to us in 1965 – enough to have bought six more cars or a small terrace house in Kentish Town.

Before *Here we Go, Round the Mulberry Bush* was published, the publisher did what most do to this day – send proofs round to established novelists, hoping they will give the newcomer a good quote which can be used in pre-publicity. I was astounded and thrilled when John Braine wrote an enthusiastic letter from his home in Bingley, Yorkshire. I had never interviewed or met him, but of course knew all about his success with *Room at the Top*.

It was quite a long letter and he seemed to see more in my novel than I had intended, which of course was pleasing.

'I think the best thing about *Here We Go Round the Mulberry Bush* is that for once someone has told the truth about adolescent sex. I personally have always felt that all sex surveys – Kinsey most of all – are completely inaccurate and are always bound to be by their very nature. No one tells the truth about sex or even tells lies according to any consistent pattern.

'What Hunter Davies has done is to show not only how adolescents are tormented by sex but also how transfigured they are by it . . . it is tremendously difficult convincingly to portray this down to earth innocence, this starry eyed lust, but Hunter Davies has very triumphantly carried it off.'

Well, wasn't that kind? Going to all that trouble. On publication, the novel did get some good reviews and was seen as quite racy for the times. Later on, I used to meet people who had been at school when it came out and they remembered reading it at the back of the bus or under the bedclothes. But it was hated by almost all booksellers. Heinemann had gone ahead with their idea of having plastic lips on the cover which did look good, especially when the book was displayed in a window and appeared to kiss passers-by. But on a shelf, with other books, it turned out a disaster. When customers took the book off the shelf, the lips came off. They would complain to the bookshop, insisting they wanted a copy with the lips stuck on. I don't think any other publisher, in the history of books, has since attempted such a daft gimmick.

The film rights to the novel got bought by United Artists, one of the big Hollywood companies, to be directed by Clive Donner. He'd recently had a big success with *What's New Pussycat?* He'd also done a film version of Harold Pinter's *The Birthday Party*, which had been critically acclaimed.

I was hired to do the screenplay, as Margaret had been with *Georgy Girl.* It was a bit difficult to fit in, while doing the Atticus column. I was used to writing in the evenings after work, and at weekends, but the film people wanted meetings at short notice and at odd times. Luckily, I had Tim Heald to do all the draggy jobs and ring-rounds. I wonder if he moaned about me as I had moaned about Nick Tomalin.

I took the script as I wrote it, scene by scene, to Clive's flat off Marylebone High Street where we worked on it together. He often had with him a young, handsome, Ivy League American called Larry Kramer. I didn't know who he was at first, or what his job was, till I discovered he had been brought in as an assistant producer by United Artists. They didn't want the film to be too British, so I was told.

I did lots of drafts, which was very annoying, especially when Clive suggested a brand-new scene he wanted me to work on. I would do it, then rush round to his flat. He would say fine fine – but he wouldn't be using it. He just wanted to see what I would do with Jamie, the film's hero, putting him in another setting.

I had hoped the film would be shot in Carlisle, where the novel had been set. I liked the idea of a Hollywood film crew turning up in Carlisle and amazing all the neighbours on our council estate, especially those who had never given me tips at Christmas when I had delivered their newspapers.

But it was felt by the film people that there had already been quite enough films set in the gritty North of England, or similar, such as *Saturday Night and Sunday Morning*, *A Taste of Honey* and others. Far better, they thought, to set it in one of the gleaming New Towns which had been springing up in several parts of Britain. Nobody had yet used one as the background to a feature film. They eventually chose Stevenage, thirty miles from London. There was another reason for this choice. Over that distance from London, according to union agreements, all the cast and crew would have had to have been paid overnight allowances during the making of the entire film.

Mulberry Bush was shot in colour, whereas *Georgy Girl* was in black and white. My film had very Sixties clothes, kipper ties, psychedelic shirts, mini-skirts, as it was supposed to be a teenage movie. It also had great pop music, by Stevie Winwood and Traffic and Spencer Davis. Margaret's, being in black and white, was seen as more arty, more intellectual than a flash Technicolor film with noisy music. My film was rather mocked by my smarter friends, and some of the critics, for being trendy. That didn't worry me particularly, but I always wished it had been set in Carlisle. It would have made it more realistic. The newness of Stevenage made it over-glossy.

Both of us having a major film out in the same year now seems amazing, if not unbelievable, but at the time, it all appeared so natural. You did a novel and it became a film, that was how it worked, how it would probably always work.

*

By the time *Mulberry Bush*, the film, had opened, I had produced two other books, both published in 1966, though one of them was an editing job.

My follow-up book to *Mulberry Bush*, again published by Heinemann, was a non-fiction work called *The Other Half*. I wonder now, thinking about it, why I didn't do another novel, as the first one seemed to go so well. Perhaps I wanted to do something worthier, as a contrast to a lightweight novel, though that wouldn't have worried me.

The Other Half was vaguely sociological – about the new poor and the new rich in Britain, first-person interviews with five of each type, demonstrating the massive gap between people in the mid-1960s. I defined the new poor as those who traditionally had needed a long education and training, who worked hard in difficult and stressful circumstances, who held responsible positions, were deemed vital to society, who at one time had been well rewarded but whose wages had now fallen ridiculously low. These new poor included a teacher, a nurse, a curate, a Civil Service clerk. The new rich, on the other hand, had had little education or training, society didn't depend on them, yet they were making small fortunes. They included a hair stylist, a barrow boy, a burglar, a prostitute, a newspaper vendor. I found some excellent people to interview and was rather pleased by how the book turned out, though the sales were modest.

At the same time, I was approached by a new young publisher, Anthony Blond, an old Etonian who seemed to have a flair for good ideas and knew lots of interesting people. His office was in Doughty Street, round the corner from *The Sunday Times*. He wasn't offering to pay much, but he appeared amusing to work with and was outrageous when it came to gossip. He wanted me to create and edit a new guidebook to London to be called *The New London Spy*. The title was taken from a scurrilous nineteenth-century London guide. I had to decide what sections of London were to be covered, find people to write them, get the copy out of them, knock it all into shape.

One of the contributors I got was John Betjeman, the poet. I had earlier interviewed him for Atticus. He was living in a little house in the East End, and appeared, in spite of his fame, to be pretty hard up. I happened to mention I came from Carlisle and immediately he insisted on giving me a two-volume 1814 edition of a leather-bound book called *Border Antiquities*. They looked very valuable, so I protested, saying I couldn't accept them. He said he'd bought them cheap from a barrow in Farringdon Road. He now had too many books and wanted to clear some out. I was doing him a favour by taking them away. I asked him to sign them which he did. 'Tae Hunter frae Iain MacBetjeman.' A rather confusing inscription which no one in the future will be able to understand.

The topic I thought up for Betjeman was the best London churches – and also the best sermons. Other contributors included Michael Horowitz, George Mikes, Jonathan Routh, Maureen Duffy, Anthony Lejeune, Gillian Freeman. Their names were listed, but you didn't know who had written which section, partly because we had a section on homosexual London, where to meet, where to pick up partners, and the author didn't want to be exposed.

Anthony Blond sold *The New London Spy* very well, and even found an American publisher. He wanted me to do another edition, finding new people and new areas and topics, but I said no. Once was enough. I always preferred a brand-new subject.

The Other Half was also published in the USA which was a surprise, considering it was such a totally English subject. And it came out in paperback and was sold to a book club, so Heinemann were very pleased.

Once *Mulberry Bush*, the film, came out, and did so well, I was offered various film ideas, but I didn't fancy any of them. But one of the results of the film's appearance, and my name appearing on it as the scriptwriter, was that I was later approached to write a TV play. The suggestion came from Tony Garnett, then one of the best-known and most admired TV producers. He asked if I had an idea for a 'Wednesday

Play', which was the BBC's big prestigious slot for original TV plays.

I couldn't think of one at first, then I remembered my stage play, written some years earlier, which never made it. I dug it out, dusted it off, changed a few things and it became *The Playground*. It had a good cast and got excellent reviews, but alas I don't have a copy. It was one of those TV plays, done live, not filmed, so it was never preserved on video. I would like to have had it, if just as proof that you shouldn't throw anything away. Recycling can work.

Heinemann wanted me to do another book on similar lines to *The Other Half*, but on a different theme – long interviews with people linked by the same subject. I decided to do it about people at universities. They were in the news, with the opening of all the new universities, such as Sussex. I would interview a cross-section of people currently at a British university, lecturers as well as students, from different social classes, at different sorts of universities, ancient and modern.

I signed the contract and in 1966 started work on the new book, which naturally enough was going to be called 'The Class of Sixty-Six'.

I was about half way through it when by chance an even better and more challenging-sounding project presented itself. I decided to drop 'The Class of Sixty-Six', for the moment at least, thinking I can always come back to it later on. After all, I can change the title to 'The Class of Sixty-Seven', or even 'Sixty-Eight', depending on what happens when I've finished this new and, so I hoped, exciting book idea . . .

Chapter Twenty

With the Beatles

I didn't take much notice of 'Love Me Do' when it came out in October 1962 but then few people did. When I first heard John Lennon copying the Americans and screaming his way through 'Twist and Shout' it gave me a headache. But I liked 'Please Please Me', 'From Me to You' and 'I Want to Hold Your Hand'.

We could hear their Liverpool accents by now and, as we learned more about them, I identified with their background, their grammar schools and council houses. They were near my age – I was just four years older than John – and they seemed to be singing songs for me, about our experiences.

Some time early in 1964, I went to watch them working on their first film, *A Hard Day's Night*, at a theatre in Charlotte Street. I was hoping to get a paragraph for the Atticus column. John made a complicated joke about a sign saying 'Sound On' which lit up when people had to be quiet. He kept on saying 'Sounds On, Sounds On', a popular phrase at the time, meaning something was good, something seemed possible. Perhaps I mucked up this not very funny remark in trying to re-tell it, but whatever I wrote that day didn't make the column. More likely Nick Tomalin or someone up the hierarchy didn't like it or did not approve of the Beatles.

Two years later, in August 1966, I was in charge of the column and I could write almost what I liked. 'Eleanor Rigby' had come out and I thought the lyrics were as good as any poetry currently being published, perhaps any that would be published that year, so I maintained, without of course knowing much about current poetry.

I went to see Paul at his house in Cavendish Avenue, St John's Wood. I presumed, from the voice singing, that he had written it, though in those days no one bothered to separate a Lennon-McCartney song.

I got on well with him, so I thought, and we talked about the background to several other of his songs. The papers were obsessed by Beatlemania, their fame and money and record sales, but I realised there was so much I didn't know. There had been only two books about them so far – both paperbacks. One was a little fan club book and the other a slice of life done on tour by an American journalist.

I was busy with the screenplay for *Mulberry Bush*, plus I'd started doing interviews for 'The Class of Sixty-Six'. I had finished two, each about 10,000 words. One was with a girl called Anna Ford, who had just become the first woman president of Manchester University Union.

In December 1966, I went to see Paul again, this time with a different hat on – as a screenwriter. Paul had already written some film music, and Clive Donner was hoping to get him to write the theme tune for our film. He was polite enough, but eventually said no . . .

Talking to Paul, I put to him the idea which had originally struck me. How about a proper book about the Beatles, a serious attempt to get it all down, once and for all, so that in the future when people ask the same old dopey questions, he could say it's in the book. He said fine – but there was one problem. 'You'll have to talk to Brian,' he said. 'He's the one who'll decide.'

There and then, Paul helped me draft a letter. Next day, I typed it out and sent it to Brian. It was on the lines Paul suggested, boasting that I had 'interviewed the Beatles' several times, which was a slight exaggeration.

My appointment with Brian Epstein was made for Wednesday,

25 January 1967. At the last moment, he cancelled, but made it for the next day. When I arrived at his home, 24 Chapel Street, in Belgravia, best part, he kept me waiting, so I mooched around his drawing room, admiring his two fine paintings by Lowry.

He eventually appeared, in a smart suit as always, very fresh-looking, slightly chubby cheeked, healthy, affluent and confident but rather distracted. Looking back, I find it hard to believe that at the time he was only thirty-two, just two years older than me. He seemed such a polished, metropolitan man of the world who had achieved so much. I felt quite gauche.

He played me the tapes of 'Penny Lane' and of 'Strawberry Fields', their new single, not yet released. He sat back with paternal pride and watched me listening. I was amazed by 'Strawberry Fields'. It seemed an enormous leap forward from juvenile stuff like 'Yellow Submarine', full of discordant jumps and eerie echoes. I wondered if Beatles fans would like it. I asked him what the title meant, but he didn't seem to know.

He locked the tapes away saying he could not be too careful. A previous Beatles tape had been stolen and it was very embarrassing. They could fetch a lot of money if leaked to a pirate radio station before the official launch date. I didn't quite believe this, not being aware that people stole tapes just to get a few days ahead of their rivals.

I eventually got the conversation round to my letter. He appeared not to have taken much of it in, though he smiled and was charming, so I took him through my proposal and he said yes, he did think it a good idea, he would put it to the four Beatles. We arranged another meeting for the following Wednesday, for him to meet my publisher and agent, by which time he should have spoken to the Beatles themselves.

The boss of my literary agency, Spencer Curtis Brown, whom I hadn't thought was alive, said he would come in person, as did Charles Pick, managing director of Heinemann. I think they just wanted to get inside Epstein's house, see how this man of the moment lived. The proposed book itself was not being considered much of a big deal. Inside Heinemann, several people had not been at all impressed. We know all we ever want to know about the Beatles, said some. Anyway, books about popstars don't sell. I maintained it would be more like sociology. Who needs sociology? That doesn't sell either.

Brian said all the Beatles had agreed and he would give me full access and facilities. I left it to Spencer to decide the financial deal. It was going to be a biography, written by me, not a ghosted work. Traditionally, the subjects of such books did not get paid anything. It would be good publicity for them – and of course they were spending a lot on publicity, through their press office and fan club. I would be doing all the work, having to travel a lot, and it would take time, be a proper hardback book, not a cheap, paperback fan club quickie. However, Spencer proposed that Brian, on behalf of the Beatles, would get one-third. He agreed at once. Brian personally drew up the contract, between me and his company NEMS, which said amongst other things he would not allow any other authorised book for two years.

Heinemann, as publisher, agreed to pay £3,000 as the advance. Even in those days, it was not considered a huge amont. And one-third of it went straight to the Beatles. Now of course it appears piddling. In 1981, a writer with no access to them received £150,000 for a biography. As I write, a Beatles expert called Mark Lewisohn, too young to have ever interviewed them at their height, will reportedly receive £2 million (from the UK and USA) for a three-volume work about them. Which I'm sure will be excellent, as he knows more about them than I ever did.

I started work on the book on 7 February 1967. That same day I got a call at *The Sunday Times*, where I was still writing the Atticus column. It was from a strange-sounding lady called Yoko Ono. She said she'd been told I was the most eminent columnist in London and she wanted to feature me in a film she was doing about bare bottoms. 'Don't bugger around,' I said. I suspected it was some drunk from the *Observer*. 'No,' she said, 'it's very serious,' and proceeded to tell me of the other films she had done.

I went along to an address in Park Lane where the filming was being done, thinking I might get a daft story for the column. There was a queue of people outside who had answered an advert in *The Stage* promising an appearance in a film, though there would be no money. Each had to step on a revolving stage, like a children's roundabout, then drop their pants. I talked to a rather distracted Ivy-League-type American called Anthony Cox who turned out to be Yoko's husband and, I gathered, had put up the money. I found it hard to believe he had fallen for all this nonsense.

Yoko tried to make me strip off but I refused. She told me the point of the film, which I've now forgotten, if I ever understood it. In my piece, which appeared on 12 February 1967, I hoped I hadn't poked too much fun at her. I worried that the headline 'Oh no, Ono' might upset her, though she had got what she wanted, which was publicity. She rang me afterwards to thank me.

I never met her again, in the flesh, until I walked into Abbey Road studios one evening in 1968 and there she was, sitting in a transcendental state with John transfixed, looking at her adoringly, while the other three Beatles exchanged bewildered glances, clearly wondering who the fuck she was.

I began work on the book with a first quick chat with each of them, not interviews as such, just to explain how I was going to work and get from them names of school friends, teachers and most of all, introductions to their parents. I sensed they must be pretty fed up being asked the same old questions, so I decided to spend the first few months going back in time, interviewing people from their past, so that when I saw them again I would bring news and observations.

John must have taken in my few words of introduction, when I'd explained who I was and what I was doing, for I got a letter from him, addressed to 'White Hunter Davies, c/o Heinemann Ltd, 15 Queen Street, London W1'. On the back of the envelope he had written the words 'JAKE MY ARSE'. He must have taken in the fact that we'd just had a baby son, though the way he stared blankly through his National Health specs I hadn't thought he was taking much in. Later on, I always made a point of saying what a poncy middle-class name Julian was.

Going to see the parents was one of the stranger parts of researching the book. I wanted to put in more about them, and how they had reacted to their sons becoming a phenomenon, but there wasn't space. Ringo's mother Elsie and stepfather Harry appeared almost stunned, caught like rabbits in a searchlight of fame, sitting in their brand-new posh bungalow on an exclusive estate, surrounded by new furnitutre, some of it still with plastic covers on. They were so nervous, scared to say the wrong thing, that I had to ring Ritchie – as they called their son – and get him to reassure them it was OK to talk to me.

On the other hand, George's mother Louise was loving it, enjoying her son's fame, welcoming fans, opening fetes, signing autographs, making little speeches. She'd met Ken Dodd and Jimmy Tarbuck and had attended the funeral of a local popstar, seeing it as her duty to represent George. She had turned being a Beatle's mum into a full-time occupation.

When I first went up to see her, early in 1967, there were rumours, yet again, about the Beatles splitting up. It was either that or one of them, usually Paul, was secretly dead. To cope with all the mail she was personally receiving about the rumoured split, she had taken it upon herself to issue a prepared statement she sent to all fans.

I stayed with Jim McCartney, Paul's dad, a couple of times at his Cheshire home, along with his new wife, Angie. One night Paul had sent up an advance copy of 'When I'm Sixty-Four,' written with his dad in mind. We must have played it about twenty times, dancing round the room, till I thought Jim might have a heart attack.

Aunt Mimi, who brought up John, was the only one who had left the Liverpool area, moving into a bungalow near Bournemouth, to get away from all the fans. Two had broken into her house one night and were sitting in her front room when she came down in the morning, going through her belongings, looking for buttons John might have worn. But she hadn't quite escaped. As I sat talking to her, on the back veranda of her new luxury home overlooking the sea, we could hear the amplified voice of a guide on one of the pleasure steamers drifting towards us. 'And over there, ladies and gentlemen, look to your left, on her back porch, and you'll see John Lennon's Aunt Mimi . . .' Did she scream.

There were two missing fathers whom I eventually managed to track down. I discovered Ringo's real dad, also called Richard or Ritchie, working as a window cleaner in Crewe. I admired the fact that despite his son's fame and wealth he had not cashed in in any way or made contact. He ticked me off, when I first wrote to him. I had addressed the letter to Mr Starkie instead of Mr Starkey. I never was hot on spelling.

It was only at the end I made contact with Freddie Lennon, John's dad, who had done a runner many years earlier. I found him in a hotel, not far from John's home in Weybridge, where he was working as a washer-up. He gave me his memories of his marriage and John's childhood, all invaluable, with stories John had never heard. 'If it hadn't been for the Beatles,' said John, 'I would probably have ended up like Freddie.'

John then asked me to tell Freddie to contact him, but not to tell anyone. Mimi would be furious as she had always considered 'that Alfred' as a very bad lot. The upshot was that John gave Freddie money for a flat. He moved in with a nineteen-year-old girl by whom he had a son.

One interview I was desperate to obtain was with Pete Best, the drummer sacked by the Beatles, just as they had made their first record. He failed to answer any of my messages and requests, but I managed to talk his mother, Mo Best, into seeing me. She had helped the Beatles in the early stages by letting them perform at a club called the Casbah she had opened in her house.

She was still furious about Pete's sacking, and convinced that as the authorised biographer I would take the side of the Beatles, not her son. I said I simply wanted to hear both sides, which I would write fairly. It took a while to reassure her. Unbeknown to me, Pete had been in her house all the time, in the next room. She eventually took me through to see him. He was very tired, having just come off shift work at a bakery, and spoke quietly, and rather sadly, but without too much bitterness. He was very helpful, especially with dates and details of their Hamburg appearances which the Beatles themselves were very hazy about.

When I next met the Beatles, I told them what their old friends from Liverpool were up to, but when I mentioned Pete Best, they were rather shifty and embarrassed, especially when I said he was earning £18 a week slicing bread in a factory.

The highlight of my Hamburg trip was meeting Astrid Kirchherr. She and her little group of Hamburg Art School friends were the Beatles' earliest intellectual and artistic fans. She had got engaged to Stu Sutcliffe who had joined the Beatles, without really being able to play, just because he was John's friend. Stu had died suddenly of a brain haemorrhage in April 1962.

I was rather shocked by the life Astrid was leading in 1967. Her room was almost like a shrine to Stu. Everything was black – the bed, soft furnishings, furniture, candles – yet she was able to talk about him without pathos or melodrama. She was working in a bar, the first lesbian bar I had ever been in, serving drinks but also dancing with customers, if required. She had a great influence on the Beatles, on their hairstyles and their clothes, and had taken what I think were the best ever photographs of them, but she had refused to make money from her memories, or her photographs.

It took me a while to realise Brian Epstein was homosexual. At first I thought it didn't matter, either way, till I slowly recognised it was a vital part of his relationships with the Beatles. His background, public school and RADA, his tastes in music, his business life and social circle, were so different from the Beatles, so what had really first attracted him? I believe it was watching John perform at the Cavern in his leather outfit. Brian was masochistic in his sexual tastes, deliberately picking up non-homosexual boys, bringing them home to his house or a rented flat, treating them to drinks and drugs. It usually ended in tears, with him being beaten up and items stolen, then he would get blackmailed, which led to depression and further pill popping.

I spent one night at his country home in Kingsley Hill, Sussex. We were joined at dinner by a well-known pop music personality of the day. After the meal, Brian decided he would like some boys to amuse them, but by this time it was after eleven o'clock on a Saturday evening. Brian had some sort of credit card which was his membership to a homosexual call-boy club. He dialled the number and gave his name. I could hear a long discussion, with someone at the other end saying it was far too late, all the best boys had gone. Brian said he would pay double, and the taxi fares. They didn't arrive till about four in the morning, by which time I had long been in bed.

Paul, I think, was upset by Brian's homosexuality, and didn't like it mentioned. John was the only one I discussed it with. He told me he'd had a one-night stand with Brian when he'd gone on holiday with him to Spain, just after the birth of John's son Julian. I mentioned this holiday in the book, but not what John alleged had taken place. He was of course happily married to Cynthia, as far as the world was concerned. John wasn't a homosexual, but he was daft enough to try anything once. On the other hand, he did say things for effect, exaggerating what did or did not happen.

I was with the Beatles in Bangor, north Wales, in August 1967, when they heard about Brian's death. By a sequence of events, their wives and roadies had got left behind at Euston so I was in their carriage with them, along with Mick Jagger and Marianne Faithfull, all of them in their flower power clothes. It was interesting to watch John and Jagger together. They seemed wary of each other, respectful but distant. I later discussed it with John. He said he wasn't at all jealous of the Stones' music but of their rebel image and clothes. He still resented the cleaning-up operation Brian had done on them, putting them into little suits. I argued that it was thanks to the Beatles, paving the way, with their long hair, that the Stones were allowed to act as they did.

On the train, when we stopped, fans shoved autograph books through our carriage windows. When John refused to sign any more, and a kid was clearly very disappointed, I duly signed John's name. I do hope Sotheby's have a way of checking the genuine ones.

Late that evening, we all went into Bangor for a meal. All we could find was a Chinese restaurant. When the bill came, I found I did not have enough to cover it. The Beatles at this stage, like the Royal Family, did not carry money and their roadies had still not arrived. The Chinese waiters were getting restless, suspecting we were all going to do a runner. The atmosphere was turning nasty when George put his foot on the table and took off a sandal. He slit it at the front with a knife and produced a £20 note, more than enough to settle the bill. Months, if not years, previously he had secreted the money away, just in case such an emergency should ever occur.

Back in London, while working on the book, the Beatles in turn visited our house for tea or a meal. When Paul and Jane Asher came, Paul insisted on walking round the corner to the local shop to buy something. I tried to stop him, knowing he would be recognised and be pestered and followed back to the house. I think he was still at the stage when he quite enjoyed being spotted – and also being seen as an ordinary guy, who could still walk the streets. When George and Pattie came, Pattie brought flowers and chocolates, being a well-brought-up girl.

Before Ringo and his wife Maureen arrived, Ringo warned me he had become a vegetarian. Margaret got out a vegetarian cook book and made a rather ambitious if complicated dish with aubergines and stuffed courgettes. Ringo took one look at it and pushed his plate away. What he meant by being a vegetarian was beans on toast, his favourite dish, or failing that, fried egg on toast. He didn't actually like vegetables.

We both got invited to the Beatles' private party to celebrate 'Magical Mystery Tour', along with various friends and relations, though we were a bit worried when we were told we had to come in fancy dress. I refused to hire anything so I went as a boy scout and Margaret as a girl guide, borrowing the clothes from neighbours. John looked magnificent at the party dressed as a greasy Teddy Boy, just as he had been, ten years earlier. He talked to Margaret for a while about books, then sat in a daze.

The most enjoyable part of the book was being in the studios at Abbey Road while they were recording. John and Paul would usually assemble beforehand at Paul's house nearby, going up to his top floor where they would try out any ideas they had had on their own, sparking off each other. In Abbey Road, John or Paul would write out the latest versions of a new song on the back of an envelope or scrap of paper, so that George and Ringo would know what was happening. At the end of the sessions, I would often pick up these scraps from the floor, ask if I could have them, as otherwise the cleaners chucked them out. The Beatles themselves had no interest in such items, concerned only with the next thing, not what they had done.

When I was interviewing them, in their homes, I would use a notebook. But in the studio, when they were working, I was more of a fly on the wall, observing rather than note taking, keeping out of the way, trying not to break their concentration. Outsiders were never allowed in the studio itself – until Yoko came along. Afterwards I would rush home and type out everything I had heard and observed as quickly as possible, before it all faded. I wish now I had made more and better notes on their music making, which I observed as it was happening, especially during the making of *Sergeant Pepper*.

Looking back, of course, I should have tape recorded all my interviews with the Beatles, as the tapes would now be fascinating, and worth a lot. But I've gone through my writing life scribbling in little red notebooks, which I buy in bulk. My theory is that using a tape recorder doubles your work. At least half of what anyone says is not worth repeating anyway, but with a tape, you have to listen to it all through again. I don't write down everything, just what I think I'm going to use, so I'm editing as I go along. I also include descriptions of faces, expressions, clothes, furniture, which you can't capture on tape. If they say don't write this down, I nod and smile and put my pen down. Later, when they tell me how they love animals, help old people across the road, I write down what they had said earlier – purely as a record, of course.

I did once use a tape recorder, back in about 1962 on *The Sunday Times,* when the literary editor, Leonard Russell, sent me to interview W. H. Auden who was staying at Stephen Spender's house in St John's Wood. I had to hand over an envelope to him first. It wasn't properly sealed, so I peeped inside – and there was £30. Auden grabbed it the moment I arrived. I thought how interesting, and yet pathetic, that one of the world's best-known poets should be so hard-up.

I'd borrowed a tape recorder, a monster Grundig, and all the way through, I worried that it wasn't working. The interview never made the paper. The fault might have been mine, or his, because he couldn't be arsed to say anything of interest, but I blamed the machine – and have never ever used one again.

I have kept all my notebooks from the Beatles book. My handwriting is awful and hard to read – and even worse now – but glancing through them recently, I found Paul had done a drawing for me, of how John looked when they first met. I also found some good notes I'd made on the photo session for the cover of *Sergeant Pepper.* In them I recorded how a cardboard figure of Hitler had stood to attention during the whole of the evening. They had wanted a line-up of heroes and gurus, goodies and baddies. John had been talked out of including Hitler at the last moment. He'd caused enough trouble by talking about Jesus.

I had suggested to them that their heroes should include some Liverpool footballer, someone they had been well aware of while growing up, even though they had never been football fans. This had been a disappointment to me, that they had no interest in the game. In the end, John had stuck in Albert Stubbins who had played for Liverpool in the late 1940s and early 1950s – but just because John thought his name was funny.

I remember leaving Paul's house in a rush for the final photographic session, with Paul telling me to take along any ornament lying around his house which might fill up any gap in the tableau. I picked up a little statuette of what looked like an egg with a circle round it on a plinth and shoved it in a space at the front, amongst the flowers. You can see it in the middle of the letter L in the word Beatles, if you put your best specs on. I often boasted about this to my children when they became teenagers, but they were not at all impressed.

I didn't really want to stop working on the book, in the sense of interviewing and researching, as I was enjoying it so much, watching the Beatles at work. Things were still changing all the time and I feared that bits in the book might date by the time it came out. It had grown enormous, to around 150,000 words, so I had to stop.

I hacked out a large amount, mainly some poncy chapters I had done, trying to put the Beatles in perspective, evaluating their social and artistic significance, which included listening to the views and theories of people like Ken Tynan and William Mann, the *Times*' music critic. It was quite interesting, but I personally never like reading that sort of stuff. Anyway, I had first-hand material, from them, while it was happening. Why add to it?

I then had to get their agreement, as it was their so-called authorised biography. I sent copies to the four of them. Paul and Ringo had no worries. George did twit on a bit, saying he would have liked more about his spiritual side, but I said there just wasn't room. John said it was fine – but then a few weeks later he sent me a letter asking me to cut out a reference to a Welsh boyfriend of his mum's. He also said his Aunt Mimi was 'worried sick . . . she must see the book before publication . . . Do yer duty Hunt, lad, don't let me down – Love John.'

So I rushed down to Bournemouth to see Mimi. She said she didn't want him swearing in the book, or stealing. As a boy, he'd never done that. I said these were John's memories, I couldn't change them. But I calmed her down by adding an extra paragraph, right at the end of the first chapter, saying that Mimi and his other aunts always found John 'as happy as the day was long'.

Technically, Brian Epstein owned my contract, as he had signed it, so I had now to deal with his brother and mother. Queenie, his mother, always denied he was homosexual. He was now dead, so I could have said something, but to keep the family happy, I made no mention – except I did describe him as a 'gay bachelor'. Most of the population, including Queenie, did not, at the time, appreciate the reference.

One of the staff at Apple, Peter Brown, drove my agent Richard Simon mad over various aspects of the contract, being decidedly unhelpful but at long last it was all sorted out.

We got lots of impressive-looking copies of the manuscript run off for Heinemann to work on and for Richard to start trying to sell the overseas rights. By which time I felt ready to collapse.

Chapter Twenty-one

Legal Matters

Before I had finished working on the Beatles book, I had given up being Atticus. In my farewell column in July 1967 I did a jokey paragraph about payola, which was in the news that week, after certain DJs were being accused of taking bribes and presents from record companies. I said the only thing I had taken in my journalistic life was a second-hand suit from Teasy Weasy Raymond. Har har, was the implication, call that a bribe.

Teasy Weasy was a celebrity hairdresser whom I had interviewed for the *Sunday Graphic*, not long after I had come down from Manchester. He clearly didn't think much of whatever I was wearing and took me into his bedroom and opened a massive wardrobe, filled with his suits. He insisted I took one he said he wouldn't wear again, a hideous tweed suit in a loud check, like a high-class bookie's. When I took it home, Margaret was appalled. I never wore it and she gave it away to Oxfam.

In that little Atticus story, I finished by saying that if you ever saw a refugee dressed as if for Ascot, you would know where his suit had come from. Teasy Weasy didn't think it was funny. A writ was issued against me and the newspaper on 22 December 1967, and I was summoned to appear at the High Court, Queen's Bench division. The legal documents, sent to me by Theodore Goddard, acting for the paper, informed me that the case would be between Raymond Peter Carlos Bessone Raymond (which was his real name) and Hunter Davies and Times Newspapers Limited.

What had done the damage was not the story itself, which he didn't deny, but linking it to the word payola. That was my big mistake. But I had used the word, as it was in the news, in a topical joke, so I thought. I never imagined that anyone could consider the gift of a second-hand suit as a bribe.

It all seemed laughable, but all the same, there were big-deal legal persons making a meal of it. The court hearing might be very amusing, and attract a lot of attention for its Justice Cocklecarrot overtones, but on the other hand, it could be the sort of trivial incident which gets out of hand and turns into a very nasty and expensive case. I had to get together all my notes and memories of the day in question and what did happen to the suit. Margaret did a letter, under oath, confirming I had never worn the suit and she'd given it to Oxfam in Kentish Town.

Anyway, just a few weeks before I had to appear in court, it got settled. The *Times* lawyer never told me how much they had to pay, if anything.

In 1967, *The Sunday Times* had got a new editor – Harold Evans, my friend from Manchester, who had also been at the same Durham college as me. I was one of his main contacts on the paper when he had arrived the previous year from Darlington, where he had been editor of the *Northern Echo*.

When he took over as editor, he immediately began to have an enormous effect on all departments. I told him about my Beatles book, which I was by then in the middle of. He was immediately keen to have it for the paper, to serialise it, and we made a deal. I had managed all my previous books, bits and bobs, while still a full-time journalist, but the Beatles book was entailing far more work, time and travelling than I had expected. It was agreed with Harry that I would become chief feature writer, not too onerous a position, able to fit in my Beatles work with interviews for the paper. When I went to New York, for example, and interviewed

U Thant, Secretary-General of the United Nations, then flew on to Canada to interview Marshall McLuhan, I managed at the same time to see people in New York who were part of the Beatles saga.

It was fortunate that Harry had arrived when he did, and I was able to make these arrangements which suited both of us. I realised, probably for the first time in my working life, that actually, here was me, who had moaned for years about feeling an outsider, with the wrong accent and wrong background, using my own friends and contacts for my own benefit. So it goes.

I therefore, in theory, had more time at home, when I wasn't rushing around interviewing people, and was able to contribute a bit more on the domestic front.

I suppose I had, until then, been rather neglecting my wife and two young children. I certainly didn't pull my full weight when Caitlin and Jake were babies, although I did always boast, and still do, that I delivered Jake. He was born at home, in a little downstairs back bedroom we had converted from an outside coal cellar. He arrived so quickly, before the midwife had appeared, and emerged with the cord twisted round his neck. I managed to untangle it, before he'd strangled himself, with the help of the midwife who had turned up by then. He was born on 24 May 1966, the day before Margaret's own birthday. What a nice present.

The midwife handed me the placenta, to dispose of, but I fried it with onions. I had read in some alternative health magazine that fried placenta was as good as liver, so I thought I'd try it, purely of course to get a 1,000-word article, which I did. It tasted awful.

When either baby cried in the night, I always managed to turn over and snore, pretending I hadn't heard. I could change a nappy, and did so now and again, but very badly. On holiday, that was different. I took equal shares in looking after them when we went away, but at home, I always seemed to be rushing off somewhere. Nor did I do any cooking or housework. A sign of the times or just a selfish chauvinist pig?

We did arrive at an arrangement that I would be in charge of them on a Monday, my day off from the paper, when I was at home all day, in theory, giving Margaret a chance to get down to her own writing. This carried on for many years. I would take them to Kenwood, go in the café, or to Golders Green, look at the animals.

Margaret always refused to have any help in the house, either a cleaner or an au pair. She didn't want to have someone coming in to do her housework, or have a stranger living with us. She liked doing everything herself. I tried to persuade her, but she refused. I was thinking selfishly of course. Having help would mean she had more time for her writing – and for me. She said her own writing didn't matter, not compared with her children. My work did matter, so she would say, only half satirically, as I was the breadwinner.

By 1968, our part of the house was becoming cramped, with two young children, aged four and two. Mrs Hall, still living on the top floor, now had proportionally more space than we did, yet it was our house. We had no privacy either. She entered through our front door, went down our hall, up our stairs to the top floor, which wasn't separated, having no door of its own. At least she was fond of children. We used to pretend to be upset and apologise if we found Caitlin had gone up the stairs to Mrs Hall's flat, knowing she would be getting a biscuit and watching children's programmes on TV. We didn't have TV. We were quite proud of that, like many professional middle-class people in the late Sixties. We prefer to talk to our children, oh yes, not stick them in front of a goggle box. I used the term middle class half seriously, but we knew by then that in a sense it had become true.

I offered Mrs Hall money if she would move. She refused to name her price or even discuss it. Instead we put a lavatory in her floor, which gave us a bit more privacy.

I would like to have known how the house had been arranged over the decades, how the various families had used it, back to the 1860s. When we had some building work done, because of subsidence, they dug a seven-foot hole. Before they filled it up again with concrete, I put in it a biscuit tin filled with various contemporary mementoes. I included that day's newspaper, photographs of the four of us, what we had done that day, and a plan of the house and how each room was used.

I did my writing in our drawing room on the first floor, at an old Victorian inlaid bureau, which we still have, at my little manual, portable typewriter. Each time when I finished for the day or evening, I had to clear all the papers and books away as either Caitlin or Jake, especially Jake, would come and wreck the place. I longed to have a room of my own where I could scatter my things around and not have to tidy up after every session.

Margaret, woman of the house, did her writing downstairs at the kitchen table, which of course women writers have traditionally done, since Jane Austen and the Brontës. Jane Austen's room had a squeaky door so she would always hear if someone was approaching and quickly hide her stuff away. Margaret was much the same. For her, writing was and is a private act. She didn't want to discuss it and preferably not even admit she was doing it.

She wrote in pen and ink in longhand on unlined sheets, as she still does. No mess, no papers, but then not much space is needed when you are doing fiction, unlike non-fiction. In six weeks to three months each year, despite everything, she produced a novel.

Looking back, it is remarkable how she did it. I was cosseted, allowed to be selfish, using the best room, able to keep myself away from most of the household hubbub while she was single-handedly running our little domestic empire. No wonder she went to bed each night absolutely exhausted.

Jake was what mostly exhausted her, and all of us. Caitlin was a paragon of all the virtues from almost the moment she was born – obedient, biddable, reasonable, sensible, neat and tidy. Jake was a nightmare. First of all, he never slept. He was in our bed most nights, insisting on lying between us, thrashing away.

During the day, he was mostly in a frenzy, doing the most stupid things, like putting his fingers in the electric sockets or playing with the kitchen knives. If you dragged him away, screaming, he would go right back. The only way was to forcibly restrain him.

Getting him dressed and ready to go out in his pushchair on the Heath was always a physical fight and it took the two of us to manhandle him. He wouldn't listen to reason, was totally contrary and wilful. Having arrived in a bad temper, with the cord round his neck, it was as if he was now determined to get his own back and impose his will on the whole family.

We worried what it might be doing to Caitlin, with so much time and attention focused on Jake. We didn't believe in corporal punishment, being good Sixties, Dr Spock parents, but we often longed to throttle him.

He was also very clumsy and accident prone, unlike Caitlin. He wrecked almost every toy he played with, every room he walked into.

He was once playing with a tin of Elastoplast, which he had been told not to touch. We thought we'd hidden it, out of his reach, but he'd somehow clambered up and got it. He ran around, waving the open tin, till he fell, the tin almost slicing off his thumb. It was hanging, half off, and needed many stitches. Just the memory of Jake's wilfulness gives me a shudder.

His speech was awful as well, even after he had started school. He was very slow to read and write and we feared he might be backward. Caitlin talked early, and beautifully, and could recite reams of poetry, beginning and ending each one with a little cough and then she'd give her full name and exact age, to the month, and I would tape record her and send copies to the grandparents.

We could not have done so many books if we had followed Nick Tomalin's advice and done constant entertaining, but we did have a dinner party, perhaps twice a year, and on Christmas Eve we started a tradition of having all the neighbours in, with their children, for food and drink, games and entertainment. I played my violin, so badly it encouraged others to show off their skills. We did have one neighbour who could actually play a musical instrument properly, Wally Fawkes on his clarinet.

The Sixties, then, for us, was a time of work and babies and domesticity, not sex and drugs and wild parties, though Ringo once gave me a reefer. We kept it for a few weeks and then one evening we thought we should at least try it. We closed the curtains, made sure the children were asleep, took the phone off the hook, then lit up. Neither of us has ever smoked, so the sensation of smoking was new in itself. We sat and waited. Nothing happened.

The next time I saw Ringo I told him all this. 'It was cabbage leaves,' replied Ringo. I don't know whether that was true, or whether it was just a lousy reefer.

Margaret always gave brilliant birthday parties for the children, right from the beginning, with a different theme each year and always imaginative and creative. For Caitlin, we had a back-to-front party, like *Alice in Wonderland*. You entered the front door backwards, then went down a tunnel. The food started with ice cream and finished with sausages. Margaret invented a new game called Strip-On which they all loved. She collected a large pile of our clothes, and split the children into two teams. The team who ended up with most clothes on was the winner.

I captured all these trivial family happenings on my Super 8 movie camera. Its blank films lasted three minutes each. I sent them away to be processed, then showed them on a large white screen fixed to a tripod stand which had to be erected each time.

I never really got the hang of showing the films. When we had visitors, I would promise everyone a show, and they'd all be excited, seated in the dark, waiting impatiently – and I wouldn't be able to even start the projector. When I did, there was usually some smoke, or the smell of burning, indicating I had somehow buggered up the precious film. The films were all silent, of course, so I always insisted on giving my own, terribly amusing, commentary, so I thought. All the same, and despite the problems, it did seem like a minor miracle that you could capture such precious family moments on film for ever. Our own parents only had a few small black and white snaps of us as children. Today, everyone is a star in their own digital, computerised film.

I still have all my old Super 8 family films, but now at least I have converted them to video, complete with burn marks.

Chapter Twenty-two

Home Thoughts from Abroad

The Beatles book was published in the UK in September 1968. I wasn't there. For the previous few months, Richard Simon at Curtis Brown was in a state of high excitement as offers came in from foreign publishers all over the world. In the USA, there was an auction, with most of the leading New York publishers saying what they could offer or provide in the way of promotion, if they got the rights. It was eventually won by McGraw Hill with a bid of $150,000. It seemed a totally incredible sum. My share was a lot less than that, as the Beatles got one-third, then there were the UK and US agents who took their percentage. All the same, it was embarrassingly huge and I hoped it wouldn't leak into the papers or everyone would think I was mega-rich. Which I was, compared to most people, but then I'd always thought that anyway.

I had had an accountant, Anton Felton, recommended to me by Clive Irving, since my first book, *Mulberry Bush*, three years earlier. My *Sunday Times* salary was of course taxed at source. But we were beginning to have an increasing amount of other, free-lance, income, thanks to the success of *Georgy Girl* and *Mulberry Bush*, from their subsequent films and paperback sales. Combined with the Beatles book, it meant we were going to have a massive income in an eighteen-month period – something we were not likely to have ever again in our working lives. Super tax in 1968 was up to 98 per cent, which we had already started to pay. If it was charged on the whole lot, it was going to dramatically reduce our earnings. We could end up with very little extra, for all our work. We had been very lucky. Getting the Beatles to agree had been pure good fortune. Getting a film made, never mind two in the same year, is a lottery, with so many forces outside your control.

There had been a flight of tax exiles ever since the tax rates had risen so high, amongst writers and filmstars. Noel Coward had spent most of his working life abroad, to escape the punitive British tax system. I did a whole Atticus column once on Switzerland with interviews and a map showing where all the many tax-exiled Brits were based. Recently, Desmond Morris, after the success of his *Naked Ape*, had gone to live in Malta, while a friend of mine on *The Sunday Times*, John Pearson, had gone to Italy after the success of his Ian Fleming biography.

We didn't want to go and settle abroad, whatever the tax advantages. We felt totally British and as good Labour Party supporters, so we told ourselves, we believed in paying tax, as we had had so much out of the state in the way of health services and education.

I'd always argued against the notion of money as an incentive, saying it was only a sign of success, not an end in itself. All the wealthy, successful people I had interviewed maintained that money was a by-product. And I believed them. People who work hard, work hard. All the same, a maximum tax rate of 98 per cent did seem pointlessly over the top. It must be taking away the incentives for many people to sell more, make more money.

At one meeting with Anton Felton, he pointed out that in fact you only needed to go abroad for a year and a day, in order to save some tax. You didn't have to flee for ever. If you thought your income was never going to be this high again, why not go for a year, then come back and pay the normal taxes for the rest of our lives? This was a one-and-only chance to amass some capital.

He was doing this with several other authors and said he would consult a QC, an expert in tax, to make sure it was all perfectly legal. We were by then half way through a tax year, and a lot of money had already come in, such as £20,000 for the film rights of *Mulberry Bush*, plus some of the Beatles advances. So our tax bill was going to be huge anyway. But leaving for a year, as soon as possible, would save quite a bit.

Margaret wasn't at all keen, but the more I thought about it, the more attractive a year abroad became, for its own sake. I was now planning to become a full-time writer, not a journalist. Margaret was a novelist. In theory, we could now live and work anywhere in the world, unlike normal couples. Caitlin and Jake were four and two, not yet at proper school. It would not upset their education to have a year abroad.

This might be the most convenient, best ever time. If we waited any longer, it would be more complicated. We had been presented with the opportunity to indulge the fantasy of going off to the sun which most people, especially most writers, dream about. The few that ever made it were usually twice as old as us. Why not do it now, when we were still aged only thirty-two and twenty-nine? If we didn't like it, we'd get it out of our system, early doors, then carry on with the rest of our lives. On the other hand, we might find we loved it so much we might never come back. Hence the earlier we got off the better. By not going, now, we might regret it for the rest of our lives.

As for the children, they would be bound to benefit by such a stimulating, healthy, outdoor year. Even Jake might act like a human being for a change. It would help my asthma to be in a sunny climate, which is what the experts during all my childhood had been telling me, though in fact it had not been too bad in recent years.

All this rationalisation did of course disguise feelings of guilt. I didn't actually want to admit to my friends and contemporaries that our decision was motivated by tax reasons. I decided I would deny that, maintaining it was mainly a long holiday, a year abroad in the sun, lucky us.

But then I fell ill with what turned out be pneumonia, brought on by exhaustion, weakened by doing too much over the last two years. That acted as a final sign that we should do it. In the event, I got carried on to the plane, too weak to clamber up the steps.

Our first thought had been to go to the South of France, be like Robert Louis Stevenson and rent somewhere pretty on the Côte d'Azur. Then we thought no, our French is not good enough and we might need it in an emergency if Jake does something stupid, as he is bound to do, and ends up in the local hospital. Tuscany, that is supposed to be nice, but we don't even speak one word of Italian. It would be safer and more convenient to be in an English-speaking country. So we thought of California. It was in the air, in the pop songs, a place of peace and love and flowers, tra la. And their hospitals would be bound to be good. But it seemed so far away. In an emergency, with our parents in Carlisle, we would never get back quickly.

I can't remember exactly how Malta came up. I think a friend of a friend must have mentioned this man at the BBC – a lecturer in their staff college – who owned two or three very pretty converted stone farmhouses on Gozo, an idyllic island off Malta, so we were told. The minute I spoke to him on the phone, to ask if it was true, he was straight round with his Super 8 projector and was showing us what appeared to be really beautiful, artistic Moorish-style cottages. There was a frequent ferry from Gozo to Malta, he said, where there was an excellent hospital, and of course everyone spoke English. We picked out the best-looking farmhouse, situated near a nice sandy beach, and agreed a deal for a six-month rent, with the option of another six months, if we liked it.

The moment we arrived in Malta, things went wrong. The house we had picked was not available. Something to do with the present tenants refusing to move. But the owner said he had another, equally attractive one available, which he knew we would love.

It was in a little rural hamlet at the end of a long dusty road –

20 Birbuba Street in the village of Ghaab. It had been beautifully and tastefully converted by the owner and his boyfriend, cool and charming, with outside stone steps that went up to the bedrooms. But it was miles from the sea. That had been one of the prime attractions, especially with a four-year-old and a two-year-old. It meant we had to hire a car at once and get in it every time we wanted to go anywhere, either into Victoria, the main town, to shop, or to one of the beaches to swim and picnic. I've always hated driving, much preferring to walk, but it was impossible during the day in Gozo, because of the heat and distances to a beach.

However, we slowly got into a routine. There was a sequence of so-called maids who came with the house, who were supposed to do a set number of hours and help with the cooking and the children for which we paid £3 a week extra, on top of the £18 a week rent, but they were hopeless, so slow and indolent, more trouble than they were worth, proving all Margaret's prejudices about ever having domestic help.

The local red wine was brilliant. We bought it in huge glass flagons and then decanted it into bottles. I'd often be half intoxicated by the fumes and licking up any drips, before I'd even had a proper drink. The cheese was good, and the local bread, local tomatoes and melons. Basic household eating was therefore fine, but we never found any restaurants worth going to, except on occasional trips to a little island called Comino which had a nice hotel and fairly decent food.

We took equal shares in looking after the children, now that I was no longer going out to work. Each morning, one of us would be allowed to go to his or her room and work without being disturbed for two hours. Then in the afternoon, after lunch, when it was a bit cooler, we would all drive to the beach, usually Ramla, or to Xlendi or to Marsalforn, to swim and muck around.

During the week, all the beaches were quiet, the swimming excellent, yet they were often so scruffy, with empty sardine tins, rotting tomatoes left over from the weekend picnics by locals. They seemed to have little respect for their own natural heritage.

All their energies, and monies, had gone into massive Catholic churches, the size of cathedrals, which even the smallest, most impoverished village could boast.

One of the surprises on Gozo was to discover an extensive expat gay community. We got to know quite a few of them, and of course they were charming and amusing, great cooks, full of gossip. One or two made no attempt to disguise their inclinations, endlessly having fancy-dress parties with lots of music and local boys dressed up. But mostly they were very discreet, respectable, middle-aged, upper-class bachelors who had retired early from their profession, or their families, to live their lives privately abroad in peace and quiet.

After a very short time on Gozo, probably about six weeks, despite all the sun, the swimming, the food and wine, the peace and quiet, the escape from the rat race, we found ourselves waking up each morning, looking out of the windows and saying, 'Oh no, not another perfect day.' Six weeks, that's all it took to become blasé and just a bit bored. Each morning, when we came out with those words, it was partly satirical, but partly we meant it. We had begun to miss the variety in the weather, the variety in our life.

We had several media visitors while in Gozo. An editor from *Life* magazine in New York, which had bought the US serial rights to the Beatles book, asked to stay with us for a week. He was doing the editing, so he wrote, and needed to discuss things with me. I couldn't see the point, as any queries could be answered by letter, till he arrived. We soon realised it was his little perk. All he did was sit around and drink and irritate us.

Jonathan Aitken arrived to interview us for the London *Evening Standard* and stayed with us for a few days. Any harm I had done to his career, over the Oxford Union vote, had long been forgotten or forgiven. Before we'd left London, he had interviewed me for a book he was doing called *The Young Meteors*.

In the evening, over a few bottles, I tried to get him to confirm whether or not he'd been having an affair with Antonia Fraser, which was a rumour all over London before we left. He refused to comment, saying he never discussed personal things concerning women. What a gent. He asked me how much money the book had made, in total so far, and I estimated about £150,000 but asked him not to mention it as it gave the wrong impression. The Beatles had a share, and several agents, so I would personally get a lot less. However, when the article appeared, the headline stated I had 'earned myself £150,000', a figure which dogged me for years. And of course wasn't true.

He quoted me as saying we had no intention of moving to a bigger or better house, and that if we had any money left on our return, I would give some away. Margaret is quoted in the piece as saying 'at least the Beatles book has got Hunter over his inferiority complex'. Cheek. I have no memory of her saying or thinking that, but she probably did.

Margaret's parents, Arthur and Lily, came out to stay with us, their first time ever in an aeroplane. Arthur loved the fact that the bars were open all day long and they had names like Trafalgar Bar. My mother also came out and we taught her to swim. I have them all in my Super 8 collection, which includes a shot of Prince Charles, arriving in Gozo on some official visit, looking about fifteen.

One day, Trevor Nunn arrived on holiday next door with a girlfriend, having just been apppointed Artistic Director of the Royal Shakespeare Company at the incredibly young age of twenty-eight. He'd decided to get away, the minute the news was out, and avoid all the press attention. Our backgrounds were very similar, working class, council house, football loving. So that was a welcome diversion.

But after the first six months were up, we had had enough of Gozo and were determined not to sign up for any more. But where were we to go, for our final six months?

Chapter Twenty-three

Portugal

I never did finish that book about universities, the one originally called 'The Class of Sixty-Six'. It became the class of Sixty-Seven, then Sixty-Eight, then it got forgotten, overtaken by events, such as the nature of students, once sit-ins and protests had begun.

While in Gozo, we both worked away on novels, taking it in turns, while the other looked after the children. I'd now done three non-fiction books so I fancied going back to fiction. I always look upon it as the highest literary art. Non-fiction takes skill, experience, craft, hard work, but in the end the book is only as good as your material. When it's going badly, or you run out of ideas, or get bored and frustrated, then you can always go out and do more research, or just talk to people. With a novel, you are on your own. You have to drag it out of yourself. Margaret can do it. She has that sort of imagination. I haven't, always knew I hadn't, and yet during that year abroad, I sweated and struggled away on a novel.

Writing a novel suited being in that remote farmhouse in Gozo, cut off from all sources, people and inspirations. It started off well, as I had what I thought was a good idea, then it became a pure slog, pushing myself every day once Margaret had gone off with the children, trying to resist walking round our courtyard, reading the paper, counting the baby aspirins in the bottle.

I didn't have a commission. Novels don't work that way, not

for most people, unlike non-fiction where it's vital to get some sort of advance as you are likely to have travelling and other expenses. Margaret is different. She doesn't care if her publisher takes it or not, so she maintains, nor how much or how little they might be prepared to pay. She's had the experience, done what she set out to do. She's interested in what the publisher, reviewers and readers think about it, but not affected by their opinions. She believes that whatever they might think is correct, because all views are valid.

The novel I started in Gozo was inspired partly by the character of John Lennon, partly by John Bloom, who was a whiz-kid washing machine millionaire, a household name for a while in the Sixties, and partly by a paperback publisher friend called Gareth Powell. I didn't take anything from their lives, or real things that had happened to them, except they had all experienced enormous success and had come from poor or humble backgrounds. What fascinated me was that none of them really cared about success. At least that was how I imagined it. It was a laugh. They didn't give a bugger, really. I projected this attitude further by having my hero looking forward to failure, to ending up in gaol. That would then complete the cycle, having experienced the whole gamut. It was a very Sixties notion and Jake my hero was a very Sixties character. There were quite a lot of people like him, especially in the new areas of pop and media but also in the world of property, where a new breed of flash-git developers were having huge success.

I called it 'The Rise and Fall of Jake Kelly' – till I was almost finished and realised there was a real Jake Kelly, who lived in Cumbria, who was PR at Sellafield nuclear site, someone I had actually met, so how could I have been so stupid as to use a real person's name, when of course it had nothing to do with him? But by the time we had arrived in Portugal, I had changed it to *The Rise and Fall of Jake Sullivan*.

Yes, after Gozo we fetched up in Portugal. Someone we met one day, moaning on about Gozo's scruffy beaches, the poor quality of life, said the Portuguese were lovely, proud and dignified, not noisy like the Spaniards. The beaches in the Algarve were sensational, the best this person had ever seen. She gave us the address of what she said was a converted sardine factory at a place called Praia da Luz, just outside the town of Lagos. We wrote off to the owner who was a Belfast doctor. He had a local agent who looked after his house, a jolly-hockey-sticks, ex-Army officer called Rosemary Reynolds. We agreed to rent it for six months.

It sounded weird, a converted sardine factory, and we wondered if it would be smelly, but the situation sounded ideal, right on a beach. It turned out even better than we had hoped. There was a massive walled garden, cutting us off from the world, but with a secret door, leading right on to the beach. The house had four bedrooms, all large, and an enormous main living room. Outside our little door, the fishermen landed their catch, then sat around all day, mending their nets. The house was called Casa des Redes, which was a reference to the fishermen's nets.

It came with a full-time gardener, as the garden was enormous, full of vegetables and flowers, and there was also Fernanda, the housekeeper. She was an excellent cook, introducing us to Portuguese dishes and new ways of cooking ordinary things like chicken and pork. *Lombo de porco*, that was my favourite. Plus of course fresh fish, straight from the sea.

We arrived in the late autumn, so we had the beach to ourselves each day, apart from the fishermen. The Luz Bay Club, and other horrid modern tourist developments which now totally dominate Praia da Luz, did not exist. Faro Airport had not long opened.

Our nearest neighbour was an English lady in her late fifties called Alison Hooper who lived alone in a pretty little cottage backing on to our house. She appeared fearsome at first with her clipped prewar upper-class accent and haughty intellectual manners. And she certainly did not like children, all of whom she referred to as ankle biters. She wasn't keen on Portuguese maids either. She recommended that one way to deal with them was a bash over the head with a frying pan. That usually worked.

She was a Cambridge graduate, which must have made her one of the earliest women graduates, and also a literary lady who had had an exotic private life, having had affairs or been involved with several well-known personalities in London's prewar literary life. Her honeymoon with her first husband had lasted six months during which they had travelled across Europe to Russia and met Trotsky. Back in London, she had become editor of *Lilliput*, when it was a serious literary magazine, before the pin-ups appeared, and had written a well-reviewed novel under a pseudonym. She was an avid reader, getting all the latest literary novels and the main literary magazines. Alison and Margaret hit it off at once.

She was incredibly generous, always giving us presents of books, pottery, chairs, bits of furniture, and was so hospitable, inviting us to her parties and soirées. She introduced us to all her friends, both ex-pat and Portuguese. We had met nobody like Alison in Gozo. Otherwise we might have enjoyed it more.

Alison knew many of Portugal's leading poets and writers and artists who would visit her when they came down from Lisbon. Many of her close friends were leading communist intellectuals who were having a hard time, as Salazar was still in power and Portugal was run as a fascist state. We had been told about this, before deciding to come to Portugal, but everyone said that in the Algarve, you would not be affected by or aware of the political situation. It was too remote.

What we did see were lots of nasty-looking leather-uniformed soldiers on horseback who often appeared on the beach and scared the hell out of Jake, for which we were very grateful. What was depressing was the large number of otherwise fit young men who were hobbling around crippled, minus legs and arms, cannon fodder who had been drafted from their farms and villages to fight Portugal's unwinnable colonial war in Angola.

We discovered there were far more ex-pat Brits living along that stretch of the Algarve coast than we had first realised. They moaned about the awful Harold Wilson, England going to the dogs, bloody socialists ruining everything, no one had manners any more, these awful screaming, long-haired pop singers. They were mostly colonials, who had never actually lived in Britain, apart from time in boarding school. They'd spent most of their working lives in Africa, in Rhodesia or Kenya or South Africa, till of course those countries got ruined as well.

In England, they were the sort of right-wingers we would have run a mile from, but cut off from normal English intercourse, and not having enough Portuguese to communicate properly, if you kept off politics, some of these colonials turned out quite amusing, cultivated and generous.

I did in fact try hard to learn Portuguese, buying myself a complete set of Linguaphone records, which weighed a ton, and did my lessons every morning. My vocab was quite good in the end, but my accent atrocious. All I wanted really was a grasp of kitchen Portuguese, which of course all Brits needed, in case they had to do any bashing with a saucepan.

Over the months, we explored the whole of the Algarve coast, right down to Sagres and Cape St Vincent, finding empty beaches to ourselves or little villages like Burgau. We explored inland as well, up into the hills to Monchique. Alison gave us addresses of peasant restaurants which we would love, darling, they make the best chicken piri piri, and of buildings and churches, hidden villages and secret eucalyptus forests we simply had to visit.

Lagos itself, just four miles or so away, was still undeveloped, with little cobbled streets, quiet squares, some nice restaurants and an excellent fish and vegetable market, though even in 1968, you had to get up very early to be able to park anywhere near it.

Then of course there were all the beaches, some enormous like Armaçao de Pera, or little bijou ones like Carvoeiro, all with marvellous yellow sand, orange cliffs and strange rock formations. We loved the Algarve, right from the beginning. We only wished we had come to Portugal six months earlier.

One night, in December 1968, we were wakened by a tremendous hammering on our front door, the little wooden one, leading from the beach into the garden. I thought at first it might be some drunken fishermen, on their way home. Then I realised someone was shouting out my name – in a Liverpool accent. 'Wake up Hunter Davies, you lazy bugger.' It was so raucous I thought it might be John.

I had been in correspondence with all four Beatles, from Gozo and then from Portugal, telling them what I was doing, what I was working on, just chatty letters. In turn, they often sent me postcards, from wherever they were. I had issued a general invitation, to come and visit us, but I'd forgotten that.

I got up and opened the wooden door in the wall. There was Paul in a big dark beard with a blonde American woman I had never seen before and a little five-year-old girl. They were standing beside a battered black Mercedes with a pissed-off driver, tapping his fingers. Paul had no money, so he said, which was why the driver was suspecting the worst. I paid off the driver, with a struggle. We were 80 kilometres from Faro and I had to search the house to find enough cash for the taxi fare. Our children had awakened, on hearing all the noise. Caitlin was charmed to find that a little girl about her own age had arrived out of the blue in the middle of the night. Margaret made them coffee and something to eat and then made up beds for the three of them.

We slowly discovered that back in England, earlier that evening, Paul had decided on a whim that he would like to come out with his new girlfriend, plus her daughter, knowing we had a daughter of the same age. Neil Aspinall, their road manager, now head of Apple, was dispatched to book a plane, but they'd all gone for that night. Paul, like all the Beatles, could not wait. When they desired something, they wanted it now.

Neil had to hire a private jet which landed in the dark in an empty Faro Airport. Paul wandered around, looking for help. He had had the sense to bring some money, £50 in British currency, which he had handed to the first official-looking Portuguese, asking him to change it into escudos. Almost immediately afterwards, he'd spotted a taxi driver, so they all jumped into the cab – forgetting to collect the escudos. Paul had remembered one thing – a bottle of whisky which he handed over to me as he got out of the taxi.

They went to bed fairly soon, all being exhausted with their adventure, so we still didn't know who this American woman was. Last time I had seen Paul in London, eight months earlier, he was engaged to Jane Asher whom we had got to know and like and who seemed so good for him. This American, Linda, appeared at first to be a yes woman, clinging on to Paul, agreeing with everything he said, as if scared he would leave. Nerves, probably, being landed in this strange situation, with two people whom Paul knew quite well but she didn't.

They stayed for two weeks and we did have one or two fraught moments, mainly arguing over the upbringing of children. Heather, Linda's daughter, had had a rather disturbed few years, being sent back and forth between Linda and her father and being allowed to run a bit wild, so it seemed to our more staid, traditional eyes. Paul was excellent with all the children, and they loved him, but he did allow them to do things we did not approve of, such as letting Caitlin, aged four and a half, sit on his knee in his car and drive it, which we considered very dangerous. He would also let Jake play with a kitchen knife, refusing to take it off him, saying he would learn it was sharp when he cut himself.

But mainly we all got on very well. We took them on outings to all the places we had discovered, such as up into the mountains at Monchique. Walking down a remote hill one day, back to the car, Paul spotted an old man coming towards us with a donkey. He persuaded the man to let Heather and Caitlin each have a go, riding the donkey, which of course they loved. When we were saying farewell, and thanking the old man, the donkey stepped back – straight on to Caitlin's foot. Her screams were terrifying, and we could see lots of blood. We were convinced one of her toes was broken.

Paul, ever resourceful, set off running down the hill, towards the village of Monchique, to find help. He managed to flag down a car and persuaded the driver to come back and take Caitlin to the local cottage hospital. Fortunately, nothing was broken, just badly cut and bruised, but she was given a tetanus injection, just in case.

Afterwards, Paul went into a little craft shop in the village and bought Caitlin a purple shawl, as a present, to cheer her up. Naturally, Heather burst into tears, not understanding why she had not got one also. So Paul bought her one as well, to keep it fair.

Almost from the day Paul and Linda appeared in our house, people were arriving from Lagos bringing flowers, baskets of fruit, bottles of wine, all from shops and restaurants, wanting him to visit. I couldn't understand at first how they had found out who he was. It was all to do with the £50 he'd given away at the airport. A story had gone round about this idiot Englishman giving money away – then one person had said, 'Oh no, I recognised him, he's not an idiot, he's a Beatle.'

On their third day with us, the press arrived from Lisbon. Paul was very good with them. He agreed to an impromptu press conference outside our front door, on the beach, on condition that they would not bother him again on his holiday. Which they stuck to. After that, when wandering round the Algarve, he never got pestered or bothered. It was of course December, out of season, though there was not much of a season in those days.

While he was staying with us, Paul started a novel, probably inspired by the fact that Margaret and I were each bashing away. He borrowed my typewriter, when I wasn't using it. I did try to sneak a read at the odd page, behind his back, but didn't manage it. (I have asked since about his aspirations to write a novel, as he has now done a book of poems. He says he has completed a work of fiction, but it's locked in a safe while he decides whether to have it published or not.)

Despite that last-minute dash from London, Paul had not forgotten one vital thing – his guitar. In odd moments, including going to the lavatory, we could hear him playing away. It happened to come out one day that my first christian name is Edward, which amused him, though I don't know why. His first christian name is James, not Paul. He went off to the lavatory and when he came back he played us a little song which went 'There You Go Eddie, Eddie, Eddie; There You Go Eddie, Eddie You've Gone.'

He had only got the first part of the song, the first few bars, but I thought it was charming. Some years later, I heard it on one of the bootleg tapes, recorded during the 'Let it Be' sessions, and it was clear he had worked on it a bit more. He is singing and playing it to John, who seems quite impressed. But it never appeared on any album. What a shame. I would love to have been the inspiration and subject of a Beatles song. Even if no one had ever known it was me.

During their stay with us, we did get to know Linda much better. Our first impression of her was totally wrong. She turned out a much stronger, more creative person than we had first imagined. They got married the next year, in 1969, and she proved an excellent wife and mother and did so much for Paul during their long and happy marriage till her tragically early death from breast cancer in 1998.

Before we left Portugal, we bought a house. One day Alison took us a couple of miles along the coast towards Lagos, then down a side road we'd never noticed before, which ended in an empty beach called Porto de Mos. The beach was enormous, leading on to another secret beach which you could walk to at low tide, or along the cliff path which led to a lighthouse, and then into Lagos harbour. The other way, going west, you could walk at low tide all the way to Luz. We were enchanted by it.

The beach appeared totally empty, unused, but there were a couple of tatty beach restaurants, popular on Sundays with locals from Lagos and in the summer with families who came down every year from Lisbon. But there were no modern developments, no houses or hotel. The only development was up on the cliff, overlooking the beach, where four little houses in a row, architecturally designed, were being built. The Portuguese architect, José de Veloso, was a friend of Alison. His family were well known in Portugal as his brother, a noted communist, had escaped the clutches of the Salazar regime by taking refuge in the American embassy in Lisbon.

The houses would not be ready for some months. None had yet been sold, so we were given first choice and bought number one, at the far end. The price was £4,500. It was very complicated and time-consuming importing the money, which we wanted to do legally, although we heard stories of Brits arriving with suitcases full of cash. In those days, there was what was called a dollar premium, whereby you applied to the Bank of England who charged Brits a premium to transfer their own money out of the country. You paid one-third more, but they did promise you would get it back, if and when you imported the money again.

We loved being in Portugal so much, and had fallen in love with the Porto de Mos beach, so I went through all the boring legal process of buying the house, and coping with the equally complicated Portuguese laws. We loved the idea of having our own holiday home, to keep returning to, as our family grew up, for ever. And of course we would be able to keep in touch with Alison and our other Portuguese friends.

The house was quite small, just two bedrooms, but it had a most interesting, open-plan design with lots of bare pine wood. The garden led into an olive and fig grove, then on to a cactus-lined cliff path which we walked along to get down to the beach, just five minutes away. From our back terrace, as I cooked fresh sardines on our barbecue and drank the delicious red wine, we had an uninterrupted view of the sea, all the way down the coast to Sagres.

When I bought it, its address was Number One, Quatro Chaminees. In consultation with José de Veloso, I decided to give it its own special name – Casa D'aviz. This was meant to be a bad trilingual pun. In Portuguese, the royal family's name, like the House of Windsor in the UK, was Daviz. In French, it could mean house of note. In English, it was our surname. Well, it amused me, even if the postman was totally bemused. It made a nice present to ourselves, after the end of our year abroad.

Chapter Twenty-four

Back to London

We were so pleased to return. Caitlin had already started at the half-day nursery class at Brookfield Primary School before we had left London. Now she was ready to start full-time school, in the first year.

At the time there were no other Brookfield parents in our street. The two other professional-type parents of around our age had sent their children to private schools – one to Highgate and the other to St Paul's. The latter seemed totally mad. Condemning a child to spend most of its childhood travelling right across London.

The rest of our neighbours were either elderly, working-class couples who had lived in their house for decades, their own children long gone, like the Holloways, next door, or they lived in houses divided into flats and were mainly single people, coming and going. One of the houses opposite, where a famous musician now lives, and another further along, were like rabbit warrens and we never worked out how many were living there. It was typical of so many London streets of the time.

Today, the houses which were in flats are single homes, almost all of them lived in by professional couples, such as lawyers. And they sell for at least £1 million, compared with £5,000 when we moved in. Who would have imagined it? The traditional working classes who once lived here, such as train drivers and electricians, haven't a chance of buying a house in our street any more.

We thought we were slumming, when we first arrived, waiting for our fortune to change, our savings to creep up, so we could live in a really nice place, such as Hampstead.

On our return to London, we could now do it, fulfil that particular fantasy, before we all got settled down again. In theory, we had enough money to buy our dream house in Downshire Hill, although the accountant had warned us that the Inland Revenue could come back at any time over the next seven years and say, 'Oh, you forgot to do this, you were technically not abroad, so pay up.' So for seven whole years, I left all our accumulated savings – which in the end came to about £50,000 – in five building society accounts, not daring to touch them.

Round the cocoa in the evening, feeling awfully virtuous, we decided that as we did not believe in inherited wealth, either receiving or giving it, we should start giving some of our money away. We had been so lucky, out of all proportion to the efforts we had put in, when we thought of the back-breaking working lives our parents' generation had put in. OK, it was Margaret who suggested it. I nodded, said, 'Good idea, pet, yeah, of course, I agree, but let's just wait a bit, not be hasty, the sort of luck we have had might never happen again, we could end up in need, if something awful happens, with no income, just think of my dad, all those years bedridden. Let's just wait a bit, see how the financial situation pans out.'

We were of course earning again, each of us, and paying the normal taxes, which had started to go down. We could easily have afforded to go at least one notch up the housing ladder, without making too big a dent in our savings. But in the end, after not too many discussions, we decided we preferred to stay where we were. We liked our house, our garden, our area, our friends and were very happy with Caitlin's school, impatient for the day when they would take Jake, if of course they agreed. They might not, as he was still driving us mad, still not sleeping, demanding endless attention.

When Jake got to five, I did an article about him for *The Sunday Times*, headlined 'Jake the Wake', about the fact that he had never slept all night through in his life. I got the biggest postbag for that article I have ever had, before or since. One of the common themes, from parents who had had similar hyperactive and demanding children, was to hold tight, don't worry too much, it will all come out right – their child, who had displayed similar behaviour at that age, had turned out to be clever and original and also very caring. Huh, I scoffed. Some hope. He can't read, far less speak properly.

But what we desperately needed was to have our whole house to ourselves, otherwise we would be forced to look for something else in the area. Before we had left, Mrs Hall was resolute that she would not be bought out. What would she do with the money, so she said. She still had to live somewhere. So that left only one alternative.

After working on her for some months, she finally agreed that she would move if we bought a flat for her to live in, paying the same rent, for ever, until she died. She had realised that with this deal, she could not lose. She wanted to be in a new block, so it took quite a few months, contacting all the local estate agents and developers, and at last we found a very nice new block going up in Swains Lane, very near the bus terminus, only minutes from the Heath, in an up-market, middle-class area. Its postcode was N6, as opposed to NW5 where we lived, and was considered to be much smarter.

There was a security entry phone, private car parking at the front for residents, full central heating, the latest kitchen and bathroom fittings, all the sort of stuff she had never had before. The price was £7,500 for her two rooms, k and b, on a 99-year lease. I was appalled by the price. It was 50 per cent more than we had paid for our own house – yet we were paying it just to get rid of Mrs Hall and gain access to the whole of our own house.

Not long after she'd moved in, I got two interesting phone calls. I had bought the last vacant flat, not knowing that every other flat had been acquired by Russians. The Russian Trade

Delegation had a big presence in Highgate at the time, in a large, high-security residential block overlooking the Heath's boating pond. There had been a funny story in the papers about a window cleaner who had been hired to clean the Russians' windows, who had spied on them and sold his story.

Mrs Hall's little block, four storeys high, with eight flats in all, was not far from their main residence. Handy for their overflow. When I looked at the various deeds and joint things I had to sign as owner, I could see that the Russians living there were all from Sovrac, which was apparently some sort of trade body. I wonder if they're spies, was my immediate thought. We were at that period in Cold War relations when every few weeks the Russians would chuck out ten British diplomats from Moscow, claiming they were spies, then we would do the same.

I once played for *The Sunday Times* football team against the Russian Embassy in London which was a very exciting occasion as we used one of the royal pitches behind Kensington Palace Gardens, Millionaires Row. (It was on 2 May 1971, for I've just found the programme.) We had real nets and corner flags and an excellent pitch, so that was exciting in itself. Brian Glanville was our captain but came off with a pulled muscle. We won 2–1. (I scored the winning goal. That's why I kept the prog.)

Afterwards, the Russians provided food and vodka for the teams, plus families and supporters who had come along to watch. They were surprisingly hospitable, despite their reputation for being dour and suspicious. At that time, if you came across any Russian families walking on the Heath, they would stop talking to each other the moment they saw you, and not continue till you were well past, and then only in whispers. Today when you meet them, they are all yelling on their mobiles and clanking their bling.

One day I got a phone call from a very well-bred English gentleman asking me if I was Mrs Hall's landlord. He appeared to be an official, from some government department whose name I didn't quite catch. He said it was just routine checking. I asked him what he wanted to know. Well, was Mrs Hall English?

I said yes, at first, not thinking, then of course realised she was not. She had been born in Dublin, as I happened to notice on some of her documents one day, though for some reason she looked down on the Irish and would not admit to being one of them. She also went by a different christian name from the one I had seen on the document. As for Mr Hall, she never ever mentioned what had happened to him. The caller then asked her age. Again, I didn't know. She kept that a secret as well, but I estimated seventy. Once I mentioned her age, the man on the phone – and by then I had decided he was working for MI5 – immediately lost interest.

About two weeks later, I got a similar call, asking similar questions, from a Russian, saying he was from Sovrac. His line was that he was on the property side, and wanted to know if I would ever sell, but his questions were really about Mrs Hall – who was she, why was she there? I explained I had moved her there to give ourselves more space, and she'd pay the same rent for ever. He couldn't understand this and clearly suspected she had been planted. When I mentioned her age, he too lost interest.

Personally, I think Mrs Hall would have made a totally excellent spy. I could easily see her fixing bugs to walls, using a hidden camera, dropping documents in tree trunks on the Heath. Behind her Old Mother Riley, doddery demeanour, we knew she was as cunning as a fox, saw everything, missed nothing. Perhaps, now I think about it, she was in fact working for the Americans. That could explain her three months every year in the USA.

On our return, I polished up and then handed in my novel, *The Rise and Fall of Jake Sullivan*, to my publisher, Heinemann. By now, they'd had huge sales with *The Beatles* and they hadn't done too badly with *The Other Half*. There was silence for some weeks, then I heard they were turning it down.

One of the reasons, so I picked up, was that Charles Pick, the chairman, had taken exception to all the bad language. I had made a point of my hero still being the lout he had always been, behaving as he'd done as a labourer on a building site. In board meetings, he farted and grabbed other directors by the balls. Charles thought this was all totally unnecessary. I maintained there was a new breed of entrepreneurs who ignored all the polite social conventions, didn't agree with acquiring polish along with their wealth. I refused to tone him down. Perhaps, of course, they didn't think the novel was very good anyway. The upshot was I was left without a publisher.

Richard Simon, my agent, had by now left Curtis Brown to set up on his own, working from his own little bijou Georgian house in Islington, with an excellent assistant called Vivien Green. He decided to send it to Weidenfeld and Nicolson where a new whiz-kid, Tony Godwin, had taken over. Tony read it in a matter of days and liked it, so I was told. By the time I went to see him, he had read the manuscript twice and made notes and graphs. These graphs charted the flow of the plot, the changes in the character. I have never seen a publisher put such thought and work into a manuscript, before or since.

I had quite a bit of work to do, and came home moaning to Margaret, but I was so impressed by Tony that I was willing to do whatever he said. He had praised the bits he liked, which every editor should do, before coming to the stuff which hadn't worked and needed attention. I remember him saying that his only object as a publisher was to get out of an author the book the author was trying to write.

He once invited us to a dinner party at his top-floor flat in Gloucester Crescent, Primrose Hill. He was living alone, having separated from his wife, Fay Godwin (who became a very eminent photographer). He had done all the cooking, after a long day at the office, for about six of his authors, plus partners.

Towards the end of the meal, Margaret happened to voice some criticism of Antonia Fraser. Antonia was not at that dinner party, though she was one of Tony's authors. I can't remember exactly what Margaret said, but she is always more than willing to give her honest opinion, especially a literary one, whether asked or not. The conversation had turned to Antonia's biography of Mary Queen of Scots. Margaret said it was of course an excellent story, Antonia had done some good research, but she, Margaret, personally had found the writing clumsy and unreadable . . .

It was this last bit that hurt Tony. In fact he was absolutely furious. He said he would not allow any of his authors to be insulted in that way in his house. He would be obliged if Margaret either retracted what she had just said, or left his dinner table.

There was silence. Even the other guests couldn't believe this passionate outburst had been caused by the sort of generalised, offhand remark that authors often come out with about other authors, especially over a convivial meal.

Margaret said fine, in that case she would leave. So she got up to go. I finished my meal, hurriedly, and then joined her outside where she was waiting by our car. Tony followed me downstairs and out into the street, clearly surprised and disturbed by what had happened. He said he was sorry, he hadn't meant to dismiss Margaret, and had not expected her to stand up and leave the table. It was just that he was always over-protective of his authors. Margaret mumbled her apologies, saying she should not have used the words she had, but of course he must agree that all authors can be criticised. We all parted as friends. I think.

Tony rose to great power at Weidenfeld and Nicolson, which was not easy, given that George Weidenfeld was still running the firm, which he'd helped to found, and had his own idiosyncratic and secretive ways. Tony was also very helpful with young editors, people starting out in publishing. I personally thought he was the best publisher I have ever met and went on to do many other books with him.

Thanks to Tony, *The Rise and Fall of Jake Sullivan* did pretty well. It caught a mood of the moment and we sold the paperback rights, the US rights and the film rights. Beryl Vertue was running the film company which bought the rights but it was owned by Robert Stigwood whom I had met by chance when doing the Beatles book, as he was a friend and one-time colleague of Brian Epstein. He had had a lot of success with the Bee Gees and latterly with Cream.

He found and hired a brilliant young director, Tony Palmer. I don't think anyone who has seen his excellent TV programmes about famous classical composers would deny that Tony is an original talent. At the same time, so many people who had worked with him maintained he was an egomaniac, over the top, someone who moved from extreme elation to manic despair, always having rows, always threatening to sue people. I personally found him vastly entertaining. Everyone said I was so lucky to have him. He was the most creative young TV director of his generation and was clearly going to end up a star in Hollywood.

This was going to be his first feature film, just as it was going to be Robert Stigwood's first venture into film production. I worked for several months with Tony on the script till he was satisfied, which wasn't too hard, as he was more interested in visuals and emotions, shock-horror scenes, than in polished dialogue. Then he started holding auditions.

I went along to the studio he had hired on the day he was doing tests for the part of Jake, our hero. The person who really stood out was John Alderton who had turned up for his audition in a white suit with a red rose, a scene from Jake at the height of his success. He therefore appeared smooth and polished, but of course Jake then starts effing and blinding like the lout he was.

Then, as the months went on, nothing happened. Actors and actresses who had been lined up went elsewhere. Robert Stigwood apparently had the money, but didn't want to do it on his own and was trying to interest a major film company. In the end, Stigwood's first feature film came later – *Saturday Night Fever* – and that did turn out to be a Hollywood blockbuster.

Meanwhile, I had finished another novel, *A Very Loving Couple* – this time a shorter, more sensitive novel, with no bad language or nasty people, certainly not, about the marriage of a young couple with two young children. I was quite pleased with it, but I got a nasty review from Auberon Waugh, taking the piss, which did depress me.

That novel was a first for me in that I gave all the money from it away – to the Multiple Sclerosis Society, thinking of course of what my father had endured. Over the subsequent years, we each did it with several books.

One didn't at the time go around boasting about this, and I shouldn't be doing it now, how vulgar, and the normal reader was never aware of it, as the charity's copyright was always in very small print, but one day I got a letter from John Fowles. Someone in publishing must have told him, or he'd spotted the small print and realised the charity was genuine, not our Swiss bank account. He wanted to know what the legal format had been, as he was thinking of doing something similar with one of his books.

Chapter Twenty-five

Journalistic Jobs

I didn't fancy working at home, full-time, all round the year. I had the freedom to do so, either in London or in the country, anywhere really, but I felt I would miss being in an office, in a team.

When you work from home, you have to be self-motivated, self-reliant, able to live and work on your own for a year, perhaps two years, with no one knowing or caring, no one aware of when you are skiving, when you've got stuck, become bored, or done a really, really good bit.

A publisher might have commissioned the book, but he or she is busy with other stuff, perhaps even been moved on or moved away. A good editor keeps in touch, takes you out to lunch once or twice a year to ask about progress, but mostly these days they haven't got the time, or the expense account, not unless they have a massive advance tied up in you. It's like a footballer when he's injured. He feels he doesn't exist any more.

Then there's the lack of social contact, if you work all on your own. Being in a team, if it's going well, and you all get on, is fun in itself, for the laughs, the gossip, the lunches. I always looked back fondly to my days on *Palatinate*, even though there were no lunches.

Margaret can't understand all this. In fact she thinks it's pathetic, this dependency on other people. She has no interest in what other people think. She has never worked in an office, in a team, apart from those couple of years teaching, which is not quite the same.

Something else you miss, working on your own, is the aggravation. And the main source of aggravation, which all team workers experience, is the boss. It can be very liberating and relieving, having a boss to complain about, their stupid decisions, their daft ideas, their nasty character, suspected vices. You can say it's all their fault, when things go badly. At home, you have only yourself to blame. You got yourself into whatever it is you now wish you had never got into.

Thinking about all these pros and cons, I decided I wanted the freedom to be able to work at home on a book when I wanted to, but at the same time, I quite fancied doing some journalistic job for at least part of the year. If I'd been a plumber or a teacher, a bricklayer or a policeman, who had made a bit of money, I still think I would have wanted to go back and do a bit of ordinary work.

I always felt I was lucky meeting Tony Godwin. Being Harry Evans's friend, having known him for a long time, coming from the same roots, was also fortunate. I admired him more than any other journalist I've ever met. In some ways, Denis Hamilton was a more successful editor, buying all those major wartime serials, introducing new elements, increasing the circulation, striding ahead of the *Observer*, the old rival. But Hamilton wasn't a journalist, not by my definition. He was a leader.

The thing about Harry was that he could do all the jobs on a newspaper, most of them better than the incumbents. He could write first-class leaders, economic features, political analysis, sports journalism, sub-edit complicated copy at speed, edit any section of the paper, run campaigns and create series. Unusually for a national newspaper editor, he also understood all the nuts and bolts and technical stuff, how to crop photos, lay out pages, design the whole paper.

Most of all, he was an enthusiast, always open to ideas and suggestions. Sometimes to his own detriment. He would often say 'Yes, yes, yes, great idea', when someone wanted to do something, making them feel highly flattered, forgetting that someone else might already be doing it. Which is what happened to me when I arrived to edit the Look pages in 1970.

I decided that I would go back to journalism full-time but half-time – in other words I'd work for the paper for six months of the year, going on half pay. I would do whatever job Harry wanted me to do, wherever he had a problem or wanted to try something new. I wouldn't hang on, after my six months, so therefore I would not be a rival to anyone. I would be doing what was thought best for the paper, not for myself, because I considered myself no longer a career journalist, as once I'd been.

Harry explained that his current problem was Ernestine Carter, OBE, the *grande dame* of British fashion pages. She was an American, small, bird-like, fearsome, with an enormous reputation in the fashion world, great contacts and huge power.

Harry, however, considered she was holding back the paper's progress. She was only really interested in the top end of fashion, high-class couture stuff, and when she did agree to write about ordinary items, like a plastic raincoat, they would turn out to be some enormous price. Harrods adored her, as she was always featuring their items, and in any disagreement with Harry about the contents of her page, she would get her friends at Harrods to threaten to withdraw all their advertising.

She jealously guarded her domain, maintaining she was women's editor, not just fashion editor, so all features or articles for a female audience must be controlled by her. And she certainly didn't want to feature any of the low-class, popular, vulgar, street fashions, health or sordid social stuff, or first-person articles about one's awful personal gynaecological problems which other papers, such as the *Guardian*, were beginning to feature.

Harry's plot was to surround her, in two senses, so she would be engulfed and might well give up in disgust. He agreed she was fashion editor, and would certainly not want to change that, certainly not, she was an icon in the industry, the paper was proud to have her, but he was going to introduce what would be one or two domestic pages for younger families, aimed at men as well as women readers, unlike Ernestine's pages. They would of course not interfere or clash with her wonderful fashion spreads.

The new section, just part of a page at first, was called Look – a nice, asexual title, which would not put anyone off, or overtly annoy Ernestine. The page had been going a few weeks, under the control of Mark Boxer, who had been the editor of the colour magazine, where he'd done an excellent job. But Mark, who was a bit of a dilettante, rather waspish and superior, was also looking after a few other bits. Harry decided Mark's heart was not quite in the idea of Look.

Harry's brief to me was to take over Look and turn it into a proper section. I could have a proper staff, expert writers, be gradually given more pages, and eventually the Look pages would in fact become the women's pages – but a brighter, more modern, younger, more family-orientated section than Ernestine's version. It would eventually attract new readers to the paper, so I hadn't to worry about upsetting older, more traditional readers, and could run articles about sex and ailments which the paper had not touched before. Nor had I to worry about Ernestine. He would deal with her, once she sussed out what was happening and naturally started complaining.

On my first day as editor of Look, I found two other people sitting in the same office, as if they were its editor too. Mark was there, as Harry had forgotten to tell him the new arrangement. He wasn't at all put out when I explained things. In fact he was glad to have one less thing to do.

Also in the office, or the Look suite, as I liked to call it, was a strange-looking young woman with an enormous purple turban, monster platform heels and lashings of black around her eyes. This was Molly Parkin. She said she had been hired by Harry to help edit the Look pages. 'Ooh, he's lovely,' she said in her flowing Welsh accent. On cross-examination, I discovered she was not a journalist, never had been, either as writer or editor. In fact she couldn't even type and had never written anything. What the hell was Harry doing?

When I said, 'Actually, I'm in charge here,' she wasn't at all upset. On reflection, she admitted that Harry might have told her she would be fashion editor of Look, which sounded more likely, though of course that would have infuriated Ernestine if she had found out.

Molly's fashion spreads turned out to be pretty amazing, for *The Sunday Times* in 1970, and they included a huge feature on monster platform shoes which I personally thought no one would ever wear. I learned from Molly that the extreme mad-looking unwearable new fashion ideas she featured, which she came across by going round the art colleges, getting to know the new young designers, were not meant to be worn by ordinary readers, as such. The best, most acceptable, would be watered down, altered for High Street consumption. Which is what came to pass. Well, in many cases.

We would sit in the Look suite, surrounded by all the frocks and stuff she was featuring, her chosen best photos spread out, and she would talk the story and captions to me, what had been in her mind, what had attracted her. I would sit there, listen, typing out what she was chuntering on about, trying to capture her voice. Eventually, she did manage to learn to type out her own stories.

She was such a good talker, so colourful and distinctive, and also, in due course, she proved to be such a good writer that I encouraged her to do non-fashion stories as well. I sent her to interview Cyril Knowles, the Spurs footballer, when the song 'Nice One Cyril' was being sung by everyone. She took a top fashion photographer along to produce an excellent photo of Cyril at home with his family, which was unusual for the times. She did ordinary people and their clothes, which of course Ernestine rarely did, comparing North with South. In Bradford, Molly stopped people in the street and asked them how many pairs of knickers they had. One girl had thirty-two, which was thirty more than Molly.

Molly was single at the time and her love life was very complicated – but not at all private. She would disappear and return and regale the whole office with her sexual exploits. This might feature John Mortimer, George Melly, a famous architect, a well-known barrister who loved being spanked, or perhaps a young taxi driver who had picked her up in his cab at the front door of *The Sunday Times* and whom she then invited to go with her to Brighton for the night. Molly would tell us all the details and have the whole office hanging on every word.

The Look pages eventually grew to four, then to six, and the staff increased accordingly. Lucia van der Post was the home editor, doing kitchens and gadgets and stuff – later going on to be a distinguished editor in her own right on the *Financial Times*. Caroline Conran, wife of Terence, was our cookery writer, whose immaculately typed copy arrived by taxi. I was allowed to hire a new feature writer and offered the job to Valerie Grove – or Jenkins as she then was – of the *Evening Standard*. She eventually declined, using it, I suspected, as a way of getting promotion from the *Standard* editor, Charles Wintour. Instead I interviewed various other young women writers and chose Lesley Garner, who was then on the *Daily Herald*.

The person who became the best-known, best-loved writer on the Look pages, and in fact the whole paper, much to the fury of some of the heavy brigade, was Jilly Cooper. Her column became the paper's single best-read feature. I remember discussing her with Cyril Connolly, the literary critic, who just could not understand her attraction. He had been writing for the paper for decades, and was a household name in educated households, along with Harold Hobson, the paper's drama critic. Yet Jilly had come from nowhere, as a failed secretary, and quickly dwarfed them in readership recognition and popularity.

Jilly, despite her jolly persona, could be a mass of worries and insecurities, but she was willing to be guided, which at times I worried about doing, once she became so vital to the paper and once Harry was scared she would be tempted away. I tried to get her to alternate the frothy stuff with more serious topics, such as being a second wife. (Leo, her husband, had been married before.)

When the pages got bigger, I started a policy of cutting back every feature by four lines, the theory being that all journalism has too much fat. Instead, I inserted a four-line poem. They were mainly of a domestic, social, romantic or topical nature, meant in the beginning to reflect the concerns of the pages. To do them, I hired Roger McGough, whom I had admired since his Mersey Beat poetry days. He did a neat Spanish holiday one which went:

Olé to bed,
olé to rise,
only the tourists
outnumber the flies.

He also sent me a football one at a time when it looked like Liverpool might win three trophies:

Liverpool Love Poem
I think of your hips
Slinky as silk
I think of your lips
Drinky as milk
I think of your breast
Smooth as a pebble
(But more often than not
I think of the Treble)

His poems became so popular that readers started sending in their own four-liners, many of which were excellent and we used them as well. (A later Look editor did them as a book.)

I did bits and pieces myself, such as what happens when your underpants go yellow. That was done awfully tastefully with some high-class artwork by Michael Roberts, one of Molly's protégés, but it didn't stop letters of outrage, saying it was disgusting, what is the paper coming to, which of course was what Ernestine Carter thought. She stormed into Harry's office to complain and he pretended to be shocked. It was around this time that *Private Eye* got it in for me, caricaturing me as Oonter Underpants Davies. They always had me speaking in a joke Northern accent, which I maintained I never had.

On 1 April 1970, which was a Sunday, we did a huge fashion spread on headscarves for men. Molly hired a top fashion photographer, and it was done very professionally in a studio, with me and a bearded sub as the male models. Our headscarves for men included a J-Cloth. On the Monday there were hundreds of enquiries from people wanting to know where headscarves for men could be purchased. All a joke, of course, but not long afterwards Mick Jagger appeared on stage in what looked very like one of our headscarves.

While editing the Look pages, I came up with a book idea, a round-robin sort of novel, with different chapters to be written by different people. It was partly a bonding exercise, to get our new team established, but it expanded to include the best writers then working on *The Sunday Times*, such as Alan Brien, Philip Knightley, Francis Wyndham, Jilly Cooper and Irma Kurtz.

The plot I thought up concerned an unknown female photographer who has suddenly become world famous. She then disappears, goes into hiding, leaving the world's media desperate to talk to any people who knew her – relations, teachers, lovers, bosses. The title of the book was *I Knew Daisy Smuten,* her name being an anagram of *Sunday Times.*

The reason for Daisy's instant fame was that Prince Charles had got engaged to her. So this unknown woman would be the next queen of England. It seemed far-fetched at the time to suggest that the world's media would be obsessed in such a way, till of course Diana, not Daisy, came along.

I didn't tell the writers what the plot was, why Daisy had suddenly become famous. I said 'Put your hands up who wants to sleep with her, who wants to have bullied her at school, who wants to be her brother?' Peter Wilsher had a good idea – he said he would be her tax accountant. I gave some broad guide-lines such as her age, where she was born, her general appear-ance, but let people create their own image of her. As we know, in real life, three people can know the same person intimately, yet recall three different characters. I did the final editing and polishing, just to iron out any blatant inconsistencies.

Tony Godwin at Weidenfeld loved the idea and gave us a good advance. The only slight embarrassment was that when all the copy came in, and I had done my subbing, he took against Molly's chapter. He said it was disgusting and sordid. The book had begun as a Look exercise, yet Molly of all people was not going to be in it. That was hard to explain to her. (Later, Molly published several novels, on her own, with great success.)

We sold the paperback rights, the US rights and even the film rights, though that never got made. We had equal shares so we all made quite a bit of money.

Tony talked George Weidenfeld into giving us a big launch party, to be held at George's own house. Something I'm sure George has always regretted. There were so many people, so many gate-crashers, so many drunks, so many feuds and fights, so many of George's precious objects got damaged or disap-peared.

Daisy Smuten, the book, was forgotten in about a year, and quickly remaindered, but Daisy Smuten, the launch party, passed into publishing lore. For the next ten years, in the publishing trade press, I was constantly reading references to it. Either as a classic literary thrash, long remembered by all who were there. Or as a dreadful warning, to all publishers . . .

Chapter Twenty-six

Family Affairs

In 1972, we were driving up the M1 to Oxfordshire one Friday evening. We had bought a country cottage in the village of Upper Wardington, near Banbury. It was what people like us did, what people still do, though at the time you think it's not a cliché but a truly original, independent, deeply felt desire. How nice to get out of awful London at the weekend, give the children some real fresh air. They'll love it.

So every Friday afternoon Margaret packed the car with all the food and stuff for the weekend, as we didn't want to waste valuable fresh-air time shopping. We had a standing order for meat in the village, from a wonderful little butcher, and Mr Thompson, our marvellous ancient gardener whom we had inherited, always had some vegetables ready for our arrival, either from our garden or his. Mmm, Mr Thompson's new potatoes, I can smell and taste them now, good enough to eat all on their own.

There was always a mad panic before we left London, sitting outside Brookfield school, wishing Caitlin and Jake, especially, would not hang around, or be kept in, or forget totally that it was the weekend. It was so vital to get on to the North Circular and roar up the M1 before the hordes of other middle-class professional couples belting off to their weekend retreat, many of them spending the time with other London weekenders who just happened to live nearby.

Even though I really can taste those potatoes, it all seems like another life. I can't believe we did it, every weekend for four years, plus Xmas, and Easter. In the summer, we went to Portugal, of course, our other retreat from London. It can be so exhausting, being a member of the London middle classes.

If you are fortunate to find yourself going through life on a certain social and economic conveyor belt, you acquire, without realising it, certain must-have fantasies, like a country cottage, that little place in the sun, so it's vital to realise some of them when you can. Otherwise they hang over you, or get dangled before you, or you read about them, as the same articles appear every year, and you fear you are missing something. Once you've done them, you know the reality.

Margaret still doesn't know how she put up with it – the provisioning, cooking, cleaning, all that packing and unpacking, just to come back again on Sunday night. I of course was a total wash-out, purely a passenger in this rural idyll. She was exhausted so much of the time. Looking back, I think this could have been a contributory factor when Margaret later fell ill.

I had decided that after a week slaving over a hot typewriter in London, what I needed was some proper physical exercise. So when we moved to Wardington, I signed on for Wardington FC, the village football team, who played in the Banbury and District league. The first thing I did, on arrival in Wardington on Friday evening, was rush round to the village notice board for the team sheet and see if I'd been picked.

Saturday lunch time, I did do my bit, taking Caitlin and Jake to our village pub for fish and chips, purely so I could watch any football preview on the pub's useless, flickering black-and-white TV which the bad-tempered publican would often switch off, if he was in a nasty mood. Then I would roar off in my car to whichever village we were playing against.

A lot of the players were farm labourers, plumbers and electricians, muscle-bound hulks, so in almost every game I ended up injured or at least knackered, dragging myself home, then I spent all Sunday moaning and groaning with ice packs or hot water bottles on my legs, until it was time to crawl into the car and roar back down the M1.

It did roar because it was an MGB GT, in orange, very flash, a great car for arriving to play football, showing off to the lads, but utterly stupid for a family of four with a weekend cottage, making it even harder for Margaret to pack. I've never been interested in cars, so I don't know why I bought it. Another fantasy, I suppose, which I had picked up from somewhere. While we were abroad, I told myself that when we get back, I must have a sports car sometime in my life.

This particular model had only two proper seats as the rear space was little more than a low bench. Caitlin and Jake sat there, or crouched there. I used to think, watching them in the rear mirror, This can't go on much longer. Not only am I going to stunt their growth but they're going to end up with flat heads.

One Friday evening, on the way to Wardington, we announced to the two of them that something exciting was going to happen in the Davies family. Jake, then aged six, immediately said he knew what it was. 'Bunk beds!' Caitlin, who was then eight, thought for a while and said, 'A dog?'

The big news, in our little nuclear family, was that Margaret was pregnant. They were therefore going to have a little brother or sister. After a gap of six years, we were going to have a third child. They were both delighted, as we were.

Flora was born on Halloween, 1972, so that made her special for a start. Her birthday party theme could stay the same for ever. Margaret was working on a biography of Bonny Prince Charlie at the time, and had liked the name Flora McDonald. We let Caitlin and Jake have one choice each for her second names, for which Flora has never forgiven us, or them, as she hates her other christian names, Abigail Jessica.

After the birth of Flora, I decided that the daft sports car had to go. Naturally enough, we got what every North London family like us was buying at the time, or thinking about buying – a Volvo estate. In orange.

*

We were still going up to Carlisle once a year at least, to see my mother and Margaret's parents. We'd always done this, even before we had children, and grew to hate the freezing cold and cramped conditions of their council houses, where of course we had grown up and hardly been aware of the discomfort. So after we came back from Portugal, we bought a bungalow for Margaret's parents in Morton, a suburb of Carlisle – where I used to work as a hod carrier.

Not long afterwards, the bungalow next to Lily and Arthur's came on the market. We saw that as a sign and bought it for my mother. This was not such a good idea. I don't think my mother liked living next door to Arthur, who was an expert gardener with very strong views on how grass should be cut, hedges cropped and all windows and woodwork kept in sparkling condition. This was not quite my mother's way, never having been the most organised of people. We did it really for selfish reasons. Having them next door to each other meant we didn't have to travel across Carlisle all the time.

My mother loved her bungalow, especially her little summer house which came with the property. She sat in it in the summer with a large pot of tea, her feet up, a volume of Dickens and her back to Arthur bending over his immaculate rows of potatoes and sweet peas next door, no doubt going 'Tut tut, just look at the state of that woman's lawn'. There was one slightly worrying moment when I rang her once and said 'Hi Mum, it's Hunter here.' I could hear a pause and an air of some confusion and she said, 'He doesn't live here any more.'

My twin sisters had stayed at home in Carlisle, looking after my mother, till they were into their twenties. They had both left school at fifteen with no O-levels and gone into local offices. Annabelle then came to London, worked in the Guildhall in the City of London, met and married Roger Priestley, a Yorkshireman. He'd gone to grammar school, got A-levels, then joined the Civil Service at eighteen, working in a tax department. He rather languished at first, as in the Civil Service there had always been strict officer-class demarcations, with the

Oxbridge types being fast tracked. But then there was a positive move to open the higher grades to everyone and he shot up the ladder, becoming for a while one of the senior civil servants helping Shirley Williams when she had to answer trade questions in the House of Commons.

And then, what excitement, he suddenly got moved to California on a two-year posting. Not exactly the place you expect civil servants to go. He had been made British commercial consul in San Francisco, one of his main jobs being to organise a forthcoming British trade fair which Princess Alexandra was to open. It was all a great success.

They sailed back from the USA, on the liner *Oriana*, and during the voyage Roger entered a general knowledge quiz and won it. From then on, everyone in the family, including his two children, Ross and Lindsey, addressed him as Oriana Champ.

And then tragedy struck as history repeated itself. Annabelle and Marion had taken the brunt of my father's last years at home when he was suffering from multiple sclerosis – by which time I had got well out of it. Roger started to suffer from dizzy turns, his walking began to suffer, all the usual early signs, though they took years to be diagnosed properly. He too was found to be suffering from MS. There was far more support in the 1970s than there had been with my father in the 1950s, and Roger bravely managed to carry on. Being a civil servant, he knew all the rules, how facilities for the handicapped now had to be installed by law, and he made sure this was done. For about two years he travelled by train, in his wheelchair in the guard's van, from the family's home in Leighton Buzzard to London. I don't know how he did it. His determination was incredible, but eventually he had to give up work and retire. He was honoured with an OBE and then, despite becoming house-bound and then bedridden, he did an Open University degree. He died in 2003.

Marion got married in Carlisle to Jeff Pitt, a male nurse who became a sister tutor, teaching other nurses. They had no children. After ten years at Tyre Services, doing unskilled, routine, boring office work, Marion was presented with a model tyre, for her years of loyal service. It made her suddenly think, 'What am I doing here, what am I doing with my life?'

In her spare time, she began to study for her O-levels, and then A-levels at the local tech and then, amazingly, in 1974 at the age of thirty-five she got into Oxford, to Ruskin College. It was a two-year social studies course. She could then have gone on to do a degree course, but left to start work as a social worker, back in Carlisle.

While at Oxford, she was seduced by a female lecturer. She discovered something she had never known or realised, that she was a lesbian. She immediately came out, telling all her friends, and of course her husband, with whom she always remained friends and from whom she never divorced. But she didn't tell our mother. I was partly to blame for this. Not through shame. Just that there was something going wrong with our mother, her memory becoming more hazy, her actions stranger. I thought it could make her more confused.

Life for a lesbian in 1970s Carlisle was rather limiting, though there were little groups who had social functions, spread out across the country, which meant a lot of travelling. We encouraged Marion to come to London, which she eventually did.

To help ease her arrival, I bought another house which had suddenly come up for sale in our street. There was only one floor vacant, which Marion was able to move into, with sitting tenants in the other two floors.

Margaret was strongly against the purchase. We should not be influencing Marion's decision to come to London in any way, and we were doing so by providing her with a flat. Also, taking on two lots of tenants would lead to a lot of grief, so she warned . . .

Which it certainly did and I quickly regretted it. The house was in terrible condition and I inherited two old sisters in one of the flats who drove me mad, just as Mrs Hall had done. Every time I moaned, Margaret reminded me of what she had predicted. But it was typical of my wilful attitude. We had agreed that major decisions in our life must be taken jointly. One would always have the power to veto the other. But in this case, I had gone ahead, regardless of her objections, despite our agreement.

Johnny, my young brother, went to one of the poorest schools in Carlisle, and also left at fifteen with no qualifications. My mother pulled strings – a phrase which makes me smile even now, as if my mother ever had any strings of influence with anybody – by asking a neighbour on our council estate if he could give Johnny a job. He was an electrician and he agreed to take Johnny as his apprentice. After five years, on rubbish wages, just when he had qualified, he was laid off. However, he got a job with Carlisle's State Management company, who owned all the pubs in the area.

Then by chance his career changed, just as had happened for Marion. He got a job in a local approved school, as an electrician, but part of his job was to look after the boys, teach them basic electrical work. He did this so well that he was soon spending all of his time with them. It helped that he is very big and strong, unlike me. It was then suggested to him that he become properly qualified and he went to Newcastle Polytechnic – now part of Newcastle University – to train as a residential social worker. He found having to write essays a bit of a shock. For twenty years, since he'd left school, the only thing he had ever written was his time sheet.

Once qualified, he came back to Carlisle and rose to become manager of the educational welfare department for North Cumbria, with a staff of thirty. Meanwhile my sister Annabelle, just before Roger became homebound, had re-trained and become a teacher of commercial studies at a comprehensive in Leighton Buzzard. Marion, her twin, had joined Camden Social Services and eventually became a team leader.

So it came to pass, by the end of the 1970s, that my three siblings, who in theory had had none of the educational advantages I had been lucky enough to receive, all of it for free, and instead had gone to poor schools, passed no examinations, had now ended up as properly trained and qualified professionals.

And all of them were doing worthwhile jobs, of use to the community. Unlike me. Writing books about a pop group, or journalism about underpants, isn't exactly saving lives or helping people . . .

Chapter Twenty-seven

Football

After we gave up our Wardington cottage, and I stopped playing football in a proper team in a proper league, I missed it so much that I decided to begin my own team, with my own rules, the most important of which was that we would never have to travel away to play a game. We'd always play at home. And so was founded Dartmouth Park United, a proper club, registered with the Greater London Council to whom we paid money every year.

It was a joke club, of course, just a muck around really, and I didn't begin it on my own but with two or three other dads of around my age who lived in neighbouring streets and who, like me, had played football in their youth, but now, approaching forty, either weren't up to a proper game or didn't have the time. So every Sunday at 11 o'clock we turned up on Hampstead Heath and picked two teams. Sometimes it would be seven a side. Sometimes fourteen a side. Two people, different every week, were captains and took alternate picks, just like a school playground. One side would then play in shirts, just whatever they'd turned up in, and the other in skins, i.e. no shirts. Oh, we were tough. In the football season, having registered with the GLC, we had proper goalposts, which we had to get out and erect ourselves, as well as a dressing room and showers.

One of the unique selling points about DPUFC was that we did not recognise seasons. We played every Sunday at 11 o'clock, all the year round. Even when Xmas Day fell on a Sunday, at least half a dozen would turn up. Out of season, it was coats on the ground, not proper goalposts. In and out of the season, people were always having terrible arguments, storming off, going home in a huff. I loved it. Not just the playing, but the rows, the letting off steam, the shouting and swearing, all the things I never ever do in my normal life.

Two of the founder members were lecturers at LSE, John Carrier and Bernard Donoughue. Then there was an architect, Derek John, my next-door neighbour but one, and Alan Aldridge, the artist who lived nearby and had drawn the cover for my Beatles biog. In turn, they brought along people they knew who fancied a game. I introduced my dear chum Melvyn Bragg who played for many years. It was very handy for him, being able to walk down the Hill from Hampstead. Martin Amis made one appearance, changing his gear in our house. He wasn't much cop, but awfully keen.

I first met Melvyn properly on the day that President Kennedy was assassinated. Margaret and I had known about Melvyn for some time as he too came from Cumbria – not from the big city of Carlisle, but from Wigton, out in the sticks, so we city slickers liked to think. By chance, Melvyn and I acquired the same agent, Richard Simon, and he and Margaret had the same publisher, Secker and Warburg, though we had never met till 22 November 1963, when all four of us – Melvyn with his first wife Lisa – were brought together for dinner by Anne Graham-Bell, a noted literary figure who was doing some PR work for Secker and Warburg. We heard the news about Kennedy's death as we left the Arts Club, where we'd had dinner.

Melvyn was bigger and stronger than he appears on television. He wasn't a naturally gifted player, but he played sensibly, doing what he was told, not trying to be flash. I was the flash one, and also the bossy one. Well, it was my ball.

As we progressed, other people joined in, having seen us playing, and not very well, in fact pretty uselessly. If they watched for a few weeks, then asked for a game, we usually said yes. We had a bloke who worked on the dustcarts for Camden, a scaffolder, two waiters, two musicians, a photographer.

We also attracted a lot of foreigners, people in London for a year or two, who found themselves aimlessly on the Heath on a Sunday morning. Over the years they included South Americans, Nigerians and a Portuguese. We had a hard core of thirty members who remained faithful to the team for the next twenty-five years. In due course, sons played along with fathers, which was one of the aims when we began.

I did love those years playing Sunday-morning football, especially when Jake joined us. I continued, stupidly, till I was fifty, despite two cartilage operations. It got rid of so much of my hidden bad temper and irritations. But in the end, I was spending the whole of the week recovering from Sunday morning, swathed in heat pads and ointments, just in order to play again the next Sunday. I called it a day when I realised I was fit enough to play football, but not fit enough to recover from it.

In 1972, I wrote *The Glory Game*, a book about a real, professional football team, Tottenham Hotspur FC.

I had followed Spurs since I first came to London, just because I wanted a London team to go and watch. Arsenal's ground was slightly nearer, but Spurs were better, more entertaining and successful, winning the Double in 1961, so I started going along to White Hart Lane, queuing up to get in and stand on the terraces. Most of their games in the 1960s were a sell-out.

I even took Margaret along once. A sign said All Tickets Sold and she said, 'Good, that's it, let's go home.' I never pay attention to such notices, or to signs saying One Way Street or No Entry. They are for other people. I walked round the whole ground and I did eventually find a turnstile still letting people in.

In 1971, when I first thought of trying to do a book about the inside life of a football team, I naturally wanted to do Spurs. I wrote to them, but got no reply. I later spoke to Brian Glanville who said I was stupid to approach Spurs – their board was the most unhelpful and old-fashioned and Bill Nicholson, their manager, was dour and uncooperative. So I contacted Arsenal, with no luck, and also Chelsea, where I was invited along to talk to Brian Mears, the chairman and owner. But that came to nothing.

My idea was to follow a team, a professional team, over a year, and then shape it so there was a narrative, a development. Along the way, you would learn how a top club operates, about the apprentices, scouts, coaches as well as the star players. Tony Godwin was very keen on the project, despite his lack of interest in football. Other people at Weidenfeld, and in the book trade, thought that a book about one specific club would have limited interest. Who would want to read about Spurs, outside London N17? There would be very few sales in Manchester or Liverpool.

In the end, I went back to Spurs and got their agreement to do a journalistic piece about them, for *The Sunday Times.* This was a trial run, to see if they liked me and if I could get inside, secure access. Nobody at the club objected when the article appeared, so at the beginning of the 1971–2 season, I just turned up on the first day, 15 July 1971, for their four weeks of pre-season training at their training ground at Cheshunt, in Herts.

I had no contract with the club – either with the chairman or with Bill Nick, the manager. I just gave the impression to each of them that the other had agreed to my project. But I had promised each that they could read the finished book, before publication. I had also told the nineteen in the first-team pool that they would share 50 per cent of the book's proceeds, so there might be a few bob in it for them. This had Richard Simon, my agent, moaning and groaning, thinking of having to constantly divide up piddling sums by nineteen.

At first, I stood on the touch line at the training ground, watching Bill talking to the players about the season ahead, then doing a few exercises. I followed them afterwards into the changing room – and no one stopped me. Next day, I went straight into the changing room. That day, they were going on a cross-country run. To my delight, Bill threw me a Spurs training kit, with a number on, just like the rest of them, and told me to join in their run. Which I did, with a struggle. Quite a few of the players also struggled, or moaned and groaned. Most players anyway hate running any distance, especially without a ball. And as with any group, even professional sportsmen, there are always the skivers, cutting corners. At the time I was thirty-four, the same age as some of the more senior players. So, I didn't stand out too much. Playing Sunday-morning football had kept me fairly fit.

I came back, had a shower with them, and carried on like that during the rest of the pre-season training, even making up the numbers on the pitch for little ball exercises. By the time the season started, I felt accepted. I'd got to know each of the players, and the coaching staff, finding out who were the influential ones, who to be careful with.

When the season proper began, I was thus able to insinuate myself into the dressing room before and after most matches, walking in as if I were part of the squad. On away games, or when going abroad, I travelled with the team on the train in their reserved section – teams did not use luxury coaches in those days – or on their specially chartered plane. It was much easier abroad, as all the foreign officials assumed I was a player. In a game against Nantes, I am described in a photo, which appeared in the Spurs programme, as one of the Spurs players. That was a highlight. At the San Siro stadium, for their UEFA game against AC Milan, I sat on the bench, along with Bill and the real subs.

Over the season, there were times when I thought my game might be up and I could be ejected, such as at half time in one game where Bill Nick was absolutely furious with Martin Chivers, Spurs' centre forward. In the dressing room, a glass got smashed, by accident, but emotions were so high that I expected Bill to suddenly catch sight of me, an outsider, standing in the corner of the dressing room, and take his anger out on me, ordering me out.

During the year doing the book, I was aware of this possibility, but at the same time, I used to tell myself that at least I will have been inside the dressing room of a top team, something I had always wanted to do. Even if the book fails, and never comes out, I will have had that experience.

While I was doing the book, boasting about all the access I was getting, Dr John Carrier from my Sunday-morning football team, a sociology lecturer at LSE, said I should do some proper surveys of the first-team pool. I was in a unique position, so I should use it. He helped me work out a series of questions about the players' social, domestic and political habits, apart from their football life. I tried to gauge their pleasure in playing and found to my surprise that all of them had enjoyed the act of playing football more at fifteen than now, at the top of their career, because of course of all the stresses and pressures. Almost all the players said they would never want to coach or manage. They had seen the state Bill Nick got into and wouldn't want to be like him. (Despite what they said then, eight later did end up as managers.) On the political front, almost all the players said they were Tory, except three, one of whom, Steve Perryman, assumed all players must be Labour, because of the background they had come from.

These surveys and appendices took up forty pages of the finished book – and over the years have attracted more letters from readers than the book itself. Other writers, not necessarily writing about football, have used the surveys to compare and contrast with other groups.

The book was serialised by *The Sunday Times* and also *The People* who naturally took out the juicy stuff, such as it was. One player, Alan Gilzean, was described knocking back a few lagers and Bacardi on the train home. One coach was quoted swearing and shouting and making racist comments. Nothing out of the ordinary, and nothing compared with the misdeeds that get reported today, but some of the club directors were furious, saying the club's good name was being tarnished. I got a letter from Lord Goodman, of Goodman and Derrick, the most feared firm of libel lawyers at the time. Fortunately, both Bill and the chairman had indeed read the manuscript – and I could prove it. The chairman had even made odd pencil marks in the margins. I was also able to prove that each player had read the bits about himself, and had not objected. I never heard anything further.

The book was popular with football fans all over the country, not just among Spurs followers. Foreign rights were sold in Denmark, Norway and Sweden. It was even sold in the USA, where soccer was not played professionally.

After Tony Godwin had left, Weidenfeld let the book go out of print, much to my fury, but I managed to get the rights back. I then sold them to Mainstream, the Edinburgh publisher, who have kept the book in print ever since, with regular updates. It's now even back in print in the USA. It's considered something of a football classic, according to polls in various football publications, such as *FourFourTwo*, despite the fact that in the book, the players are on £200 a week, live in £20,000 houses and wear flared trousers.

Today, such a book would be practically impossible. All Premiership clubs and players have hordes of lawyers, accountants, agents, plus endless corporate deals and sponsorship arrangements. They wouldn't or couldn't say hello to you, without charging a fortune. But they probably wouldn't be bothered anyway with a book like mine, as they are all so rich.

Football is now a totally different game, a huge industry, with a massive TV audience round the world, billions of pounds swishing around and players like Beckham becoming one of the most recognised and richest young men on the planet.

And yet, at heart, I like to think that the sort of feelings and emotions, training and rituals, pressures and pleasures which I tried to capture and convey in 1972 are still true and believable. I also like to think, in my fantasy world, that playing the game itself is not really totally different from playing with Dartmouth Park United. Except of course we never had proper strips.

Chapter Twenty-eight

Famous Persons

On my return to *The Sunday Times* each year, if I didn't have a specific executive job for my six months, I did interviews. In theory, I could go anywhere in the world, as there was little penny-pinching in those days, interview anyone I fancied, which sounds attractive and easy, but of course is much harder than it appears. Why should famous, rich, successful people give interviews, even to *The Sunday Times*, if there's nothing in it for them? Which is why almost every celeb interview, then as now, has a hidden agenda, with something being sold or pushed. An interviewer always longs for an interview with a writer between books, or a filmstar not in a film, to meet them at their own home, not in a hotel or office with a PR present.

In 1969, I went to see Noel Coward at his home in Switzerland. He wasn't promoting a play or film or book or anything of that sort. It just happened to be his seventieth birthday. We managed to talk him into giving just one newspaper interview, to us, to celebrate this lovely event, honour his achievements. That was our slob stuff, softening him up, which I'm sure he treated with amused and probably obscene cynicism. When he heard it was me, author of the recent Beatles biog, he had not been so keen, so I was told, as he was not a fan of the Beatles, though I didn't know why.

However, being a trouper, he not only agreed to me doing the

236

interview but he invited me for dinner at his home, Les Avants, near Montreux. I booked into the Montreux Palace Hotel which was an experience in itself. It was vast, dripping with chandeliers and receptions which disappeared into the distance like something from Marienbad. It seemed totally empty.

About half an hour before I was due to see Noel Coward, and when my taxi had already arrived, Cole Leslie, his secretary, rang to cancel. Cole Leslie had been born Leslie Cole, but Noel hadn't liked it and changed his name around. 'The Master is indisposed,' so he informed me. He really did refer to him as the Master. And not as a joke. But not to worry, he said. I could join the Master for dinner tomorrow night, same time, same place.

I therefore had 24 hours to put in, which annoyed me. I was still at that stage in life when I hated being abroad, wanting to get in and out quickly, then home for tea.

Next morning, hanging around reception, wondering what to do all day, I happened to glance at what appeared to be a directory, full of names, just underneath the reception desk. Seemed strange, so many names, if the hotel was empty. I then remembered I had been told there was a private wing where a handful of people kept permanent suites, presumably mega-rich international financially dodgy types, keeping a low profile. When the receptionist was busy elsewhere, I leaned over and quickly read down the list. I noticed that one of the names was Nabokov. Could it be Vladimir? I memorised his internal phone number, went back up to my room and rang him. A voice answered. 'Mr Nabokov?' I asked. 'Who is it?' a voice replied. Which I took to be confirmation.

I then spoke as rapidly and amusingly as possible, so he wouldn't hang up on me. I told him the truth. I was waiting to see Noel Coward, who had put back our dinner till tonight. I worked for *The Sunday Times* but I was also a book writer. I was a great admirer of his work, his style, his use of English. I had read several of his books. Which was true. It was one of the reasons I was planning to give up writing novels, realising how useless I was.

There was a long pause and he said, 'Do you know Alan Brien?' It appeared that he'd had a recent correspondence with Alan, who at that time was film critic for *The Sunday Times*. He was checking me out, just in case I had been lying. Alan Brien was in fact one of our neighbours, living in the next street. I knew him very well, and could give his address and the names of his children, one of whom, Jane, was in Caitlin's class at school.

When I'd convinced Nabokov I was who I said I was, he said OK, he would meet me at reception in an hour. We would go and have a coffee in town. But there was one condition. I could not write about him, or anything he might say, in *The Sunday Times*, or any other newspaper. I agreed.

We walked round the town for over an hour, stopping for a few coffees. As we talked, he pointed out certain well-known locals, telling me who was having an affair, who was up to some dirty deed, all libellous, or perhaps it was all in his imagination. It was a fascinating hour, and I played fair. I never wrote about it. I didn't even make notes afterwards, which is what I normally do when a conversation is supposedly off the record.

When that evening I eventually turned up for dinner at chateau Coward, he and Cole Leslie were involved in a slight argument about a smell. I mentioned this in the piece, inferring it was to do with some new paint. In reality, one of them had farted, and each was blaming the other. Cole Leslie was then sent to fetch an air freshener, and went round spraying. 'It's like a fucking Turkish brothel in here,' said Noel.

He swore all the time, but in 1969, one just didn't repeat bad language in a newspaper. Twenty years later, when for a while I did a series of interviews for the *Independent*, I could have used every fuck. Nor did I mention the fart in the *Sunday Times* piece. It was supposed to be a nice birthday tribute and it would have made me look vulgar and nasty, by going on about it.

It was a very pleasant dinner. Noel performed well, telling me lots of amusing theatrical stories, and not all of them were in the cuttings. I did manage to get one unusual and most interesting item of information out of him – that he had a passion for watching people in hospital on the operating table. Whenever he was in hospital himself, he would ask the surgeon if there were any good ops he could observe. He'd seen a hysterectomy, childbirth, death. I found this faintly creepy and alarming, but a fascinating insight into his personality. When I started pushing him for more details, or to offer an explanation for his unusual hobby, I must have appeared too eager, and he clammed up.

We did, though, get on to the Beatles. And it was true he was not a fan of them personally. For some reason, I'd happened to mention the incident at the Royal Variety Performamce, when John Lennon told people in the stalls to clap and those upstairs to rattle their jewels. I said I'd found it quite funny.

'I thought it was the height of bad taste,' said Noel, suddenly going all serious and ungiggly. 'It must have put the Royal Family at a terrible disadvantage.'

I then asked him if he had ever met the Beatles and he said yes, after he'd been to watch them perform in Rome.

'I enjoyed their concert and went backstage. I met John McCartney who was very charming. I said I wanted to come to their dressing room. He came back and said the others did not want to meet me. I marched straight in and told them what I thought of them. Would I have come to their dressing room if I hadn't liked their work?

'I deplore the bad manners of today. If you are a star, you behave like one. I always have.'

Which was true. He gave me more than ample time, told some good stories, was amusing, charming, hospitable. And he didn't complain or comment afterwards about my article, either about anything I might have got wrong or by objecting to some cheeky comments I made about his chintzy furnishing.

In 1970, I interviewed someone who wasn't famous, wasn't pushing anything, whom I'd come across through personal connections. He had seen Margaret's photo in her publisher's catalogue and written her a letter. David Farrer, her editor at Secker, had asked if she would like it passsed on and Margaret said of course, she always wrote back to everyone, loved writing letters. All she didn't like was meeting people.

So for six years she had corresponded with Christy Brown, a thirty-seven-year-old man living in Dublin. His letters were so witty, erudite, obscene, literary and incredible – particularly considering he was writing them all with one foot.

Sixteen years earlier, aged twenty-one, he'd had published a long-forgotten book, *My Left Foot*, a happy, heart-rending story about his life as a cripple. In his letters, he now rubbished it, saying it was not the book he wanted to write. It was the one he'd had to, in order to get published. Since then, he'd been struggling to do a second, but he was now working on a book he was really proud of, to be called *Down all the Days*.

Throughout these six years corresponding, Margaret was adamant she didn't want to meet him. Not because of his condition, but because she wanted their relationship to continue to be purely on paper. She liked the artifice, the artificialness, the amusement of playing games and performing on paper. Meeting in real life would spoil the fun, shatter the images, on either side.

Now and again he had written to me as well. Unlike Margaret, I was keen to meet him. One day he told me he was coming to Shepherd's Bush, to stay with some of his Irish relations, so I drove across to meet him. His condition was far worse than I had expected – his brain damage was so severe that he couldn't walk, stand, feed himself. He shook and slavered and grunted and I couldn't understand one word he was saying.

The house was full of Irish labourers, who picked him up bodily and carried him when he wanted the lavatory, or helped the Guinness down his throat. He was a bit drunk when I arrived, which didn't help my comprehension. One of his relations, a nephew, Joe, translated for him. He told me that all Christy wanted in the world was to meet Margaret. He went on and on and in the end, I thought, Why not? I'll take him home, just for a few moments, so he can see Margaret, then I'll bring him back to Shepherd's Bush.

Joe carried him to my car, and got in with him. All the way through North London, Christy stared out of the window, grunting and groaning, turning to tell me some long story, make some sharp observation, but I still couldn't make out what he was saying. Joe translated, half listening, as if Christy himself was speaking a foreign language, of which he knew the words, but not the meaning. One of the things Christy said in the car, according to Joe, was 'Nabokov's tragedy is too much language and not enough feeling.' I suppose I must have boasted about my chance meeting with Nabokov.

We got home, and Joe carried Christy into our house, where he was immediately sick all over the floor. The excitement had been too much, plus being thrown about in my car and of course the drink. The noise woke Jake, then aged four, who came down and was much intrigued to see this strange-looking, slavering, shaking body. In the way of four-year-olds, he proceeded to ask direct, personal questions, such as 'Why are you shaking?' He'd recently asked Lily, Margaret's mother, when she was going to die. She had replied, 'Soon, I hope.'

Margaret, despite being caught on the hop, and of course furious with me, was immediately hospitable. She fussed over Christy, helped clean him up, and had a long conversation with him, when he'd sobered up a bit. She was much better at working out what he was saying than I was.

During his brief visit, I did manage eventually to make out quite a few things, one of which was about this book he was working on. I asked what it was going to be about. 'The truth,' he said. 'That's all.'

Before its publication, I did a piece in *The Sunday Times* about Christy, telling the story of his correspondence with Margaret, about his condition and his life so far. I used quite a chunk from his own letters. It received an enormous response from readers.

Down all the Days became an international success, making him about £70,000, enough to buy his own house outside Dublin. Most remarkable of all, two years later, in 1972, he got married, to Mary, a nurse from County Kerry. She had first been attracted to Christy's paintings, also done with one foot, which she had noticed on the wall of his brother's house. The film version of his life, with Daniel Day -Lewis, *My Left Foot,* came out much later.

Christy died in 1981, aged forty-nine. In 1989, I suddenly heard again from Mary, his widow, who was now living in Brighton. I went down to see her, and wrote a bit about her. She was then working for the British Nursing Association, specialising in the elderly, particularly those with Alzheimer's disease.

She'd had one relationship since Christy. 'It didn't work. In fact it was awful. I don't know what to do. Christy is a difficult act to follow. Unless I have someone to look after, I don't exist . . .'

I think she moved from Brighton not long afterwards. Since then, I've heard nothing about her.

In 1975, I began my last ever proper journalist job, editing the *Sunday Times* Magazine. This was Harry's idea. It sounded interesting, until he said I had to do it for two years. Turning it round, in the way he wanted, could not be done in six months, which was the maximum I'd been doing as a journalist for the last few years.

The Colour Mag was a much more important, flag-waving part of the paper, financially and circulation wise, than it is today, now the paper has so many other supplements and mags. I agreed to do it, but at the same time I told myself this would be my last hurrah as any sort of editing or office journalist.

The best fun in journalism is writing, seeing your name in the paper. But I had also discovered, over the years, there's a secondary fun in thinking up ideas, deciding who will do them, then seeing them into the paper, sitting back and taking a quiet satisfaction when it's worked out well, even if no one else knows. This is what I'd hoped to achieve on the Mag.

Harry had told me what he thought the problems were, and his plans to solve them, all of which I agreed with, but he hadn't made them clear to the Mag staff. So I had to do it, at my first staff meeting. In effect, I was criticising what they had been doing so far, which was a mistake. I thought I was being honest and open, and they would all understand the rationale, but they saw me as brash and destructive.

The main problem, which the existing staff refused to accept, was that readership reports were constantly saying the same old thing: 'There's nothing in the Mag.' By this, readers meant there was little to read. There was indeed a huge proportion of adverts, something like 60 per cent, but the concentration of so many picture stories, spread after spread, meant that there appeared to be little editorial content, stuff to actually stop and read. This was already being noted by the advertisers who of course were paying huge rates on the basis of reaching a large number of contented readers. Research showed they were not very happy.

The Mag staff loved and were proud of their big picture spreads, especially the ones from far-off exotic lands. That was the Mag's *raison d'être*, so they believed, making a unique contribution to British journalism. I said, 'Hard cheese. From now on, we are going to cut right down on the foreign stuff.' I wanted more home stuff, which people can relate to.

Harry's main idea was to introduce a Mag inside the Mag, a separate section which would be filled with lots of hard-working, informative stories, about things like health and education. We called it Lifespan. I brought Del Mercer from the paper's newsroom to edit it, which he did brilliantly, despite the old lags on the Mag being set against it. He had to bring in his own staff, just to get anything done.

I found I had inherited three or four freelance feature writers on long contracts. They got something like £2,000 a year, just to be available, to work for us when needed, plus generous payments when they did any actual stories. One of them was Jeffrey Bernard. I looked in the files and found he hadn't actually produced a word for about four years, despite getting £2,000 a year. I talked to him, gave him some ideas for stories, and he said yeah, he'd do them. He never did. After six months, and endless potty excuses, I stopped his contract.

Another star writer, who had done lots of well-received

features for the Mag over the years, was Bruce Chatwin. I made it clear to him I wasn't keen on foreign stuff, or very long reads. He later wrote that when he realised I was about to sack him, he had sent me an abusive telegram, which finished with 'Gone to Patagonia'. I don't remember receiving it, though the story appeared later.

There were two other contract writers I kept on, because I thought they were so good, so talented, and so productive, and these were Russell Miller and Gordon Burn. Gordon was not quite as productive, working more slowly, but he had a very individual approach, in his writing and the subjects he wrote about.

I fought a continuous battle with the picture department, who of course hated all these changes. One of the minor things I tried to insist on was pictures having accompanying captions. Sounds obvious. But they were in love with big photos which were bled – i.e. they ran all over the page, to the edge, with no margins or space left for a caption. You had to work it out, or turn over the page. I also hated joint captions – when perhaps captions for six different photos were crammed into one little awkward space in the corner.

Some of the assistant editors were not very helpful either. There was one each week at our editorial conferences who always said the same thing whenever I had what I thought was a bright idea – 'We've done that.' He would then rush off, self-importantly, look in the files and produce a similar feature done ten years earlier. I might not have been a natural editor, but I'd always had one rule since I had been charge of anything – there's no such thing as a bad idea. What matters is when you do it, how you do it, and who does it.

Introducing and creating Lifespan – which was swiftly dropped by a later editor, after all the sweat and rows and agonies – was one way of making the Mag appear bigger than it was. The other way, which I personally tried to solve, was to open up the back of the book.

When I arrived, the Mag just tailed off, the last twenty or so pages being advertisements. People knew this, expected this, so many readers would just chuck the Mag away, before they'd even got to the end.

What was needed was a self-contained one-page editorial feature, simple and straightforward, with one photo, which would be of interest to all and could run and run. It would go on the inside back page, so the advert opposite would be a premium ad, for which there was a higher rate.

I started off with a series called Home Town, in which a well-known person went, or was taken, back to the town where they had grown up. I did the first one, whose subject was Edward Heath, and I went with him to Broadstairs. It was pretty boring. We then did Eric Morecambe, about his life in Morecambe, and that was slightly better. After six of these Home Town columns, I dropped it. The problem was quality control – the person, the place, the quality of the writing, was so variable.

I then started a new series called Sacred Cows – in which well-known writers or experts could sound off about things or people they thought had been overpraised. It would be easier this time to control the standard of writing – but the problem was the tone. It turned out to be much the same each week, people moaning on.

I had an idea for a third series which would be about people in their ordinary lives, as opposed to their working lives, well-known people as well as unknown. It would always be written by journalists, not the subjects themselves, so we could keep it at the same level. There was a bit of scoffing when I first outlined what I had in mind, as it sounded so trivial.

Over lunch one day, when I was describing how it would be done, what questions would be asked, I turned by chance to the chief sub, Patrick Nicolson. I asked him what time he got up each day, did he have tea or coffee, who made the breakfast, how did he decide what clothes to wear. It was the answer to this last question which made everyone stop yawning and looking bored. 'I consult my diary,' so Patrick replied.

Now Patrick, as far as most people who had worked alongside

him for many years were concerned, was a perfectly ordinarily dressed bloke, usually in a suit, collar and tie, as befitted his status as chief sub. But it appeared that he had never worn the exact same outfit twice over a two-week period. To make sure he didn't, he always recorded his clothes worn each day in his diary.

It was this piddling piece of insight into his character that made everyone realise that inside the humdrum, domestic life of everyone, there could be little fascinating nuggets.

I called the series 'Life in the Day', which was a pinch from the column I had written in 1957, all those years ago on *Palatinate*. In those days, I had made everything up. Before I finished the Mag, I did write a made-up Life in the Day – which was about Guy the Gorilla at London Zoo.

I did my two years as editor, as agreed with Harry, and did all the things he required, but I can't say I enjoyed it, apart from the chauffeur-driven office car which took me to the office and back home each day. I never fitted in with the Mag ethos, or felt at home or accepted. I realised I'm not really a visual person. I always prefer words to pictures and layout.

However, 'Life in the Day' continues to this day, over thirty years later, one of the longest-running features in modern British journalism. So, I suppose I didn't quite waste all those years in journalism . . .

Chapter Twenty-nine

Back to Books

Giving up on journalism after the Magazine meant I was at home all the time, while I tried to think of what sort of book to write next. I was so relieved at not having to go to an office every day, not having to try and affect a caring, serious face while idiots and skivers, bigheads and ranters moaned on about the size of their desk, the size of their expenses, their lack of a by-line, their lack of a secretary, their amazing idea for a story which meant flying to Cuba, this very moment. The only thing I really truly missed about being a journalist was lunch.

I was chuntering on about this one day when Margaret said, 'Why don't you organise your own? 'My own what, pet?' 'Your own lunch. You've got your football team, pathetic though it is, playing at the same place all the time, with your friends, so why not do the same with lunch?'

So I sat down and in an hour I had made a list of thirty writers I knew, or knew of, who lived within a two-mile radius. They were all working from home and would doubtless be in need, now and again, of a chance to go out and have lunch with some other writers who worked from home. Only two out of the thirty I contacted said nah, not for me. David Cornwell (John Le Carré) wrote to say that he hoped it went well but he personally would rather meet his fellow writers in the next world, not this. A. J. P. Taylor, the historian, who lived just two streets away, said

247

excellent idea, but he never ate lunch. If I could make it dinner, he would certainly come along.

Everyone else was keen, depending on where and when and how often the lunch took place. I talked to Margaret Drabble, Bernice Rubens, Eva Figes and one or two of the other keen ones and after some discussion we decided to have our first lunch on the last Wednesday of the next month, and then, if enough people turned up, on the last Wednesday in the month, for ever.

I wanted it to be in Hampstead, so I could just walk back across the Heath, whether I'd had too much to drink or not. Margaret Drabble, who lived right beside the Heath at the time, in Heath Hurst Road, which would have made it incredibly handy for her, thought Hampstead might put some people off, make it appear elitist for younger, more struggling writers. We compromised on Camden Town and chose a Greek restaurant, Koritsas, near the Tube, which we reckoned would be cheap and handy enough for everyone. The restaurant agreed we would have a side room, to ourselves, but I couldn't guarantee how many would turn up.

Almost thirty people came to that first lunch. I got everyone to sign a list, so I knew who was there. They included Kingsley Amis, Margaret Drabble, John Hillaby, James Cameron, Bernice Rubens, Eva Figes, Gillian Freeman, Melvyn Bragg, Bernard Kopps. We agreed basic ground rules. That you had to be a published author, but it didn't matter how few or how many books you had written. No publishers were to be allowed, or agents. After all, we were mainly going to be slagging off publishers and agents, when we weren't slagging off our fellow authors. Membership had to be by invitation, but any member could invite along any other author. We were keen to invite authors from abroad, who might be in London.

It was very noisy, jolly and great fun – except when we came to pay the bill. I had suggested at the beginning that we just divvy up the total by the number of guests, regardless of what each person ate or drank, to keep it simple. What I hadn't reckoned on was that Kingsley Amis had ordered a whisky the moment he sat down. He then proceeded to drink whisky all the way through. The average bill therefore shot up.

There were shouts and objections from some of younger, poorer authors who had had nothing at all to drink, yet been presented with what seemed to them a huge bill. I remember one young writer being asked to pay I think £5, saying that her weekly personal spending allowance was only £3. She would therefore never be able to come again.

Kingsley of course didn't want to change the rules, which he had gained by, but at the next lunch, which was equally well attended, it was agreed that from now on we would divide up the food bill, but each person had to pay for their own drinks.

Over the next year, we got a good turn-out every time and lots of other authors came along, such as Martin Amis, Salman Rushdie, Beryl Bainbridge, Victoria Glendinning, Fay Weldon, Deborah Moggach, Shiva Naipaul, Gillian Tindall and Jessica Mitford who was visiting from the USA. After two years or so, the numbers settled down to around a dozen at each lunch, most of them women, and most of them living in Hampstead. The venue was then moved to a restaurant in Hampstead High Street, Fagins, to be handier for most members.

I greatly enjoyed all the Literary Lunches. They developed a life of their own, but were totally informal, with no officials or rules. There have been similar literary lunches over the centuries in London, meeting in places like Soho and Bloomsbury, but those have tended to be smaller, more exclusive. And many of them have ended in rows, if not fights. After that first argument over money, ours was always amicable and friendly and relaxed. You didn't need to go for months, could miss a year, live far away or abroad, yet you would know that some fellow-hacks would be meeting to have lunch at a certain place at a certain time.

After a few years, there was a change in my life so I personally couldn't go as often. I started doing some radio work and the recording day was always Wednesday. The Literary Lunch itself went on for at least ten years. By which time, on the rare occasions I went along, I didn't know any of the people. And then it slowly petered out when it got down to just two people having lunch together. It was amusing, while it lasted, and it spawned similar literary lunches in other parts of London, such as Kew and Richmond.

It was useful for me in particular, helping me to acclimatise in that first year of being home-bound, while I tried to decide what sort of books I was going to write from now on.

I fancied another 'Year in the Life of' book, a bit like *The Glory Game*, following something, some group, some person over a whole year. I liked the neat format. You fall in love with a subject you know very little about. You work away for a year, acquiring loads of stuff you don't know if you'll use, or how, then you have to shape it, give it a narrative and momentum so that readers have to read on, picking up lots of information along the way but are not aware of the joins. I hate research which shows, where you can see the shuttering where raw concrete has just been poured in.

I discussed with Tony Godwin at Weidenfeld the idea of following a group of Grand Prix drivers over a year. I'd start with, say, ten and by the end of the year, one of them would probably be dead or badly injured. I had met Graham Hill and Jim Clark and Jackie Stewart all those years ago, after Nick Tomalin sent me to Le Mans, and they seemed pretty helpful, interesting blokes. The Grand Prix world has a global audience, so there would be lots of foreign rights. I would make sure I followed at least one driver from each of the main book-buying countries. In the end, I decided against it. I just couldn't work up enough interest in motor cars.

I then thought of a trade union, picking one with an interesting, dynamic general secretary, following all the rows, problems, development, from one TUC conference to another. Hard to believe now, but trade unions were of mainstream interest and importance in the late 1970s. Then I thought, No, boring

boring. I could be stuck in smoke-filled rooms all year.

Instead I decided to spend a year on Hadrian's Wall, walking from one end to the other. I now can't remember how the idea came up, yet it combined two things I so enjoy doing – walking and talking. All my London life I have walked for two hours on Hampstead Heath each day, give or take dodgy-knee days.

Ironic of course, picking on such a subject, when all the time I was at Durham, supposedly studying Roman British history, I was bored stiff. I decided to see it as a Living Wall, alternating the past and present, telling the story of how the Wall was built, how the legions operated, what life was like in a fort, along with people and activities on the Wall today.

I spent a whole year over it, and walked all the way, from east to west, from Wallsend to Bowness on Solway, but of course I fiddled things, making sure I arrived in places at good or opportune times. And I didn't do it in one consecutive walk. I split it into roughly ten-mile sections, researched each in advance, digging out interesting places or people in that area, then ringing ahead to make sure I would just happen to meet them. Once a month I went up to the Wall, spent three or four days walking, poking about, then came back to London and spent the next three weeks at home, writing it all up. What fun, what self-indulgence.

I enjoyed it so much, became so fascinated by all the Roman remains, especially at a place called Vindolanda, which is a privately owned fort, not part of English Heritage, where under Robin Birley they had made a big effort to re-create elements like the turf wall and build displays of interest to children. I decided to give them the proceeds from the book. The contract had been drawn up, in the normal way, but luckily I hadn't been paid anything as yet, so we tore it up, did a new contract, in the name of Vindolanda, so they would get all the advance.

Out of *A Walk Along the Wall* came another book – a biography of George Stephenson, the father of railways, my first biog since the Beatles. I had come across his birthplace, Wylam, which is near the Wall, and followed his tracks, physically and metaphorically, all along the route. In Newburn church, just outside Newcastle, I discovered he had been married twice, which was new to me, something I hadn't learned at school.

The most fascinating, if slightly fanciful, fact connecting George Stephenson and the Roman Wall concerns the gauge that George chose for his first railway line – 4 feet 8½ inches. His great rival Brunel built the Great Western line with a broader gauge, 7 feet wide, but George's triumphed and became Britain's national gauge, and the world's, to this day.

So why did Stephenson pick 4 feet 8½ inches? It does seem a very odd width, and it puzzled me, till I discovered that the width of the entrance to all the Roman forts, on Hadrian's Wall and elsewhere, was also 4 feet 8½ inches. Was it a coincidence? Or had George pinched it from the Romans? Not quite. Most British horse-drawn carts had subsequently adopted a width similar to the Roman one, presumably from the carts which had gone in and out of the Roman forts. In the early nineteenth century, horse-drawn carts were being used to carry coal along the early tracks laid down at the collieries. Naturally the track had been laid at a width to suit the existing carts. When George came to perfect locomotives capable of running on reliable tracks – his two great achievements, thus creating railways – he stuck to the same width.

I didn't do too much on the technical side, wanting to concentrate on George, the man, and his battles. I loved the fact that he had never been to school, eventually teaching himself his letters on a slate while driving his locos. He was a rough, rude Geordie, whom the establishment figures all hated and he got horribly humiliated in the House of Commons when trying to bring in a railway bill and the clever clogs, Southern smoothies, mocked his accent, his grammar, his incoherent arguments.

I felt I had a bit of a mission, to re-establish his importance. He was one of the few people who, in their lifetime, can honestly be said to have changed the world. After George, thanks to his railways, suburbs were created, fresh produce became widely available, transport was transformed and life generally was quickened up. Until George, life had moved at the speed of the fastest horse. Afterwards, it was never the same again.

People like George, horny-handed craftsmen and engineers, rarely seem to feature as the subject of mainstream biographies from our leading general publishers. There is, so I believe, an Eng Lit conspiracy. Publishers tend to have English or Arts degrees, and so do the literary editors, the literary critics, book-shop managers and most writers, come to that, so they gravitate to what they know about. That means you can suggest a new biog of Keats or Wordsworth on the hour, and it will probably get accepted and widely reviewed. Try it with an engineer and see the difference. It seemed to me that poor old George Stephenson had been forgotten and overlooked since Samuel Smiles in Victorian times had turned him into a national if rather unreal hero.

The George Stephenson biog didn't sell all that well. So much for my mission. (Though I'm pleased to say that today it is back in print.) But the success of *A Walk Along the Wall*, which had sparked off the Stephenson biog, did lead to several other books, with similar formats and titles.

A Walk Around the Lakes, which came out in 1979, did even better, and has never been out of print. The Wall gave me an easy, linear route, all laid out for me, and also a running subtext, writing about archaeology. With *A Walk Around the Lakes*, which I was desperate to do, wanting an excuse to explore all the Lakeland bits I didn't know, I had a struggle at first to decide on my route and my angle.

In the end, I walked roughly in a circle, writing about people I met along the way, while the secondary running theme was literary. I made a point of visiting all the literary sites, places associated not just with Wordsworth, but with John Ruskin, Beatrix Potter, Arthur Ransome and A. Wainwright. I managed to get the first proper interview with A. W., on condition I used it in the book, not in any newspaper or magazine.

As with the Wall book, out of the Lakes walk came a biog, this time on Wordsworth. In researching him, I found endless lit crit biogs, giving acres of analysis of his poetry, most of them very hard going, not to say unreadable, but no straightforward one-volume biography for the general, educated public. I decided to fill that gap. I was pleased with the result, and it got very well reviewed, even by the lit crits, but I vowed never to do another biog of someone who lived to such a great age and wrote so much. There was a vast amount to get through, and no widow or children or friends still living to go out and interview.

I later did three other walking books, on the same sort of format. *A Walk Along the Tracks* entailed walking along ten disused railway tracks, in different geographical areas of Britain, from Somerset to Aberdeen, meeting people today and telling the story of the different railway companies in the past.

In 1948, when British Rail had come into existence, there had been 19,000 miles of railway. By 1982, when I set out on my walks, they were were only 11,000 miles left, mainly thanks to the Beeching cuts. That meant there must be 8,000 miles of disused track out there, waiting to be explored. It seemed a brilliant, original idea for a book, and you don't get many of them in a writing lifetime. By the time the book came out, two other authors had had a similar idea, though they were mainly interested in the railway history, not in people today.

One of the people I met, by chance, was Dr Beeching himself who turned out to live along one of the disused lines I had chosen to walk – East Grinstead to Three Bridges in Sussex. He was by then retired and was jollier and more forthcoming than his bogeyman image had suggested. Some years later, when he died, Lady Beeching wrote to me, asking if I'd be interested in writing his biography, but I declined. I'm not sure if anyone ever did it.

A Walk Around the Parks was my idea, and a poor one really, from a sales point of view, but it gave me an excuse to walk around ten London Parks, including Richmond, Epping, Greenwich, Hyde Park. On reflection, people don't want a book covering so many different areas. Those living in Richmond have little interest in Epping. Whole books about each of them might have done better.

I did the Parks book for Hamish Hamilton, for whom I did several books in the 1980s, when it was being run by Christopher Sinclair-Stevenson. He took over from Tony Godwin in my life, in that he was always encouraging and enthusiastic, and also excellent on lunch.

He found a photographer to work with me on the Parks book, Mark Fiennes, who appeared at first to be uptight and aristocratic but turned out to be a bohemian with little money who'd lived an unusual nomadic life. He also had lots of children, two of whom have gone on to be well-known actors.

A Walk Around the West Indies, which I did more recently, is probably the last in that little series of Walk Around books, now that my knees are so poorly. It was pure self-indulgence, giving me an excuse to visit twenty-seven different Caribbean islands. It was published by Weidenfeld, under Ion Trewin, for a puny advance, but I was pleased to have it accepted.

When the first of the Walks books came out, on Hadrian's Wall, I did a TV documentary about it, made by Tyne Tees, and it was shown on the network. I was the presenter, walking along the Wall, chatting away. It was quite an interesting experience – except it all took so long. They used big crews in those days, eight people at least, and it was all such a palaver, setting up, re-doing shots. It took all of eight weeks to make, just for a one-hour film.

I did another, made by Border and Tyne Tees, also for the network, based on my Lakes book. I later did a much more ambitious TV prog on George Stephenson, made by Andy Wonfer, who later became one of the leading women executives in TV. I also did a two-part series on Beatrix Potter for BBC TV, based on a book.

The publishers were always keen on these tie-ins, as it helped publicity for the book, but it grew more and more boring. I found myself revisiting places and people I had been to for the book itself, asking questions to which I already knew the answers.

It all seemed so false, a waste of time, when I would rather be getting on with a brand-new subject. I also wasn't very good at it, though I suppose I might have improved, with more practice.

While working on one of the Tyne Tees films, flying up to Newcastle, I met Melvyn Bragg at the airport. He was doing some local arts programme I didn't know existed, just in the NE region. For weeks and weeks, he had been flying up and down. I couldn't understand how he stood it. He said he was doing it for the experience, learning the craft of appearing in front of a camera, as opposed to creating programmes, which he already knew about. He was using it as an opportunity to make his mistakes well away from London. I thought, How wise, how smart, but I wasn't tempted. I could never have done it as well anyway. It's not just his looks, and lovely hair, he's an actor. All TV presenters are good at acting, even if all they are acting is themselves.

In 1976, I did *The Creighton Report* about a year in the life of a comprehensive school. I had become an activist for them, attending meetings in our area and joining protests. I wanted to do a book about a real comprehensive, which had been fully comprehensive for seven years. They didn't yet exist in Camden, our borough, but they did in Haringey.

I picked the Creighton School in Muswell Hill and wrote to the borough's education department and then the school's head teacher, Molly Hattersley, wife of Roy. She had only just arrived at the school, so it was good of her to let in an outsider.

During the year, I even did some teaching, which of course I could legally do, having got a Diploma of Education at Durham, all those years ago, when I'd done it to keep my mother happy. When I told her I was now going to do some teaching, she was very pleased. She thought I had come to my senses at last. I would now get myself a proper worthwhile job with a pension at the end. As for her own senses, she was, alas, beginning to lose some of them . . .

Chapter Thirty

Domestic Matters

My mother started wandering when she got to around the age of seventy, the age I am now. This would be in 1978. She'd never had a good sense of direction, or a good memory, but it had seemed funny rather than worrying. Despite all her years in Carlisle, she never knew her way around, unless she stuck to the main streets.

In 1977, we bought a cottage near Caldbeck, John Peel Farm, about ten miles from Carlisle, as a holiday home. This time we would not be bashing up and down the motorway every weekend but using it purely for school hols and half terms. The cottage was very small, basically one room up and one room down, but it did have a big derelict barn which we slowly renovated into a playroom and an upstairs area where the children could sleep if they had friends staying. It came with about twenty acres, which was let to a local farmer. The cottage was very genuine and ancient, dating back to the seventeenth century, in other words very dark and very damp. It was so small and the contents of such little value that we usually left it empty all winter, but as we gradually made it better and more comfortable, we began to let some local young person, such as a teacher, have it over the winter, for free, to keep an eye on it. The vicar's daughter had it one winter, and moved her boyfriend in, which didn't thrill the vicar.

I was doing my *Walk Around the Lakes* book, and used the cottage as a base, so that was one reason for buying it. The other was a desire to have a stake in Cumbria, to return to our roots. With age, these unexpected feelings creep up on you. It was also tied up with the old folks, my mum and Margaret's parents, becoming increasingly fragile. Having the Caldbeck cottage meant that for many weeks of the year we were only twenty minutes away from them. And we didn't have to actually stay with them, which was a blessing.

Ideally, we would have liked to have been in the Lakes proper, but the Caldbeck fells did have a wild, empty, untouched charm. There are no lakes, so very few tourists, but lots of atmosphere. Chris Bonnington has lived there almost all his grown-up life, and much prefers it to the more glamorous, famous, honeypot Lakeland sites.

Caitlin hated it, of course, but by then she was a teenager. The last place on earth she wanted to spend the summer was a damp little isolated cottage up on the remote, barren fells. But Jake and Flora for a good many years loved it, or at least they got a lot out of it, enjoying our long walks, ticking off all the Wainwright fells as we climbed them. They used to compete, along with their cousins Ross and Lindsey (children of my sister Annabelle), to see who was first on the cairn on the top. We had to bribe Jake, being older, to let Flora win the race, now and again. In the evening, by the log fire, we would record the achievements on a huge green sheet of art paper. Ahh. Even at the time, I was aware of the happy domestic family image-making. But I still loved it.

Caitlin had moved on from Brookfield Primary to Camden Girls, in its last year as a grammar school when she entered. Jake went on to William Ellis, an all-boys school, just three minutes away from our house, in its first year as a comprehensive. Flora, like them, also went to Brookfield Primary.

By that time, I was working from home, so I spent more time with her than I had done when Caitlin and Jake were at that age. I took Flora up to school most days, and got involved in school things, such as starting a school newspaper, the *Brookfield Bugle*. Wally Fawkes, another parent, did us an excellent cartoon cover. I then became a school governor and eventually chairman of the governors.

To finish off the happy domestic picture, we had eventually bought Caitlin a pet – a tortoise, for her eighth birthday in 1972. Not very exciting, but totally worry free. We got Tortee from a pet shop in Parkway, Camden Town. She came with some instructions about how in the autumn, when she grew sleepy, we had to put her in a stout wooden box, with straw, in a garage, high up, so rats won't get at it, which we did, as instructed, for two years. In the third year, when October came, we couldn't find her. That's it, she's a goner, either eaten by some predator or wandered off. We completely forgot about her, till one day in April she suddenly appeared on the lawn and staggered across the garden, all covered in soil. Since then she has put herself to sleep every year, somewhere in the garden.

Her favourite sport is getting into the house, clambering up over the back step, which you would think impossible, given her build, then she flops down in the kitchen, very pleased with herself, and starts exploring, sliding along the polished floor as if she's ice-skating.

This so amused the children when they were young that I wrote a story about it – and sold it to 'Jackanory', the children's TV programme. It was read and semi-dramatised by Patricia Routledge. It was well received and I thought vaguely about trying more children's stories, but at the time, I had more than enough with my walking books. But it's another example of the first rule of hackery: anything and everything can be turned into copy.

We still have Tortee, now over forty years old, and she delights the next generation. And she still requires no care or attention, help or money. Oh, if only children were like that.

Caitlin was a paragon of all the virtues till she was about fifteen or sixteen. She wore what was put out for her, did what she was told, was excellent at all school work, conscientious and law abiding, causing no problems, no worries. And then, oh help, as my mother used to say.

We agreed to a teenage party when she was fourteen, and the house got wrecked. It happens with every generation, yet we all still get caught, never expecting our lovely well-brought-up daughters, and their lovely friends, to suddenly behave like yobs. Some boys gatecrashed it. Same old story. I did the same at that age, but I'm sure I didn't do any damage. I hope. I think. These boys did really stupid things such as throwing raw eggs at all the walls. I had of course hidden all my drink, and Margaret had emptied the fridge, but she'd overlooked a dozen eggs on a wall rack.

Then Caitlin began raking round the pubs, and clubs and dumps of Camden Town till the small hours of the morning, with us lying awake, blaming each other for having allowed it. We worried that she or her friends were taking drugs, of some sort. Then of course there were all the unsuitable boyfriends we dreaded coming to the door.

In the Upper Sixth, she moved out, left home and went into a squat off the Caledonian Road with the boy we thought the most unsuitable of all. But what do you do? You warn them, you make it clear what you think, but by that age, you can't force them. You just have to love them, give a safe haven, hope they won't totally wreck their lives and their future.

She did somehow still manage to keep up her studies, though we feared she might leave school and never sit her A-levels. And while she got very thin, and scruffy and dirty from living in that awful squat, she never seemed to us spaced out, drugged up, or in need of medical attention.

She in fact sat her A-levels, got good grades, and went to Sussex to read American Studies. The dreaded boyfriend remained around. He followed her down there, and no doubt helped her spend her money, which wasn't hard as she was always totally hopeless with any money. When she began at Brighton, I gave her her term's living allowance in her hand. It had disappeared in a week. I then doled it out every half term, and then week by week.

She lived on campus at first, in what appeared to us a very nice modern block, but she hated it. After just a few weeks, she moved into a slum in Brighton, a flat shared with several other like-minded students. We went down one day, had a look in her kitchen, opened the cooker, and a rat jumped out.

After a lot of soul searching, agonising about spoiling her, behaving like a rich middle-class flash dad, we bought a little flat in Bedford Square, overlooking the West Pier, for her to live in. At least we then knew her living quarters were respectable, if nothing else. Oh, the years and years we seemed to lie awake, arguing with each other, worrying about Caitlin, wondering whatever was going to happen to her.

She was of course a heroine to Flora. When Flora was eight, and Caitlin sixteen, Flora would literally be in tears of jealousy on a Saturday evening when Caitlin was out, raking about, having good times, while she, Flora, was sitting at home with me playing Scrabble, having cocoa and going to bed at eight o'clock.

I'd tell Flora her time would come. When she got to Caitlin's age, she would be doing much the same. She would probably have a Saturday job on Camden market, making badges and selling them, going to pubs and clubs, having boyfriends, just like Caitlin.

'But I want to be sixteen NOW,' so Flora would sob.

To amuse Flora, I made up a story about a little girl called Flossie, which was one of Flora's nicknames. By a piece of magic, Flossie is able to go from eight to sixteen, in an instant, then go off out and have all the adventures that a sixteen-year-old might have.

I then decided to write them down, as little stories, and let Richard, my agent, see them. Almost at once he had found a publisher, Margaret Clarke of Bodley Head. She loved the idea, the character and the jokes, but thought I had the tone wrong: I was too knowing for the market she had in mind, eight- to twelve-year-olds, so I had to work on them.

The first one, *Flossie Teacake's Fur Coat*, was published in 1982.

The name 'Flossie Teacake' came from Margaret's mother Lily who used to describe, quite affectionately, any little girl looking unkempt or wild, or simply needing her hair brushed, as looking like Flossie Teacake.

The fur coat was based on a real garment, an old and tatty and smelly fur coat which Caitlin – known as Bella in the stories – had found on a skip and insisted on wearing for a while. In the book, Flossie creeps into Bella's room when Bella is out, puts on the fur coat, and by magic she becomes sixteen. Flossie then is sixteen, so she thinks, but she still thinks and jokes and reacts like an eight-year-old.

Margaret Clarke found an excellent artist to illustrate the stories, Lawrence Hutchins. He came to our house, when Caitlin was out, and we showed him her bedroom – which was much as it appeared in the Flossie books – a dump, filled from floor to ceiling with old clothes, broken ornaments, rubbish from skips.

I went on to write five Flossie Teacake books and they were very successful. They were a particular hit in Japan. In one of them, for the Japanese version, I got a request to have Flossie going to a ballet class, not a disco class, which was easy to do, just altering one word. It was explained that the Japanese publisher wanted Flossie in ballet clothes on the cover as all Japanese girls of eight to twelve had a passion for ballet.

For the next twenty years, I wrote a children's story every winter, most of it over the Xmas hols, when normal life goes limp after Boxing Day and you get peace and quiet. Apart from the Flossie books, I also did two series for boys. One was about Ossie, who like Flossie used a bit of magic to suddenly grow up. The other was a series about Snotty Bumpstead who is a boy living on his own in Camden Town. His mother has disappeared, but she's left him with her credit cards. He can feed himself, pay bills, but when she doesn't come back, he knocks the whole ground floor into one room for indoor football.

The Flossie books received lots of interest from TV and film companies, but no one could work out the best way to play Flossie – should two actresses do her, or one? – as of course when

Flossie is sixteen, she is still Flossie. Nothing ever came of it. But for several years, I used to get so many fan letters about Flossie, often from whole classes at primary schools where the teacher had read out the latest Flossie to them, that I had to have printed a standardised reply. Can't say that's ever happened with any of my adult books.

I did think now and again about writing about the oldies, about either my mother or Arthur, Margaret's dad, who became a widower in 1981 when Lily died. They were both such strong and interesting characters, but I couldn't quite face it or find the skill to capture them. Margaret eventually did, particularly in a novel called *Have the Men Had Enough?*, sparked off by my mother's illness.

We didn't know it was Alzheimer's at first, as it happened so slowly, stage by stage. Around 1980, while she was still in her bungalow in Carlisle, we hired help to come in for an hour or so a day, see she was OK, make a meal for her. We always worried she'd set fire to herself. For three winters, we brought her down to London – staying with Marion in the house I'd bought in our street.

Then in 1985 we brought her down full-time. I managed to buy out the tenant on the top floor of the house. Marion moved into it and my mother took over the ground-floor flat. We organised a corps of helpers, plus meals on wheels and other social services back-up. It was never enough of course. At one time, we had seven different helpers doing shift work, seven days a week, who all had to be paid in cash, in their hand, including a sister from a convent. She was very kind and caring, but also desperate for the money. I suspected she either had a secret drinking habit or was putting it on the horses.

For about ten years, in the late 1970s and through the 1980s, we seemed to be continually pulled two ways – worrying either about the children, their problems, their futures, or about the oldies, their problems, their futures. We also became financially liable for both lots.

I suppose this is bound to happen with the first generation of working-class families going to university and becoming reasonably well off. We felt we wanted to look after our parents, give them holidays, their own home, things they'd never managed in their own working life.

But there was also another huge difference between us and them. Once we'd left home, we felt somehow unconnected with our parents. We loved them, visited them, but we never felt close to or intimate with them. We would not for a moment have moaned to them about our personal or family life, told them what was really going on, or asked for help or advice. Which was why Margaret, while a student, had written pretend letters from foreign places, so as not to burden her parents with any worries.

And yet we haven't the same relationship with our own children, I'm glad to say. We have felt, rightly or wrongly, involved in what they were doing, give or take a few dark secrets I'd prefer not to be told. We have always been in touch, regardless of what was happening in their lives, treated like equals. But it meant of course that their problems became our problems. We were always aware of things going wrong in their lives, whereas our own parents never knew about us.

Our children were different from us in that they were middle-class, though you might not have known it from their accents. Jake at school always said 'fink' for 'think' and 'fought' when he meant 'thought'. Flora wasn't much better, glottal stopping most of her words. Caitlin, for some reason, always had a BBC accent, goodness knows where she got it from, despite the same sort of comprehensive education. Perhaps it was the effect of peer group pressure. Her girlfriends, by chance, tended to be from fairly middle-class, professional homes.

Our children were born middle-class, and lived that way, though all three would have screamed at the very idea if I had suggested it to them. They'd always lived in a private house, had their own bedroom, were surrounded by books, got taken to exhibitions and plays, were constantly being run in the car by daddy to endless out-of-school activities, got picked up from parties by the same daddy from the back of beyond in the middle of the night, had a holiday home in Portugal, a weekend cottage in England, called dinner supper, always had wine in the house – all the trimmings that middle-class children take for granted.

I used to tell them my wartime memories, of being a little boy in the air raid shelters in Glasgow, about never having bananas, till they said boring, boring, heard all that.

What really did stop me in my tracks was one day, probably about 1979, when Flora was seven. She happened to ask me about the olden days – and it turned out she meant the Sixties. The clothes and fashions and styles had already become ancient history to her, while to me it was still the Sixties. And very often I think it still is.

It was for about a decade a strange period for us, realising we had acquired children of a different social class, while at the same time feeling remote from the oldies. We felt responsible for both lots, for their health, their happiness and welfare.

We seemed to have the same conversations over the cocoa all the time about all of them. What can we do, what should we do, where will it all end? We seemed to be stuck, with no perceptible changes happening. The lack of progress or apparent movement was like being young again. For about ten years, time did seem to stand still.

Chapter Thirty-one

Life as a Columnist

I was talking to Alan Coren, editor of *Punch*, one day about my children – roughly the same age as his two – saying that the women's pages of papers like the *Guardian* were now full of women going on about bringing up their children, but you rarely read about fathers. He said try a couple of columns, which I did. They ran and ran for the next ten years, from 1979 to 1989.

The 'Father's Day' columns also came out in paperback, as collections, and then to my amazement, the film rights got bought by a TV company. I had always hoped a Flossie TV series would get made, as they were proper stories, with beginnings and endings and an original idea, but I thought a TV series based on an 800-word column was a nonsense. It would never work on TV, so I turned down the chance to write the scripts. Instead they were done by one of the most successful TV scriptwriters of the day, Peter Spence, who had had a huge success with 'To the Manor Born'. They then got John Alderton to be the star, acting the part of me, which was ironic. He of course had been cast as Jake Sullivan in the Tony Palmer film which never got made. This time it did all come to pass and the TV version of 'Father's Day' ran for two series starting in 1983.

In the *Punch* columns, I made a big thing about telling the truth – not the whole truth, not the awful things we thought

266

Caitlin was doing, but basically it was true, using real places, my real children, with their real names and ages. I've always hated those sort of domestic columns where the children are given silly nicknames, like the Treasure, or the dad is called Useless Simon. I suspect most of the stuff is made up.

But by making it real, I eventually wrote myself out of a column. As they got older, the children did start protesting about the use of their names. At William Ellis, there was a master who read *Punch* and began making references to what Jake had supposedly been doing or saying in the column – yet Jake had no idea what he was on about. He of course never read such boring stuff, but at school it did embarrass him. He wanted me to change his name. For a while I called him Jimmy, till he forgot, or the master stopped making remarks.

But by using their real ages, it meant they really did grow up, and grew away. Fictional heroes like Just William can stay the same age, for ever. If only I'd made up their names, I could have kept the column going. But soon Caitlin had left university and gone off to America.

Jake was in his first year at Gonville and Caius College, Cambridge. That was a surprise, when we remembered how he had appeared backward for so long, unable to read and write and speak properly. It was in the Sixth Form that he suddenly blossomed, showing an original turn of mind, obviously inherited from his mother. Those *Sunday Times* readers who had written to me long ago had proved to be pretty accurate. Jake's nature seemed to change totally, becoming calm and loving by the time he was a teenager. Caitlin, of course, had made an equally dramatic personality change: but the other way. I would say, based on a close examination of two people, that children change their personality every seven years as they grow up, until they become whatever it is they become.

In 1981, I began another column, which went on to run for five years, though you would need to have been in a very, very small select group of the population to ever have been aware of it.

It came out of the end of playing football. I realised at last that I was being stupid still playing Sunday-morning football in my late forties, so I got into stamps. An excellent, harmless hobby for healthy middle-aged boys. Not much chance of being injured with a pair of tweezers, though it can happen, or pulling a muscle while examining a Penny Black. I took to haunting the stamp shops in Covent Garden, the stalls under the Charing Cross Road Arches, the platforms on London Bridge station on a Sunday morning, and other hidden-away exotic venues which I never knew existed till I started collecting stamps.

I came across a new publication, a tabloidish stamp newspaper called *Stamp News*, rather different from the old, traditional, very serious and academic stamp publications, written for and by real philatelists. I was in stamps for fun, able to poke fun at myself and other collectors, and our sad obsessions, but at the same time, I did take it seriously, as I take all fun things.

I can't remember how that column came to end. Perhaps the paper closed, or ran out of money. But I wasn't sacked. I do remember that. Unlike almost every other personal column I have had over the years. Sacking is part of the process.

In 1987, I was asked to do a column for the London *Evening Standard*. They were starting a system of a column a day, written by a different person. Beryl Bainbridge, who did one of the days, was always saying she was stuck, or no one liked her column, no one at the paper had said anything about the last one. I said, 'Don't worry. As long as they print it, that's all that matters.'

One day, after just six months, one of the feature executives rang me up and said, 'That's it, you're sacked, the editor doesn't want you any more.' I think the specific thing objected to was that I'd been going on about comprehensives when I was supposed to be writing about life in London generally. Beryl, the amateur columnist, the worrier, meanwhile carried on for several more years with great success.

As a columnist or any sort of freelance writer, you have to acquire a hard skin, not expect praise or even much reaction. I once had dinner with James Cameron at Joan Bakewell's house. He was one of the most revered journalists of our times, a bit older than me, and I'd missed perhaps his best foreign work, but I still admired and enjoyed all his work.

He was at that time writing a column for the *Guardian* and he was moaning that no one from the paper ever contacted him. No one said his last column was good or bad or OK, or ever suggested any ideas. He'd met none of the people who looked after his column, or the section where he appeared, no lunches, not even an annual drink, no anything. He felt he was taken so much for granted that he might as well not exist.

About six months later he died – and the *Guardian* cleared the decks. There were pages of appreciations, reprints of his old columns, glowing accounts of how he was so much a *Guardian* man, how they were so proud of him. I wished he'd been there to enjoy it.

I moved out of my depth rather with a general opinion column for the *Independent on Sunday*, under the editorship of my friend Ian Jack, with whom I had first worked on *The Sunday Times*. I wrote it for about six months, and was enjoying it, when early one Sunday morning, before the paper had arrived, so I didn't know my column had not been used that day, there was a knock at the front door. A very nervous, embarrassed-looking Ian Jack was standing there.

Margaret invited him in, bemused by such an early visit, having no inkling what the purpose might be. I was still sound asleep in bed. Ian confessed to Margaret he was in a bit of a state, finding it very difficult to find the words he was going to have to use. Margaret just laughed, unable to believe anyone could get in a state about facing me, for any reason.

He had of course come to sack me. He said he wanted to do it to my face, as I was his friend. I like to think I took it on the chin. Smiled, said don't worry, and went back to bed.

That's easy to do, when it's a peripheral job, not your bread and butter, and it doesn't really matter. But even if it did matter a lot, I hope I'd feel much the same, being able to rationalise it.

It's only a matter of opinion. Editors always want someone new and different.

The most unexpected column I ever got offered was from the *Mail on Sunday*. I was asked to be their TV critic, appearing in their Night and Day section when it first started, when it was new and excellent. I explained I didn't actually watch TV, apart from the football. The editor of the section, Jocelyn Targett, had read my various columns and journalism over the years and thought I would bring a fresh eye to TV reviewing. Not being a TV watcher didn't bother him. He could see it as a plus.

I did it for about six months and the space grew bigger and bigger. They wanted me to do more, to include previews as well, and interviews with TV stars, but I refused. I hadn't got that sort of time, and didn't want that sort of work, writing books was my main occupation, but the reviewing itself was good fun and quite easy. I didn't in fact have to watch TV, as such. A bundle of videos arrived each week and I'd pick the interesting ones, fit them in at my leisure, and knock out my 1,000 words. For the extra bits on my page, I recommended a young journalist, Brian Viner, whom I'd been reading in the *Ham and High*, our local North London paper. I'd never met him, knew nothing about him, but I thought his copy was bright and amusing. He was interviewed, and got the job, was taken on to the staff. One of his little jobs, early on, was delivering the videos to my house.

We were in the Lake District, in the long hot summer of 1995, when Jocelyn's secretary rang to say Jocelyn was coming to see me. I said what for? She said she honestly didn't know. Was I being sacked? Oh no, she said, Jocelyn loves your stuff.

By this time I had become convinced I was about to be offered some new and amazing and important job, otherwise why would he want to come all this way when he could tell me on the phone?

It took Jocelyn about eight hours to reach us from London, mainly because the driver of his office Jaguar – the *Mail* Group know how to treat their executives – had decided to drive through the central lakes, via Windermere and Ambleside, and had got bogged down in all the holiday traffic.

Jocelyn arrived, hot and sweating. He and his driver got out of their steaming Jaguar and Margaret gave them some refreshments. There was some inconsequential chat, till Jocelyn made it clear he didn't want to tell me, whatever it was, in front of his driver, or Margaret. I suggested a walk down to the lake. When we got there, he told me I was being sacked. He then got back into his Jaguar and was driven the 300 miles back to London.

I was so surprised I didn't really ask what the reasons were. It was only some time later, on the telephone, that I found out what had happened. Apparently, David English, boss of the *Mail* Group, had taken against me when I'd written in a recent column that I had never seen 'EastEnders'. He thought this was inexcusable for a TV columnist.

The reason why Jocelyn had come all that way to sack me personally was more complicated. When he had taken over Night and Day, he'd decided to sack two people. By chance, they found out beforehand and it had led to a very nasty atmosphere in the office for several days. He vowed that next time he had to sack anyone, no one at all would know beforehand. He would tell the person in question first, face to face. I happened to be the next victim, living 300 miles away. The person who got my job was Brian Viner. And he did it far better than I had done.

When my various columns were trickling along, or trickling to an end, I also found myself as a radio broadcaster. All those years ago in Carlisle I had been told I gabbled too much, people couldn't understand what I was saying. I never thought I had a good voice anyway. And I knew from the TV progs I'd done I was useless at reading the autocue and making it sound natural.

I was rung up one day by Helen Fry, head of the BBC department which included 'Bookshelf', Radio 4's weekly book programme, and asked if I'd fancy presenting it. Frank Delaney, who does have a beautiful voice, and is a great actor and performer, was giving it up. I was auditioned, along with two or three others, and to my surprise, I was given the job.

I did it for three years, 1983–6, and enjoyed it, working with some very talented and professional producers, such as Simon Elmes, Kate Fenton, Angela Hind and a young new producer, just promoted from being a sound recordist, Andy Parfitt, who later went on to be Controller of Radio 5. It took a while for them to knock me into shape, as I had no proper experience of radio. Each week we did about three or four authors, plus a feature.

It became very time consuming – which was why I missed my Literary Lunches – partly because I insisted on doing forty-minute interviews, even though I knew we would end up with only five minutes. They were all so conscientious. If for example we were doing a fishing book, they would insist on recording the interview sitting by a real lake with a real person fishing. If it was an Arthur Ransome feature, we had to be in the Lake District, actually on Coniston. I always maintained a listener could not tell the difference and we could easily have used sound effects. Today, it's all changed. There's no time for such indulgences. Programmes have to be turned round in half the time.

I gave up 'Bookshelf' voluntarily, as it was taking up so much time, even though I enjoyed it. I always prefer radio to TV. The work is simpler, you can move quickly, with fewer people, and on the whole radio people are nicer. And you do get to ask people questions to which you don't normally know the answer.

One of the great things about being a media hack, in these modern times, is the opportunity to jump around, try out different parts of the media, see if you can do it, see if you like it. TV and radio, as they're not really much good on original, creative ideas, prefer to pinch or adapt from other media, so they are always looking to use people from the written world.

I suppose it's always happened, even when the media were small and the options were limited. Southey and Coleridge, despite living in Lakeland and supposedly writing poetry, were always knocking out book reviews or articles for the London or Edinburgh magazines. I always liked the fact that Wordsworth did some hack work on someone else's book of watercolours and then went on to write a guidebook to the Lake District – which made him more money than any of his poetry. A vicar is said to have met him one day and complimented him on his guidebook. 'And have you written anything else, Mr Wordsworth?'

I'm not for a moment comparing myself with dear William, but I always liked it, during the years I was writing my stamp column, when stamp collectors would come up to me and ask me the same question.

Chapter Thirty-two

London and Loweswater

My mother died on 8 December 1987. I missed the funeral as well as the death, as I was abroad, working on a book, a biography of Columbus. We had managed to keep her at home, in the house I had bought in our street, with round-the-clock care, till almost the end, then she had gone into Friern Barnet Hospital, in North London, for the last six weeks. This was a vast Victorian mansion-style institution, a nightmare version of an asylum, which is what it had been and still felt like, with long echoing corridors, people moaning and screaming in the distance.

What an awful way to end your life, so I always thought when I went to visit her, feeling guilty that we could have made her last months more comfortable, but by then she had no idea who she was or where she was. She was in a dedicated Alzheimer's wing, so in theory receiving specialist attention. All day long she sat in a smelly room with the other patients, none of them with any idea where they were, some of them only in their fifties, looking otherwise fit and well. When she'd been semi-well, semi-aware of what was happening to her, she had often become bad-tempered and depressed, which she had never been in her normal life. But near the end, she moved into a vaguely serene state, smiling a lot, as if she knew a secret.

She was in her seventy-ninth year. A good age considering her years of ill health, her hard life. She left nothing, not a bean, just as she'd had nothing in her living life.

I've kept lots of her letters, the ones she wrote to me each week for forty years, the ones she sent in reply to mine, confirming in those early years that my £2 had arrived. She was a witty writer, with a good turn of phrase.

I have one in front of me, written on 21 February 1960, from Carlisle, addressed to me at '6a Kingscroft Road, Shoot up Hill, Hampstead, London NW2'. I'd not long moved in, but it wasn't Hampstead of course, though I might have led her to believe it was.

'Thanks for usual. The nights are fairly getting longer. Spring will soon be "a commin in". Johnny received your shirt and thanks you very much for same. I was waiting for him to write and thank you but when I suggested it, he said "what me, oh you know me," as if it were a virtue of his not to thank anyone.'

I love that last sentence, the neatness of it, the way she handled the running quotes, when you realise how little education she had had.

Johnny, my younger brother, was still at home in 1960, working as an apprentice electrician. He had just turned nineteen on 16 February. My mother had obviously eventually cajoled him into writing some sort of thank you. At the end of her letter, he has scribbled his own few words.

'Dear Hunter, thanks very much for the shirt, your choice of present is a little better than your wit, the shirt seems to fit OK but the hanger seems a little tight Johnny'

Not so hot on the punctuation as my mother, and there are several crossings-out, but again, very amusing. I often think that there are millions of people who can write as well as the so-called professionals, who have a natural smoothness, their own style, if not perfect grammar, yet who will never think of writing more than bread-and-butter letters in their lives. Which is just as well for those of us who have somehow managed to make a living at it. There is of course a huge jump from 'she writes a good letter' to actually completing a whole book. All the same, there is nothing exclusive or special or unusual about being 'able to write'.

My sister Marion, by then a team leader with Camden Social Services, was loving her work and had a large circle of female friends, and not all of them lesbian. She eventually moved to her own flat, in Muswell Hill, and settled down with her partner, Frances.

And then something unexpected happened to her – she started writing. She was approaching the age of fifty when she began knocking out little bits for her own amusement. She did it all on her own, without telling me.

She sent off some columns to the *Guardian* and to everyone's amazement, they were accepted. It led to her having her own column in the Society pages, 'Mary Black, Leader of the Pack'. Mary Black had been my mother's mother's maiden name. The column was based on Marion's work as a team leader, but she had to do it anonymously, or Camden would have objected. She also had to make sure no real people or places were identified, but all her columns rang true enough and they were very popular with *Guardian* readers and in the social work world. Everyone tried to guess who the author was, which council she worked for.

I once went to see Glenys Kinnock, wife of Neil, then leader of the Labour Party, and when I arrived she was sitting in her kitchen with the *Guardian* spread out, reading 'Mary Black, Leader of the Pack'. She was smiling at it, saying how much she enjoyed it.

The column was sharp, witty and written in a deliberate staccato style, usually with a good anecdote or incident, plus a little moral or observation. As was typical of the *Guardian*, Marion never met anyone who looked after her column, was never called in, taken out to lunch, or had ideas suggested.

I wanted her to move on and write a lesbian column as well. I was sure the *Guardian* would have loved it, a funny one, not the usual stereotypes. But instead, she'd got it into her head she wanted to write a play.

Its title was *Who Stole your Scone?* which was a Scottish phrase my mother used. It was about my mother's life, and her death. It was accepted by a theatrical director, Claire Grove, who had it performed at the ICA in the Mall. There was a professional cast, who did it brilliantly, performed all the parts on a stage, although it was technically a read-through, for one night only, to try it out in front of a proper audience. The little theatre was packed – half of them, I suspect, were Camden social workers, the other half our family, friends and neighbours. We all cheered like mad and then a party of us came back to our house where Margaret had laid on a slap-up dinner to celebrate Marion's achievement.

The play was then accepted by the BBC and performed on Radio 4 and got good reviews. It looked like the beginning of a late flourishing but exciting new career for Marion as a writer, as opposed to social worker, what with her *Guardian* column and her play. But then she fell ill.

As with all such dreadful things, the first signs seemed trivial and temporary, then came the endless tests, the beginning of serious treatments, then awful operations, each preceded by false hopes. It seemed to go on for years before the real problem was diagnosed as cancer. Her throat and nose were operated on, so she could hardly eat, apart from ice cream. She had been a heavy smoker, most of her life, which clearly had not helped.

Marion died in 1995, aged fifty-six. She had organised her own memorial service, and had found a woman minister, decided on all the hymns and prayers. The church was packed and it was all terribly emotional, but the wake afterwards was a noisy, happy occasion, as Marion would have wished.

Margaret later wrote about Marion's death, and that of her father Arthur, who died in 1996 aged ninety-six, in her book *Precious Lives*.

In 1987, the year my mother died, we decided it was time to start preparing to achieve a little fantasy we had had floating around in our heads for a few years.

Bombing up and down the M1 and M6 to Caldbeck for short breaks several times each year had never been much fun. Just as hellish as going to Gatwick every summer for our charter flight to Faro.

I used to say I had three ambitions in life – never to go on the Tube again, never to go to Gatwick in the school hols again, and thirdly to live half of each year in Lakeland and half in London. The first was easy to achieve, once I stopped proper work. The second two depended on the children growing up, leaving us to be fancy free.

In the Lakeland fantasy, our home would have to be in the Lakes proper, i.e. with a lake in view. We'd go there once a year, live our life, and then come back, for the London half. Wouldn't that be great.

We couldn't contemplate spending six months in Lakeland until of course Flora had left school, gone off to wherever she might be going off to. Caitlin had already flown the nest, off in America, clearly with no intention of ever returning to the family home. Jake was about to graduate, and had plans to go to Europe. Flora was still only fifteen, so she would have three years presumably still at home, living with her dear mama and papa.

It was a very selfish and self-centred fantasy, but then we had had about twenty years when either the children or our parents or both had seemed, to me at least, to have been our first and practically only priority. Margaret never saw it in those terms. It wasn't a matter of putting other people first, or second. It was what you did.

I talked Margaret into it and started looking. On 7 May 1987, there was a house at Loweswater to be sold by auction. We had seen it, briefly, a few weeks before, and liked its situation. It didn't quite have a lake view, except in winter when the trees were bare, but it was on a little hill, so the views around of all the fells were magnificent. It was within walking distance of not just one, but three lakes – Crummock Water, Buttermere and Loweswater, three pearls on a string.

The auction was being held at the Globe Hotel in

Cockermouth – a single house sale, not part of any other properties being auctioned. The estate agent, Smiths Gore, had said on the phone they expected it to fetch up to £80,000, judging by the interest so far.

I decided to attend the sale in person and I set off from Euston, promising Margaret I would not go beyond £80,000. That was almost four times what I had ever paid for any property, so it seemed enormous.

I got a taxi from Carlisle and arrived at the Globe just as the estate agent, an elderly gentleman, was into his spiel. He had been an estate agent working in Lakeland for decades, so he was saying, but this house had the finest situation of any he had ever sold. I felt like turning round and going home, even though part of me was cynical, suspecting it was estate agent hype, but there again, people in rural Cumbria don't play such tricks.

The bidding was slow at first, so I entered quite early on, hoping to frighten off the opposition. Gradually it got up to £80,000, and then very slowly it reached £90,000. I hesitated, remembering my promise, then I decided to make one last bid – at £92,000. And the hammer came down. The vendors, who appeared to be three people in a corner, one of them with a clerical collar, then went into a huddle to decide whether they would accept my bid. There was a long pause, while they conferred, stared across at me, then the white smoke went up, a new owner had been elected.

I wasn't sure of the age of the house, when we bought it, but it turned out to have been built in 1860, the same year as our London house. Unlike John Peel Farm, which was much older, this house had big windows, front and back, so there was lots of light, and a pretty porch, front and back. It had originally been the village carpenter's house. His workshop, next door, had been converted into another house, then lived in by the Rev. Geoffrey White, a retired vicar of Loweswater, and his wife Joan. It was Joan's family, the Robinsons, who had owned the property.

For three years, we used it purely as a holiday home, for the school hols and half terms. It was a bit of a drag, getting in to

Carlisle every second day to see Arthur, which took an hour, but it was well worth it.

Up to the age of ninety-four, Arthur was in great fettle, still in his own house, still doing his garden, still going to the pub and knocking back two pints of beer in minutes. He had had no operations in his life. His medical notes made about a page, whereas mine, in my late fifties, could have covered a whole bookshelf.

He had been born in 1900, so his memory of war breaking out in 1914 was very clear. Aged fourteen, he'd run away to Newcastle to join up, lying about his age, but his dad ran after him and dragged him home.

When the millennium started to loom, and with the year 2000 approaching fast, I thought how interesting it would be to talk to other people like Arthur, also born in 1900. I'd look for a broad social and geographical cross-section, get down their thoughts and feelings and memories, which would cover the whole of the twentieth century. I hadn't done a book in a vox-pop style for over thirty years, since *The Other Half* in 1966. Publishers don't like such books. They think it's just a collection of pieces. I persuaded Alan Samson of Little, Brown, my new best friend in publishing, to take it, explaining it would have a proper theme, the history of the century. I would include things as well as people born in 1900 – such as the hamburger, West Ham United, Mercedes cars, Birmingham University, the Labour Party. It was good fun for me, having so many different subjects and different people to go out and research.

Arthur, alas, the begetter of the book, was not in it. He died in December 1996, before I'd even had a proper chance to interview him. As I write, there is just one of the ten *Born 1900* people in the book who is still alive, Commander Kenneth Cummins, an ex-P&O captain.

Flora got As in the two A-levels she sat, despite various educational upsets she had had to suffer, such as industrial action by teachers – and then decided she didn't want to go to university. The example of her older brother and sister, and what they had done, or not done, was not particularly attractive. But mainly she couldn't think of any subject she'd like to study, nor did she want to be surrounded by students.

Jake by this time had left Cambridge. He'd got a First, which again amazed me, not that I don't think he deserved it, just that I couldn't help thinking back again to his early years. Having achieved what is commonly agreed to be about the highest academic mark of success in our meritocratic country, he then had no idea what to do next. He said he didn't want to wear a suit, have a nine-to-five job, have a mortgage, save for a pension, and he certainly had no interest in a career. All he fancied was being in the sun for a while. So he went off to Italy, to teach English as a foreign language, play a lot of football, have a lot of girlfriends.

Caitlin meanwhile was still in the USA, doing a Masters plus a bit of teaching as a TA (teacher assistant) at Clark University in Worcester, Massachusetts. All I knew about Clark was that Freud's only appearance ever in the USA was to give a lecture there. I knew this because one of my *Born 1900* topics was a book published in that year, Freud's *Interpretation of Dreams.*

Jake had read History, and Caitlin had done English, which to Flora indicated that Arts degrees were a waste of time. They appeared not to equip you for anything. Most students were just dossers, living at the state's or their parents' expense, and she didn't want to be like that. She wasn't interested in academic education anyway, even though she could clearly do it, judging by her A-levels and all her As at GCE.

I tried to talk her into the idea of university. What is wrong with having a doss for three years anyway? That's roughly what I did. It's a chance to enjoy yourself, mess around, discover yourself, try different things. You might never get such a chance in your life. I loved Durham. But for Durham I would never have discovered journalism, nor had such fun. All of which she had of course heard before.

This argument was rather ruined by Margaret saying that she

found Oxford boring, a waste of time, she would have learned more about life and herself by three years as a cracker packer at Carr's biscuit works. She said that if Flora didn't fancy uni – a horrible word, I think, but it's what going to university was now being called – then she needn't go.

Flora decided she would follow her natural bent, which was to do something in the arts world, but something useful, such as learning a craft which might provide her with the training to take up a job. So off she went to the London College of Printing to do a two-year HND course in screen printing.

Well, it was going to provide a skill, I thought, just as my brother Johnny had left school to go and become an apprentice electrician. But somehow it didn't seem as elevated as going to university, not that I allowed such a condescending thought to seep out.

Meanwhile, Caitlin at one stage, after her two years in that squat, had been thinking of putting her name down for a council flat.

I suppose it's a sign of different social values and images today, as well as the speeding up of modern life. You can go from working class back to working class, in just three generations. Not of course that there's anything wrong with that . . .

Chapter Thirty-three
Lakeland Life

Round the camp fire, we often wonder what we would have done, if we hadn't been doing what we've been doing all these years. Margaret says if she was ever down on her luck, she would do cleaning. She doesn't mind scrubbing, brushing, washing, ironing, tidying, cleaning up of any sort. It would be no hardship to her. And she would make a reasonable living. People are crying out for good cleaners because most people don't like it or they're rubbish at it.

I would have a stall, either in a street market, or go round the car boot sales or collectors' fairs, buying and selling, rubbish probably. I'd be forced to understand and use eBay, which I'm always promising myself I will, as that appears to be the best way to sell rubbish things today, though it doesn't sound much fun. Having a stall, though, I'd enjoy that.

In reality of course, if we'd both been really, really stuck, all those years ago in our twenties, trying to have a regular income, children and a house, we would have done the sensible but boring thing and become teachers.

On the other hand, I might have gone into publishing. Which in fact I did, although not full-time. In 1984, I set up a publishing firm called Forster Davies Ltd. The company already existed, since 1966 when we set it up on the advice of our accountant when tax was 90 per cent, which is what most writers and self-employed people did at the time, turning themselves into, or creating their own little company. But it was never really used. In 1984, I decided to activate it and publish books about Lakeland.

The spark which set it off was getting a copy of my latest children's book fresh from the printers, one of the Flossie series, though I can't remember which. I was furious when I saw all the blank pages at the beginning, and at the end, making a total of eight empty pages. Bodley Head, when they did the hardback versions of children's books, always seemed to do this. One of my Snotty Bumpstead ones had fourteen blank pages in all. Fourteen! Did I scream! All those pages, going through the printing machinery, just to come out blank, what a waste. I could have filled them up with jokes, more information, plugs for my other books, not let them just lie there, doing nothing, not paying their way. Publishers, eh, how stupid they are.

At that time, I was thinking of writing a guidebook to Lakeland. On a whim, I decided I'd publish it myself – and I'd make sure there was no blank page, not even gaps in a page, anywhere in the book, including the first pages, which traditionally are always left empty. If I'm paying, I'm making every page work for its living. I'd also be able to lay out the book the way I wanted, write it in the style I wanted, criticise people and places without some editor going 'Tut tut, I don't think we can say this,' and generally chuntering on.

The main selling point of the book, apart from up-to-date information about everything a tourist or visitor would want to know about Lakeland, would be the opinions. It was and is commonplace to give stars or ratings to hotels and restaurants. I decided to award stars to everything – not just hotels, but museums, stately homes, villages, towns, even lakes and mountains. The theory was that life is too short to miss the best places, so first-timers need all the guidance they can get.

I needed a researcher to cover the Southern Lakeland, as I was based in the north, and I hired a young man called Colin Shelbourn, who was living in Grange over Sands. He was not long out of York University, and had come back to Cumbria trying to make a living by writing bits and pieces, though his real ambition was to be a cartoonist.

I got estimates from various printers, all in Cumbria, as I was determined that it would be an all-Cumbrian publication – written, researched, printed and published up here.

I got some leaflets printed, advertising the book, but they were a waste of time. Bookshops didn't put them up. I took advertising space in local publications, trying to sell copies by mail order, reckoning that was how a publisher could make his biggest profit, cutting out the wholesaler and retailer. It was surprisingly expensive – and useless. I only got about six orders.

I then decided I needed to have a proper distribution deal. A publishing friend of mine, Anthony Cheetham, was beginning a new firm called Century. I'd first met him when he was about sixteen and at Eton and I did an Atticus story about a magazine he was running. His partners in the new venture included Gail Rebuck whom I also knew because she'd been the young editor on *The Book of British Lists* I'd done in 1980. That had been a surprise best-seller, running into many editions, till I grew bored with the formula and let another author take it over.

I went to Century's small office in Greek Street, Soho. The total staff at the time numbered about six. I told them about my Good Guide idea – and led them to believe, which I half believed myself, that if it worked in Lakeland, I would use the same format and style for a Good Guide to Paris, New York, the world. This was before such modern guides as Lonely Planet and Rough Guides had got established.

I explained all I wanted was for them to handle sales. It would cost them nothing, no capital need be tied up, because I was paying all editorial, printing and marketing costs. They were very pleased to get a title on their first list, without having to spend any money or do any work. The deal was that I would get the books to their warehouse, then they would take over, get orders, delivering the books to the shop, collecting the money and paying me every month, if of course they sold any. The deal was they would take 20 per cent of the net receipts, and I would get the rest.

I got printed 11,000 copies for which Frank Peters charged me £6,923. It was a bit ambitious, as I knew that normal Lakeland books sold no more than 2,000–3,000 a year. I did a deal with Romneys Kendal Mint Cake, who gave me 1,000 bars for nothing, and arranged with the main Lakeland bookshops that the first 1,000 buyers of the book would get a free bar of mint cake.

In a bookshop in Kendal, one customer refused his bar. The shop assistant ran after him, explaining it was free, as he was a first customer, and shoved it into his hands. He threw it to the floor. It turned out he was a dentist.

I also didn't know, not being a proper publisher, that what I had done was illegal in publishing. At that time, 1984, publishers had to stick to the Net Book Agreement – all copies of a book being sold at the same price – and inducements for sale, such as freebies, were not allowed.

I priced the book very reasonably, £2.95 for a 228-page stiff-backed paperback, and all 11,000 were sold even before my launch party at Brockhole, the National Park centre in Windermere. I got another 15,000 printed, and they went quickly as well, so I did another 5,000. So that was 31,000 copies gone, on my very first attempt as a publisher.

Forster Davies was making quite a lot of money. At the end of the first year, the total income was £24,000. The profit so far was £10,000 which I just left lying in the bank. I hadn't paid myself anything, or taken anything out, as I would have had to pay extra tax. I gave two lumps away – £1,000 to the Cumbria Tourist Board to set up an annual prize for the best book on Lakeland and the same to University College, Durham, to administer an award for the best piece of journalism each year in *Palatinate*.

As a publisher, I went a bit daft after that. Not content with planning the next edition of the *Good Guide*, which I was going to do every two years, for ever and ever, I then started using the profits to publish other titles. I began with *The Good Quiz Book to the Lakes,* which did very well, followed by *The Good Quiz Book to London* – which did very badly. I published *The Towns and Villages of Lakeland,* with Colin Shelbourn as author, and I hired a photographer to do new photos, especially for the book. It was a total failure. That made me realise, just in time before I lost all the profits, that I should stick to the winning format, which was *The Good Guide to the Lakes,* and forget about publishing other books.

The Good Guide to the Lakes is still going strong – 'published by Forster Davies, Ltd, Loweswater and London', so it says grandly on the title page. I still use a Cumbrian printer, Titus Wilson of Kendal, and it's now in its sixth edition, with so far around 100,000 copies sold. I have used other chief researchers since, such as Pam Williamson, as Colin Shelbourn got too expensive and successful. He's now an author in his own right, well known in South Lakeland as the cartoonist for the *Westmorland Gazette.*

The Lakeland Book of the Year Awards are an important part of the Lakeland calendar, still run by the CTB, but now we have a big lunch, five different prizes in all and sponsors queuing up to be involved. We are the only region of England which has such an award – London used to, and I was a runner-up once with my book about London parks. I like to think the Lakeland Book of the Year Awards will go on for ever. In 2005, there were 79 books entered, all of them new, not reprints or new editions, and all about Cumbria. The majority these days are published locally, or are self-published, which was something we hoped to encourage, twenty-two years ago when the prize started.

Century turned into Century Hutchinson and after various takeovers and changes, my *Good Guide to the Lakes* is still being distributed by them, on the same terms, but now they are part of Random House. Gail Rebuck is the big cheese there, the most important woman executive in publishing. Anthony Cheetham went on to found Orion.

I think I've covered all the dramatis personae loosely connected with my little publishing venture. One of the nice things about age is being able to say I remember him/her in short trousers.

I did continue writing books about Cumbria and Cumbrian subjects, but for other publishers in the conventional way. Several have been biographies, such as *Beatrix Potter's Lakeland* in 1988. That was the idea of Warne, her original publisher, now part of Penguin. They came to me with the idea of a lavishly illustrated book about her life in Lakeland. The photos, all of them brilliant, were done by Cressida Pemberton-Pigott (now Lady Inglewood) who was brought up in a big house on the shores of Derwentwater, where Beatrix Potter's family had once holidayed.

Cressida did new Lakeland photos for the book, and also used ones she had taken over the years, which came to several hundred transparencies – most of which got lost somewhere in the Penguin building. The book had been printed in Singapore, which is what publishers do these days, to save money. When eventually the printer sent Cressida's trannies back they were apparently addressed to Beatrix Potter, Penguin Books, Wright's Lane, London.

Whoever received the package looked in the staff list for a Beatrix Potter, couldn't find anyone with that name, asked around, but still no one knew, so the package languished in a corner. It's presumed that eventually a cleaner threw them out, but the upshot was that Cressida had lost some highly valuable photographs, of personal and professional importance. After a lot of faffing, she did get some compensation.

Doing the biography of Wainwright was my idea. I had met him when doing my *Walk Around the Lakes*, when he'd said I could interview him for the book, but not use it in any newspaper or magazine. During that time with him, in 1978, I went with Betty, his second wife, to Abbot Hall where she was supervising an exhibition of his drawings.

They were marked at £10 each. I took three and got out my chequebook and began writing 'Thirty Pounds to A.W. . . .' and she stopped me. I had to make it Animal Rescue instead. Unknown to his readers, and the public, it turned out that Wainwright was giving all his money away to animals.

By this time, his books were making a huge amount of money. His seven *Pictorial Guides to the Lakeland Fells*, which I consider works of art, had sold one million copies – yet his face or biographical details did not appear on any of the books, nor did he do any signing sessions, appearances or personal publicity. The *Westmorland Gazette*, his printers and publishers, were a bit out of touch commercially. They did no marketing or publicity, and didn't even have a sales force. Bookshops had to send in their orders, and then usually come and collect.

Wainwright died in 1991, by which time he had become nationally known through a series of TV programmes and also some glossy, coffee-table books – all done, reluctantly, to make even more for his precious animals.

One of the things I liked about Wainwright, apart from his writing and his wonderful artwork, was the fact that he had self-published his early Pictorial Guides. He had wanted them done his way, with no publisher messing them up, or using printer's type. Beatrix Potter did the same, though for different reasons. She had failed completely to get a publisher interested in *Peter Rabbit*, her first book, and had been forced into publishing it herself.

Today, a copy of that first edition of *Peter Rabbit* has fetched £80,000 at a Sotheby's auction. Only 250 were printed, so they are pretty rare, and she does have a world-wide fan base, especially in Japan and the USA. A first edition of Wainwright's first self-published guide, price 12/6d, of which 2,000 were printed, sells for about £300.

I collect Wainwright books, and Beatrix Potter memorabilia; in fact I have about twenty different collections on the go at any one time. It usually starts when I'm on a book, and I want to collect as much as possible about that particular subject. It's also to do with never knowingly throwing anything away. My collections range from suffragettes and prime ministers – and I have all their autographs back to Walpole – to number ones of newspapers and magazines and Lake District postcards. These collections are relatively dormant, as I've either completed what I set out to do, or have grown bored. My main two active collections concern football memorabilia and the Beatles, two of the passions in my life.

The Beatles stuff goes back of course to doing their book, when I picked up those scraps of lyrics from the floor of Abbey Road, and also bought and stashed away in drawers lots of *Beatles Monthly* magazines, fan club material, sheet music, and assorted daft souvenirs.

I had actually forgotten exactly what Beatles stuff I had collected, till Caitlin and Jake became teenagers and showed a passing interest in pop music. I opened up the Beatles drawer, saw I had these lyrics, and hung them on the stairs. Caitlin and Jake weren't at all impressed. Some of their teenage friends were, and I began to worry that at some drunken party, someone would be sick all over them.

One day in 1983, Sotheby's held one of the first auctions of pop memorabilia. I found that overnight my scraps on the wall had become worth more than the house. I worried about their safety, should I hide or sell them, but I also thought they must be kept together, perhaps displayed for others to see.

I rang the British Museum and asked if they'd like them. I half expected a refusal, that the scraps were too trivial, but they jumped at my offer. For many years, they were on show in the BM's Manuscript Room. Now they have been transferred to the new British Library in Euston Road. They are in the manuscript gallery, along with Magna Carta, Beethoven, Mozart, Wordsworth, Jane Austen. On any one day, the Beatles display usually has the biggest crowd round it. When the Queen opened the Library, it was one of the cases she paused at.

The British Library has them on permanent loan. In my will, which I have just done, they will go to the nation. I couldn't sell them. Paul would never speak to me again. Anyway, I don't need the money, not as long as Margaret keeps writing.

Chapter Thirty-four
Gazza and Cherie

When I was first asked to do Gazza's autobiography I said no thanks, I don't want to do another football book. I'd done a football history book, a book about a club (*The Glory Game*) and two books of my collected football writings. One was called *My Life in Football* and one *The Fan*, based on my *New Statesman* football columns which I began doing in 1997 and still am, as I write.

I'd even done a football novel called *Striker* partly inspired by Paul Gascoigne, his life and character, though in my novel he comes from a remote village in Cumbria. He ends up in Italy where he's writing his memoirs while locked up somewhere, though the reader doesn't know he's been kidnapped.

I'd also done two biographies, one about a manager, Joe Kinnear, the other a player, Dwight Yorke, then at the height of his powers, playing for Manchester United and winning the Treble. I was fascinated by his life, coming on his own at the age of seventeen from the little island of Tobago in the West Indies to the winter snows of Birmingham, but alas, he didn't appear much interested in the project. He certainly didn't need the money, as he was getting about £1 million from Nike.

On our first arranged meeting, at his big mansion in Cheshire, I was kept waiting outside for an hour. I knew his address, phone number, mobile number, but I hadn't realised I needed a special security code to even speak through the intercom on his huge security gates. So I just stood there shouting. When I was eventually let in he was with a very attractive blonde whom he introduced as his interior designer, working on new decor for his bedroom, which of course I totally believed.

He messed me around, turned up late, cancelled appointments, but worst of all, which I couldn't have foreseen, he turned out to be a private person. That's how he had survived so well, building a carapace round himself, so no one could get close and hurt him. The book was a bit of a failure.

After all that, I'd decided that's it, my football portfolio is complete. I've had the experiences, and one of them I didn't enjoy and didn't want to repeat.

I told the publisher who had contacted me, Val Hudson of Headline, that if she wanted a yes or no, it had to be no. We had a family drama at the time, Xmas was coming up, then we were going away to the West Indies. Anyway, I'd done football.

Three months later, they had not found another writer and wanted to know if at least I would go and meet Gazza. I agreed to see him at Heathrow Airport. He was on his way to China with his dad and Jimmy Five Bellies, his best friend. They had all had quite a bit to drink, purely, so Gazza said, to fortify themselves for the plane as they all hated flying.

After my experience with Dwight, I wanted to ascertain three things. Would he give me the time? Apart from the fact he was flying off to China, his career appeared to be over, so there should be no problem about making time available. Did he really truly want to do the book? The answer to that was also yes. He needed the money and wouldn't get paid till it had been completed.

Would he open up? This in a way was my most important question. After three hours with him, I was saying 'Gazza, please, no more, no need to tell me that, that's awful, that's disgusting, I don't think readers will want to know that . . .' And that's when I agreed to do the book.

The first problem was connected with China. After only three months or so there, by which time he had been left on his own and his dad and Jimmy had returned to Newcastle, he went into a series of panic attacks and started binge drinking.

From China, he somehow managed to get himself to Cottonwood, a clinic in Arizona, where he had been before. Having thought he'd never return from China, I now feared he'd end up hospitalised in the USA, even before I'd begun the book. But he did return, dried out, this time admitting he was an alcoholic, promising he would never drink again.

His ex-wife Sheryl took him back and many of my early interviews took place at her lovely house in Hertfordshire, complete with swimming pool, tennis courts, big gardens. Gazza's friends and relations muttered all the time about Shel, that she wasn't right for him, but I rather defended her. Gazza had beaten her up. She'd had a lot to suffer. She must love him, or be genuinely trying to help him recover.

It didn't last long, living with Shel, and so he was on his own again. For the previous five years, he had not owned a place of his own, living in hotels or rented flats. He likes hotels, just as, in a weird way, he likes hospitals. They seem to comfort him, protect him from real life and responsibility.

While in Arizona, I had asked him to do me some notes, or tape-record answers to some questions. On his return, he pulled out a massive sheet of brown paper, the sort you use for wrapping up parcels. I wondered what might be inside. The brown paper itself was what he had brought me. On it he had done an enormous chart of his life marked PATH TO RECOVERY on which he had marked all the major events, from his birth in 1967 up to the age of thirty-six. In different colours and symbols it showed things like deaths and his twenty-seven different operations.

It's been said he suffers from Attention Deficit Disorder, but this isn't true. He could not have filled in that enormous chart without being able to concentrate. As a player, he had been first in and last out at training. For the book, he was able to sit and pay attention for three hours at a time.

He did of course mess me around now and again. I'd arrive at his hotel room first thing in the morning and after ten minutes he'd often say, 'You're doing ma' fuckin' heed in.' I would then walk round the hotel grounds, have a swim, come back later in the day. It wasn't because he couldn't be bothered. It was genuinely a case of his head not being right. He would stay in his room, playing chess with himself on his mobile phone till he felt more able to face the world, or at least face me. I can be pretty exhausting at times.

When it was all finished, he did read the whole manuscript, sitting solidly for six hours, pencil in hand, making comments, correcting my spelling. Which was useful.

Gazza's biography turned out a huge success, selling over 300,000 in hardback and winning a prize for the best Sports Book of the Year. My next biographical project was not quite as successful – in fact it didn't get off the drawing board – but then this is the nature of book writing. You always have several possible projects for your next book, either suggested to you or self-created, and you never quite know which will get off the ground. But you try to pursue or consider them, just in case.

I somehow got it into my head I'd like to do a biography of Cherie Blair. It dates back to being invited to their first cocktail party for the so-called Brit Pop stars, back in 1997, just after Tony Blair was elected PM.

We didn't actually go to that party. Margaret turned it down. We were in the Lake District at the time and I came back from my walk one day and asked, as I always do, 'Any phone calls, any faxes, any telegrams?' Obviously, telegrams don't exist any more but I say it all the same.

'Just one. From Number Ten.'

'Number Ten where?'

'Downing Street,' she said. 'Some party, but I said no, as of course we have this rule about not going to London while we're in Loweswater.'

Fortunately, we got invited to their second party in October, by which time we were back in London, and Margaret, after a lot of persuading from me, agreed to go.

I don't quite know why we had been invited, not being celebs, although I had heard that Cherie was a fan of Margaret's books. Not long previously, before the election, a newspaper had rung to say they had a snatched paparazzi shot of Cherie topless by a pool in Tuscany, reading a book. They were worried it might not in fact be Cherie, so they'd look very foolish if they used it. They had blown up the book's title and found it was one by Margaret, *Shadow Baby*. Had she written such a book? Would Cherie be reading it? Well, we'd heard she did like Margaret's books, so it was a possibility.

In the event, it was Cherie, but they never used the photo. As it became more likely that Tony would be our next PM, they chickened out, not wanting to offend him.

I had interviewed Tony on the election trail, for the *Daily Mail*, flying up to Scotland with him, spending the day, ending up in Yorkshire, a trip facilitated by Alastair Campbell whom I vaguely knew as he and his partner Fiona Miller live near us.

At the party, when it was our turn to be introduced, Cherie did spend a few minutes with Margaret, saying she had read her books. She looked far more attractive in the flesh that she ever does in her photographs.

The party was excellent, good wine and food and lots of interesting people, not all of them household faces. The Blairs seemed to have spread the invites around, to people from different walks of life, such as the law, social work, writing. I talked to Richard Branson, as I had interviewed him a couple of times, and Nick Hornby.

After the party, over the next few months, I often met Alastair on the Heath or Fiona at Kentish Town Baths and I mentioned to them one day that I'd like to do a biog of Cherie. I'm interested in her Liverpool working-class background, and also her legal career. I wrote a note to Cherie herself, saying what I had in mind. It need not be an official biog. Any help she might give could be off the record. She later wrote to me, saying we must meet.

I heard nothing for some months, and then in June 2003, when once more we were in Loweswater, Fiona rang to say Cherie would like to see me to discuss the book idea. By this time, I was in the middle of the Gazza book, and had half forgotten the Cherie idea. In between books, I'm always thinking up new projects, trying to keep several balls in the air at the same time, hoping one will fall the right way up. I explained to Fiona I was in Lakeland. Could it wait till October, on our return to London? She said fine.

My appointment with Cherie took place at Number Ten at 11.30 on Tuesday, 7 October 2003.

At the front door, I gave my name and was shown into a little waiting room. Outside, in the corridor, were lots of self-important young women with badges, floating around, chatting, being terribly important.

One of Cherie's assistants appeared, tall, slender, fortyish, blondish swept hair, debby looking, but with an ordinary London accent. She took me upstairs, past the drawing room where the party had been held. We turned left and faced double doors marked Private. She pressed a code and we entered a squarish hall with a big carpet covered with children's toys belonging to the youngest child, Leo, then aged three. Having recently done a biography of Eddie Stobart, I was amused to spot two Eddie Stobart toy trucks among Leo's treasures. She led me on into the Blairs' private sitting room and left me there.

It felt homely and real, comfy middle-class, not an official residence with official furniture. I sat on a large couch for a while, but when nobody appeared, I wandered around, making mental lists of their personal objects. I noted some guitars in their cases stacked in a corner. Inside a big glass-fronted bookcase, the middle shelf had fallen at an angle and not been repaired, so that all the books on it had slid down. They seemed mainly to be modern political thrillers or espionage. I noted several by John Le Carré.

On the wall over the bookcase was a nice oil painting by Charles Ginner, 'A view of Hampstead'. Presumably from the government collection. On a side table was a selection of family snaps, lined up in the aristocratic way. There was one of Kathryn in what looked like a white communion gown and a snap of one of the boys, perhaps Nicholas, holding a candle at his first communion. This was the only sign I could see in the room of a Catholic mother. No crosses or religious stuff on any walls.

On a mantelpiece were two snaps of Tony and Bill Clinton. In one, they were at either end of a long couch, perhaps in Downing Street, each talking on the phone to someone, looking in different directions. Bill has signed it to Tony in his bold, black handwriting, adding a *Private Eye*-type balloon caption underneath. 'Why not just hang up and talk face to face. Is this what the 3rd way means?'

No sign of Tony with President Bush, or the Queen, the Pope or any other world figures. In fact the snaps of Clinton were the only signs of Tony's day job. Every other photo was an ordinary family snap. The only evidence of this being the PM's home was a printed card on a corner table with 'Confidential' at the top. It listed the PM's engagements, hour by hour, for that day and the next two.

I was looking again at the family snaps when a Mrs Mopp woman bustled in, stopped, rather startled to see someone in the room. 'Ow, didn't know you was 'ere,' she said in broad cockney. 'No one tells me nuffink. Let me just plump those cushions for you . . .' I declined her help and she bustled out again.

Eventually Cherie arrived, only a few minutes late. She looked glowingly healthy, fit and attractive, wearing black slacks, trainers and a white battlejacket with Great Britain on the back, the sort athletes wear when warming up for a big race. She had been to the gym and feared she might have pulled a muscle.

She curled up on a sofa opposite me, drawing her legs underneath her. Coffee was brought and Cherie drank hers from a mug which had a 1930s flapper on the front and the wording 'Women – Half the Population, All the Brains'.

I'd brought with me a book I'd recently done about adoption, based on the story of triplets adopted as babies who didn't meet till they were aged sixty-nine. Cherie had become President of Barnardo's, so I thought she'd find it interesting. I also gave her the new illustrated version of my Beatles biog. She said she had a copy of the original in her own room, and had read it some years earlier. She turned over the pages, looking at the photos, and stopped at one of Yoko whom she had recently met at the re-naming of Liverpool Airport as John Lennon Airport.

I managed to drag the conversation away from the Beatles, not wanting to waste precious time, and launched into my proposed book.

Cherie made clear her main worry – that by helping me with a biography she would be accused by the media of flaunting herself, thus encouraging them to pry even more into her private life. I made the obvious response – that it was vital to set the record straight. Anyway, the personal attacks would go on, whatever happened.

She said yes, it never seemed to stop. They had both been upset by a piece by Leo Abse which had appeared in the *Mail* the week before, how unfair it had been about Tony's mum. However, she would not have asked me to come and talk about my project if she had not been interested. So what would my book be about?

I said well, hers was such a good story. She said no, she had done nothing really. I said rising in the law from her background, and a woman, with no money and no contacts, that was interesting in itself.

I knew her basic story, but didn't know what was true or not. For example, had she really come first in the Bar finals? She described in detail the day she'd gone to see the results pinned up. She couldn't find her name at first, as she was looking at the list near the middle, feeling she had done well, but not that well. Some chap standing beside her – whose name she mentioned – had a double Oxbridge first, was convinced he would be top. He had looked straight at the top of the list for his name, but couldn't find it. He was a bit miffed to see Cherie had beaten everyone.

I then asked her why she had not been kept on at Derry Irving's chambers, after her pupillage had ended. Tony had been offered tenancy, but she hadn't. There seemed at the time to be a prejudice against women in the legal profession generally. Derry's chambers did have one woman already, and perhaps he felt that was it. She said Derry always thought that she, not Tony, was the one bound for politics.

She then asked me how long such a book might take. I said a year. I'd spend the first few months, as with the Beatles, talking to friends and family, having got a list of contacts from her. How much of her time would it need? I said about two hours to get the first list, then perhaps six lots of two-hour chats later. She didn't know how she would manage that. I back-tracked, saying I'd go along with whatever time she could give.

She asked when it might come out. I stupidly mentioned it would be good to publish before the next election, which I immediately regretted, as of course it would be a mistake to tie it in with a political event. She then surprised me by saying what about coming out for her fiftieth birthday? I hadn't thought of that angle. I was pleased, as it showed she had been thinking about the book, taking it seriously.

We finished with her saying she was not against a book, but would like to think about it more. It would have to go to 'them downstairs' which I took to mean some sort of Downing Street committee. Or did it just mean Tony? I offered to put on paper what we had discussed, a resumé of the project.

At the beginning of our meeting, she had seemed rather suspicious of the idea, putting the case against it, but as our chat progressed, she seemed to warm to it more. It had ended on a very friendly, optimistic note. Or so I thought. I left at 12.20, so we'd been talking for about 45 minutes.

I waited six weeks, and then contacted Cherie's private office to find out any progress, but was told nothing had yet been decided. I sensed it had not even come up at any meeting. I waited another six weeks, and then rang again. Nobody seemed to know what I was talking about, but eventually I got a call saying Cherie was sorry, but she was not going to be able to do it.

But at least I had got inside the Prime Minister's private quarters. At Eddie Stobart Ltd, they were very pleased when I told them what toys little Leo Blair was playing with.

Chapter Thirty-five

Family Dramas

The family drama I mentioned, when the Gazza book first came up, concerned Caitlin, who had unexpectedly returned to London after almost twelve years in Botswana.

After meeting Ron at college in the USA, and getting a job teaching in his home village, they had eventually got married. She loved Botswana, the people, the language, the culture, the landscape, everything about it, and threw herself fully into being a good citizen, which is what she had become, on getting married.

Ron then got a job in the computer department of a large soda ash plant mine, not far from Francistown, Botswana's second town. It was in the back of beyond, out in the salt pans, dramatic-looking, with pink flamingos everywhere, but nothing to do for the wives and families of the workers who lived in their own compound. Caitlin put her time to good use. She couldn't teach there, so she started some freelance journalism for a paper called *The Voice* and also wrote a novel, set in Botswana, called *Jamestown Blues*. It was published by Penguin in 1996. We were so proud. She had no help from us and used none of our contacts. She made a big point of disguising her personal background, with no mention of her school or university or her family. All she gave out was that she had lived in Botswana for five years.

Ron hated the works, and his white South African bosses, most of whom were less qualified than he was, with his BSc degree in computer sciences from a well-respected US college.

He left and returned to Maun and set up on his own as a computer expert. He soon had a thriving business with three or four staff and contracts with the leading safari firms to install and mend their computers and teach their staff how to use them. He often acted as a flying computer doctor, going out in a little plane to isolated safari camps when their systems failed.

Back in Maun, Caitlin became editor of the local newspaper, the *Okavango Observer*, making a big point of training up local would-be journalists and helping them get funding to go abroad for training.

We went out to Botswana every two years to see them, while Caitlin and Ron came to us in the intervening years. They stayed with us once in Loweswater and Ron built us a dry-stone hide in our field, which was remarkable, considering where he grew up.

Ron had an enormous extended family in and around Maun. His father, who was white, had originally come up from South Africa to crop spray, and had stayed on. His mother was local, worked in the swamps picking reeds. She brought him up, in her mud and reed hut, after she split from his father. Ron was devoted to his mother, grandmother and endless aunts and uncles. As his business grew, he began to spend more and more time and money supporting them, and also helping them physically, working on their patch of land in order to build it into a proper farm.

He and Caitlin eventually built their own house, in a bend of the river, which I found pretty terrifying. When the waters arrived in Maun, and the river rose, it became full of crocodiles and hippos, so close that they were sticking their noses right up against the rather flimsy-looking wire fence around the house.

Caitlin got into certain scrapes as a crusading editor, leading various campaigns which the government was not best pleased with, and also got involved in a Rape Crisis centre.

She then had a second book published, this time non-fiction, called *El Negro*, about an African body which had been stuffed and put on display in France and Spain a hundred years ago, and was then returned and buried in Maun, becoming an all-African symbolic figure, their Unknown Soldier.

It looked to us as if Caitlin would be in Botswana for ever. She so clearly loved the country, the landscape, the culture, and identified so much with the way of life and the people, their problems and their hopes.

Meanwhile, Jake eventually got himself settled as well, though not after what seemed to me an unconscionably long time messing around, a phrase I was not allowed to use. After four years in Italy, teaching English and playing a lot of football, he then went to Spain, and spent several years there, doing much the same. He did learn both languages, broadened his horizons, improved his ball skills, and Margaret always said he was doing a worthwhile job. Teaching, of any sort, was something to be proud of, so I should not criticise. My suspicion was that most of these language schools were dodgy, they ripped off students and teachers, often went bust without paying their bills or salaries.

On his visits home, I would say to Jake, 'Why not apply to the BBC or the Civil Service? With your excellent degree, I'm sure you could get on a good training scheme.' His reply was always much the same: he didn't want to wear a suit or settle down. Eventually he did move out of TFL and for a year worked as a researcher for a British MEP, Janey Buchan, in Brussels, which he enjoyed, always having been interested in politics. But there again, it didn't lead to anything. It was short-term work, not a proper career.

But there was also part of me which thought it must be nice to be free-wheeling for a few years, not getting tied up, possibly committed to a boring job which you might quickly regret or having to worry about a mortgage and life insurance. He was in many ways typical of today's urban young men and young women, not thinking about settling down or having children till their thirties, unlike us. We didn't realise it, but we were creatures of our times, following the norms of our generation, getting married straight from university, and having children while still in our early twenties.

At last, at last, he did sit down, think about where he was going, what he could do with the only paper qualification he had, his Cambridge First, and what he might find enjoyable and perhaps, be good at. He came to the decision to go into law. So he returned home – moving into the flat Mrs Hall had once lived in, so that was fortunate – and started the long process of becoming qualified.

Even though Caitlin was so far away, her day-to-day life removed from us, I did identify with what she was doing – editing the local paper and writing books. I loved going into her office when we visited Botswana, reading her proof pages, hearing her problems, all of which I could totally understand. I was always suggesting features and stories, what you want to do is, why don't you, which of course she dismissed as stupid – what did I know?

But when Jake began to enter the law, I had no idea at all about what he was doing, or the language, or the process. He had to do a conversion year, as his degree was in history, not law, and the year was very intensive. Then he entered Bar school which together meant two years of hard study. We went to the impressive ceremony at the Inner Temple Hall when he passed out – which is not of course the correct legal word – and became a fully fledged barrister. We took photos of him in his wig, which he had to borrow from another student, as he hadn't bought one.

This was only the beginning. He then had to get pupillage – which means a position as a sort of trainee barrister, unpaid or minimally paid, who works in a chambers for a year. What a struggle that was. In the big wide world, a first-class Cantab degree sounds very impressive and you don't meet many of them, but in the hothouse world of the Bar, they almost all have equally good degrees from the top universities. Many were from legal families, with good connections. And the vast majority of them, at Jake's stage, were eight years younger.

Then came the final cliff-hanger – would he get tenancy?

Which he did, phew. So that seemed to be it, settled at last. In theory.

Being a tenant means you are officially a member of your chambers, with a position or at least a desk for life, but all barristers are freelance. There is never any guarantee you will get enough work to pay your share of the chambers expenses, which of course have to be paid, all the time.

There are occasions when he has no work coming in and we still fret, round the cocoa, wonder what will happen. As we do with all three. I don't know why I ever thought that when each of them got to eighteen, that would be it, off and away, and we won't have to worry any more. But their triumphs or setbacks seem to matter to us just as much as when they were seven, wondering if they'd make the school play, or eleven, worrying about which secondary school they would go to, or at twenty-one, hoping they would meet someone nice. I now realise that being a parent lasts as long as you are alive and they are alive. There's no cut-off point.

I liked saying my son, the barrister. And also my son, the married man. For around the same time, Jake did settle down and marry Rosa, a theatre set designer who has worked for the Royal Shakespeare Company, among others.

And in 1999, they presented us with our first grandchild, Amelia. Wonder why I chose that quaint usage, 'presented us'. As if they'd got her by mail order. It was awfully exciting, going across to the Royal Free Hospital to catch sight of her little face, her tiny fingers and toes. A new member of the planet, one of trillions which had gone before, but of course unique to us.

And then just six months later, Caitlin had a baby, Ruby, out in Botswana, so we didn't see her, in the flesh, for some time. Ruby was born in January 2000, a date of birth I rather envied, just as I used to like Arthur's birth year, 1900. Being born in 2000 seemed so symbolic, so hopeful.

It meant I entered the twenty-first century as a grandfather, with two granddaughters. Far too young of course, surely someone as young and vital and energetic as me could not possibly be a grandad. As with my own children, I encouraged them to call me Hunter or Hunt, not Dad, which my children still do, although when they want something, I notice they often revert to Father. Ruby, when she started speaking, which she did very quickly, being ever so advanced, coined her own name for me, a combination of grandpa and Hunter – Humper. I rather like it. It's now my family name.

Flora did a few short-term jobs, after realising that screen printing was not for her. She was a receptionist and then for over a year she worked as a legal assistant in a firm of solicitors in Kilburn. She enjoyed the tracking down of prospective witnesses, helping to build up a case, and also going to the Old Bailey, but soon realised she would need to get qualifications to go much further.

As with Jake, it was by a slow process of elimination that she worked out what she might enjoy doing, and be reasonably good at. She decided she'd like to be a researcher in TV.

She wrote off to lots of companies and programmes, knowing nobody, with no contacts, and eventually got a job as a junior researcher on an afternoon TV show called 'Crystal Rose'. This led to further jobs, all of them short-term contracts, but then that's the way of TV.

It took her a while to get out of daytime TV programmes and into documentaries, which is what she always fancied, the serious, searing, heart-breaking sort, about murderers, abuse, deprivation. Oh help, as my mother used to say.

When I look around today at other parents who have three or four children, you very often find one who never seems to settle to anything, who never has a proper job, gets no qualifications, just drifts around, often still at home in their thirties, to the despair of their parents. They can't understand it, when all their children have had the same background, same sort of schooling, same chances and opportunities. Even when, from time to time, at various stages, we did start to worry with each of ours, when they appeared to be drifting, we consoled ourselves by saying, 'but they're all good workers' and then smiling. This was another favourite saying of my mother, talking about her own four children.

What's the best thing you can wish for your children? Put in order the following you'd like the Good Fairy to bestow on your offspring: brains, good looks, skills, gifts, motivation, good health, confidence, contentment, happiness.

I know it's a waste of time to wish or speculate, as you can do nothing about it. I personally don't believe in the dominant power of genes, in the sense that it's a pointless exercise. Going back, you can find any character traits you are looking for, as humans are an amalgamation of all the same ones. So looking back, you can prove anything you want, identify where it's come from. Looking ahead, you can't predict or tell which elements will come to the fore. Margaret, on the other hand, is very keen on the subject of genes. She enjoys ascribing and apportioning where people's physical or emotional likenesses, virtues and vices, have each come from.

But over the years, I have indulged her on one topic. If you could pick only one, what would you rather wish for your children – being happy in a career or happy in a partnership?

Margaret always went for the latter. She didn't necessarily want them married, but settled in a fulfilling relationship. I usually went for the former. Obviously, we all want both, but I argued that at least you can throw yourself into a career, carve out a happy life, whereas being unhappy in work, or not having any, can ruin or spoil or affect even a good personal relationship.

So as well as two grandchildren, we began the new century with all three children in work, even if they were in professions without security, pensions or holiday pay. They were all doing something they appeared to enjoy and seemed reasonably good at. And two were settled in both work and their relationship. What more can any parent want?

And then, in February 2001, Caitlin on the phone from Botswana told us something awful had happened. She'd been raped. Before giving us the main details, she tried to reassure us by making it clear she was now safe, uninjured, which wasn't totally true, but at least we could hear her talking. She sounded shaky but trying hard to be controlled.

Our first instinct was to fly out to be with her, help in some way, but she forbade us from doing so. There was nothing we could do. Not now. She was coping with all the legal and medical and other matters that had to be done.

While Ron was at work, and Caitlin at home with Ruby, an intruder had got in. During the assault, Caitlin had been stabbed and received cuts and bruises, but they had been the least of the damage done to her.

The big worry straight afterwards was whether she had been infected with HIV. Lots of medical tests had to be done and the results waited for. They took some time to come through, which was agonising. Fortunately, by some miracle, when you consider the high rates of HIV in Botswana, she had not been infected.

Then came the drama and trauma of the trial. The rapist had been caught by Ron, who tracked him down in the bush, and eventually came to court, but he decided to defend himself. Caitlin therefore had to meet him, face to face in the witness box. He was allowed to cross-examine her himself, and make various accusations. In the end, he was convicted and sent to prison.

Not for a moment did Caitlin keep silent about what had happened to her. She told everyone, used no weasly words or euphemisms. She wrote and spoke publicly about her ordeal, in the African and English media, campaigned against the various injustices she had witnessed or experienced, in order to help other women. She was so brave, so defiant, so determined not to be beaten, not to let the rapist win or her life be ruined for ever. I could never have done what she did, or behaved as she did.

I felt guilty for not rushing straight to Botswana and helping, being strong, getting her through all the bureaucracy and paperwork and trial, though God knows what I could have done.

One result of the rape, if perhaps only indirectly, was that it dealt the final blow to her marriage. She had always found it hard, no matter how she tried, to bridge the culture gap between herself and Ron's family, especially his mother and grand-mother, to whom he was so devoted. They clearly had never accepted her and now, after the rape, they appeared unsym-pathetic and even hostile. Ron was caught between them, and soon resumed his old ways, spending a large proportion of his time and energies with them, on their farm, helping them when he should have been devoting all his time to Caitlin. That's how we saw it, from afar, but in any marriage, you never know or understand the full situation. Anyway, their relationship deteriorated. Caitlin decided to leave.

At Christmas 2003, she returned to London with Ruby, aged three. She had no money, no house, no job, no prospects. She appeared on the surface cool and determined but clearly traumatised, battered and bruised by what she had gone through.

They lived with us for three months, back in the room Caitlin had had as a child and teenager, then they managed to get a flat not far away. Jake and Flora rallied round, helping as much as possible, and so did Margaret, looking after Ruby.

To get some money, Caitlin started teaching at a local comprehensive school, Acland Burghley. She did not want to do any journalism. Doing it in Africa, so she said, was different. It was worthwhile. She disliked most of what she saw in British journalism.

Ruby then started having little fits, *petit mal*, going into short comas, as if spaced out, just to add to all the dramas and ill-fortune that Caitlin had to suffer. After lots of tests and spells in hospital, Ruby was put on medication, epilim.

Caitlin could no longer go out to work, teaching in the school. She needed to be at home, to be with Ruby as much as possible. But eventually she did manage to get some freelance work from home, for the Education pages of the *Independent*. She also did some examination marking.

When things had settled more, into some sort of routine, she started writing a book about her twelve years in Africa, determined to write honestly and openly about what had happened. She got a commission for it, from Simon and Schuster, for a modest advance.

So, it looked as if out of all that horror, some small bit of good might come.

Chapter Thirty-six

Fit for the Wedding

Because of a disaster with a project falling through I decided to have a new knee.

I've had arthritis for the last ten years, been on various drugs, tried all the usual remedies, consulted experts and been in hospitals in both London and the Lake District. Even tried homeopathic nonsenses, none of which I believe in, not at those prices. The worst pain has been in my left knee which I'm sure was partly my own fault, playing football till I was almost fifty.

The Royal Free consultant suggested a new knee would clear up the arthritis in that area, if not elsewhere, so why not try it? I had gone on the waiting list, planning to have it done later in the year. I was reckoning on being tied up with the project till May, when we would be off to the Lake District.

When the project collapsed, I was left with a massive hole, several months of emptiness stretching ahead as I had cancelled or refused other bits of work. When suddenly my number came up at the Royal Free, I took it and had the operation in April 2005.

I was in agony with my knee for the next two months, convinced the op had been a failure. Margaret had told me I was silly to have it when I did. I was being wilful and too optimistic about the recovery process and I would not be fit and well for the big event coming up in June – Flora's wedding.

She was getting married to a Frenchman, Richard Kingue

Kouta who had arrived in London seven years earlier with no English whatsoever. He had worked his way up from barman, to waiter, to manager of a fashionable gastro pub in Chelsea. Now he had begun his own business, Authentique, providing staff for the hotel trade, mainly managers and chefs.

The wedding was in France, so we had to get from the Lake District, as it was summer, to Nice. I was still using a stick for walking and I took with me a supply of Tramadol, a painkiller prescribed by the Royal Free. Despite my poorly leg, I threw away my stick at the reception and found myself doing my best Sixties dancing, which normally I am warned never to attempt in public. As I danced, I was conscious of the fact that my knee was no longer killing me. Was it a miracle? Was it the drink?

Margaret and I packed up first, about seven, as I was suddenly very tired. A bit merry, but I was certainly not drunk. Back at the hotel, I had a swim, then we went to bed early.

Next morning, we all went to a local beach where I had a long swim, going out to a raft and sunbathing. Jake managed to bag the last table at the beach café for us all to have lunch. As it was a Sunday, it was very busy with locals.

At 12.30, along with Margaret, my three children, daughter-in-law, two grandchildren (Richard, my new son-in-law, was taking his parents to the airport), I sat down to eat. To my delight, the wine arrived at once. I hate it when it doesn't come quickly. I took one glass, and it was delicious. I felt so happy and content.

The wedding had been a triumph. Flora looked stunning, but then she always does. I was with my own dear family. We were at a lovely beach restaurant on the Côte d'Azur. We had a good table, in the shade, under an awning. The sun was shining. All's well with the world. I was consciously thinking that, saying to myself that you are rarely aware of such moments in life, except in retrospect. And then it happened.

The next thing I was aware of was waking up half an hour later in an ambulance roaring through the back streets of Cannes, its siren shrieking, while people were leaning over me, shouting something. Margaret was telling me not to go to sleep. I felt sick in my stomach, rather dizzy, my neck was stiff, but apart from that, I could feel no pains, no aches. Slowly, I realised Caitlin was also in the ambulance, sitting behind Margaret, looking very worried.

I had no memory of what had happened. I knew who I was, why I was here in France. I just didn't know how I'd come to be lying in an ambulance. I noticed that the ambulance man was wearing big boots, too big and clumsy for working in the confined space of an ambulance. How strange, I thought. It was only much later I discovered that French ambulance men often double as firemen.

Apparently, while I was taking my first sup of wine at the beach café, Flora, who was on my right, had started screaming at the sight of my face breaking into violent spasms. Then the whole of my upper body had gone into a seizure – my limbs flailing, blood trickling from my mouth, a slight froth gathering on my lips, my eyes rolling.

Other people started screaming, calling for help, shouting out to ask if there was a doctor on the beach. Two men appeared, both doctors, still in their swimming costumes, and put their arms round me to restrain me, then lowered me to the ground. A beach lifeguard appeared with oxygen equipment and placed a mask over my face. I had passed out and was lying more still, my face turning from blue to a sickly grey. Margaret's first thought was that I had had a stroke. In her mind, she could see me as a vegetable for years, if not the rest of my life.

On arrival in the ambulance at the Cannes hospital, I was wheeled into Casualty where a young doctor with a crewcut appeared and examined me, reading the notes which had been taken down from Margaret and the ambulance men. He said I would have to go for a scan.

I waited for the result for about an hour, by which time Richard had arrived which was a great relief, having a French speaker. As in all hospitals, little ever gets explained, or the system and stages outlined, unless you can ask and pester and make them tell you everything.

The young doctor eventually returned with the scan. Basically, it was OK, nothing too worrying, but there were a couple of blips. He would like a further opinion from one of his superiors, so I would have to stay in overnight and be seen tomorrow by an expert.

I was wheeled into the Casualty ward. There was an open-plan bit, with beds shoved up against each other and some desperate, scruffy, mad-looking men and women, some of them shouting and yelling, but fortunately I found myself in a single room.

Later that evening, Flora arrived. She was soon in tears, seeing the drip I was connected to, saying she was going to cancel her honeymoon in Greece. She couldn't go away now, while I was in this condition. I said don't be daft, I'm fine, nothing to worry about. We had paid for their honeymoon, our present to them, so I certainly was not going to let them cancel it.

Next morning, I was wheeled off for an EEG exam. The woman technician did it several times, as the instrument was flickering. When she was finished, and the printer had spewed out reams of graph paper, I could tell from her face she was concerned. I asked if all was OK, but she said it was not up to her to tell me. The neurologist would do that.

I had to stay another night. I was so depressed and furious I couldn't get to sleep. Then a gang of youths from the open ward started rampaging round the corridors, screaming and shouting. I felt I was in a Kafkaesque nightmare with nothing making sense. It would appear I'd had an epileptic fit, and might well have another. Life, from now on, would not be the same. And I would be mucking up Margaret's life as well. Oh, what a fucking mess.

On the third morning, with still no sign of the neurologist, I said that's it, I'm leaving, checking myself out. A senior house doctor said I should stay, because they were only doing what was best for me, but if I decided to go, I would have to sign a form, relieving them of all responsibility.

Just after three o'clock, the neurologist did arrive – a very pleasant, intelligent-looking, middle-aged woman, Dr Catherine

Lienhard, *neurologue attachée*. She had my tests in front of her and explained, in a mixture of French and English, that the first test, the scan, had shown some blip. The EEG was more worrying. She could see 'spikes' which were signs of an epileptic seizure, indicating there might be lesions in the brain. That could suggest epilepsy, but there was always a chance they were caused by something else. I now needed an IRM scan – an MRI scan in English – to eliminate other possibilities. She wrote out an order for me to have the IRM and signed it, but I explained I was leaving, now, flying home tomorrow. I couldn't wait any longer.

She sighed and then wrote out a prescription for some anti-convulsion medication which would help tranquillise me for the journey, till I saw my own doctor and could get an MRI in England.

It took seconds to pack, as I had no possessions, just what I had arrived in. For three days, I had been in the same swimming costume and T-shirt. I had been offered a hospital smock, but I couldn't get my gammy leg through it. When I got out of bed for the last time, and pulled the sheet back, I saw a little pile of sand from the beach, the one where I'd had my fit.

The moment I got back to our hotel, I insisted on having a swim, much to Margaret's alarm. What if I collapsed, had a seizure in the water? There was no lifeguard in the hotel pool.

'You'll have to rescue me,' I told her. 'You're always boasting how you passed your life-saving test when you were eleven in Carlisle.'

So I had my swim, wondering if my life really would change from now on, not being able to climb ladders, do anything remotely dangerous, or even be alone. I hadn't been aware when I had had the fit, either before, during or after, so would I ever know it was coming on again? Then I thought, Bugger it, I'm not going to let it hang over what's left of my life.

The biggest, most immediate, single problem was not being able to drive, for a year at least, even if I didn't have another fit. I rang my brother Johnny in Carlisle and he came to meet us at

Newcastle Airport, driven there by his son-in-law Robert. Johnny then drove us home to Loweswater in my car, then Robert came to pick him up. Oh, the complications you get into, the people you have to depend on, when such unexpected things happen.

Margaret can drive, but doesn't. She passed her test ten years ago in Cockermouth, when I first began to get arthritis, as an insurance policy in case my knees got worse. She dislikes driving, is scared of it. So would it mean that living in the Lake District half of each year would become impractical?

Life, eh, bloody hell. You just never know. And yet it was nothing compared with what Caitlin had been through, or my sister Marion. What had happened was not life threatening, or so I gathered, although people do die of a major seizure. Really, it was just inconvenient, so I should get on with it. Gazza, when he gave up drink, worried that he would become a boring person from then on. I worried that life itself might get a little boring, with all the constraints, having to be sensible, which I always find very hard.

Chapter Thirty-seven

Today at Home

Six months later we were back in London, getting ready to celebrate my seventieth birthday. I took all the family to Crete, no expense spared, to a top hotel, the Elounda Beach. I'd done this only once in my life before, fourteen years ago, when I took them all to Mauritius. Caitlin was with Ron and they had a hellish journey from Botswana. The inter-family relationships became at times, let's say, a little strained. Margaret said never again. And I agreed with her, at the time. But I'd forgotten all that, as I forget all bad times.

My knee is still driving me mad, but I now hardly think about my seizure. Not had another one since, touch wood. I eventually saw an English neurologist, at the West Cumbria Hospital in Whitehaven. He sent me for an MRI – which took three months to get done, whereas if I'd waited in Cannes I would have had it the next day. As far as he could see, all the tests indicated no real problem in the brain which might have caused the seizure. The theory is that the drink at the wedding did it, combined with taking those painkillers. I should not, of course, have been drinking when on Tramadol. In the small print inside the packet, I now see that it lists amongst the rare side-effects 'convulsions (fits)'. So I'm blaming Tramadol. And of course myself.

I hope to get my driving licence back, when the twelve months are up. In Loweswater, Margaret did gather up the courage to drive into Cockermouth for our weekly shopping. The police were very kind and cleared the road every time. Joke. Which I'd better stop making as I'm still relying on her so much.

We're now back in London, in the same old house we have lived in for forty-three years. Still married to the same wife after forty-six years. And I'm still working full-time after forty-eight years. What would I do otherwise?

I went back to a Durham reunion a few years ago, for only the second time since I left in 1958, and I was astounded to find that all my contemporaries had long since retired, some of them for over ten years. They said it was the best thing they ever did and no, time did not hang heavily, they always seemed to be busy. I don't believe it. I'd be going mad, if it happened to me.

Which of course it will. I know eventually the books will dry up, as will my columns. I'll end up in Division Three (North) doing books for publishers I've never heard of, and probably for nothing. Doesn't worry me, as long as I'm occupied. I plan one day to do a biography of Canon Rawnsley, co-founder of the National Trust, who was a great Victorian activist, a friend and encourager of the young Beatrix Potter. Every London publisher I've ever mentioned it to has said no thanks, the bastards, but I know that my friend Stephen Matthews in Carlisle will publish it, whenever I get round to writing it. I can also keep doing new editions of *The Good Guide to the Lakes*, which of course I publish at my own expense. So I won't turn myself down.

And there's so much football on the TV these days, the only thing I ever watch, which I save up as a reward and treat for myself at the end of a writing day. I wonder how many more World Cups and European Championships I'll manage to fit in, before the final whistle blows.

Not that I often think that way. I just haven't the time for odes on mortality, being always so busy, so much to do. I do, though, find myself saying, when I am moaning about having to get the house painted, the roof sorted, or ordering a new washing machine, 'It will see us out.' It amuses me to say it, and is in a way quite reassuring, playing this game, pretending it will be the last time we'll have to spend money on such dreary things. But I also know it's true. Some of these things will be coming round on their final circuit.

I have of course slowed down physically, which I hate, unable to take the Lakeland walks I once loved, but you do become content with smaller dollops, shorter ambles down to the lake and back, with lots of rests. If I can keep doing that for a while yet, so I tell myself, I'll be well pleased.

I suppose in the end, if we are forced to choose, we'll give up Lakeland. London, for all its filth and squalour, speed and nastiness, has so many amenities and attractions, hospitals and facilities. And while London can be depressing, it is always stimulating. And it does contain our three children, and their families, each of them within walking distance of our house.

In March 2006, in one of my *New Statesman* columns, I rather poured scorn on the rumour that a publisher was offering £5 million to Wayne Rooney. I scoffed at the idea of a twenty-year-old doing five books, suggesting he wasn't exactly Mozart or Shakespeare. I was of course being very patronising and silly as I now know he is a young man of staggering genius and deserves fifty books, nay, a whole library to himself.

This is because just two weeks after that column appeared, I got a call from HarperCollins from their head of sports books, a person I'd never met, asking if I'd like to come along to meet Wayne. I was apparently on a shortlist of three writers, all of whom were being invited into The Presence.

My first thought was huh, don't they know who I am, at my age and stature, I am long past taking part in a beauty parade, the very cheek. Then my second thought was yeah, I'll be there.

Waiting in the atrium at HarperCollins' mega-impressive Hammersmith HQ, I suddenly wondered if a certain distinguished sports journalist might also be on the shortlist. I had been jolly rude to him, some weeks previously, and heard he'd vowed to duff me up.

I sat around for some time as Wayne was signing the actual contract that afternoon, then doing a 'walkabout', meeting certain chosen HarperCollins staff.

Eventually, I was called into the boardroom. There was Wayne's agent Paul, an elegant woman I was told was his brand manager, another person in a suit introduced as his PR consultant, plus his own personal bodyguard.

The presence of so many advisors, plus presumably lawyers and accountants in the background, made me think fondly of doing *The Glory Game,* over thirty years earlier. None of the Spurs stars even had an agent, let alone a brand manager. I dealt with the players directly, face to face, and did the book without having a contract, either with any of the players or the club. Today, a star footballer is not only a brand in his own right but a multi-million-pound industry.

Wayne himself was wearing a hoodie, trackie bottoms and trainers. He looked very young and about two inches taller than I expected, but was polite, relaxed, without a hint of arrogance.

I decided to ask him three questions. Why did he want to do the book? If he'd said for the money, or my agent thinks it's a good idea, I would have been worried. 'So much has been written about me,' he replied. 'I just want to tell my own side of it now . . .'

Would he open up, reveal himself? I was thinking of course of the trouble I'd had with Dwight Yorke. Wayne nodded, appeared to understand and agreed he would cooperate.

I told him how much time I would need, how I would work, and asked about archives – had his mam or dad kept his local cuttings, his school reports, the first letters from Everton and other personal memorabilia? Yeah, they had, he said.

I managed to work in that I did not expect to be his buddy, going clubbing with him, but that he should look upon me as a Bobby Robson/Alex Ferguson figure. I'd presumed that at least one of the others on the shortlist was probably much younger than me, so I wanted to pre-empt any ageist thoughts. I am, after all, old enough to be his grandad.

There is a well-known photo of Wayne on the beach on his hols, deep in concentration, as he reads *Gazza: My Story*. In hardback. Big spender. Paul, his agent, said they did think about sending in a bill for advertising.

I didn't mention my Wordsworth biog, as he might somehow have missed it. During the writing of it, I remember how I was moaning and groaning, telling myself I'd never again write a life of someone who gets to eighty. What a slog that was, so much to read and research. Took three years and I was exhausted. On the other hand, writing the life of someone aged only twenty might pose certain other challenges.

On the bus home, I thought, Well, if I don't get the gig, I have met him. Seems a nice lad.

Two days later, the call came. I started the book the following week, looking forward specially to the World Cup and speaking to him every day to get all the inside gen . . .

When I look back at myself, down all the years, I recognise very little. If I had to meet myself in Carlisle, going down Caird Avenue delivering the newspapers, coming home across Stanwix bridges on my bike from Carlisle Grammar School, sitting in my room at Durham Castle, or going on my first job for *The Sunday Times*, I wouldn't really be able to identify with me, understand what I was thinking, worrying about, hoping for. I look at old photos and can't believe it's me.

There's one photo in which I look like George Best, which surprises me now, because I never thought it at the time, but then looking back, with age, it's youth itself which is attractive. I also seemed to wear quite interesting clothes, and have a proper haircut, now and again, compared with today when I dress and look like a tramp most of the time. I hate buying anything new.

Thinking back to the youth I was, I wonder if at any stages of my life I had been able to jump ahead and meet me, as I am now, would I also be a stranger to myself? I'd probably have little in common with myself today, and little to say to me. Except amazement. How did I get here, from there? We all go through several lives, many phases, with often very little connection between them. Which is just as well. There wouldn't be much point in life, in living, if we all stayed the same and didn't change and develop.

Our daily routine is much the same, whether in London or Loweswater. Margaret brings me a cup of tea in bed, as she has always done, that's what wives are for, switches on my digital radio which is set to Radio 4. I do find it awfully tiring leaning over in the morning to find the radio. She brings me the *Independent*, if we're in London, opens the curtains and then leaves, ever so quietly, closing the bedroom door behind her.

In Loweswater, the paper doesn't come till later. I am part of a newspaper round, taking turns to deliver. So I'm a paperboy again, just as I was fifty-five years ago. Life has come round in a circle, only this time I do it in my Jaguar, when I'm allowed to drive it.

Our children find it shocking that Margaret should have brought me tea in bed all our married life, especially as she also does all the cooking, provisioning and cleaning. I can make a cup of tea, if I have the recipe in front of me, but that's about it.

Margaret considers herself a feminist, but she just smiles. She's always been good at getting up in the morning, unlike me. She knows it matters so much to me. She does get lots in return. Of course she does. I'll just have to think for a bit. I do the garden, in both places, except when my knee is very bad, and look after all bills and financial matters. I normally do all the driving. In most marriages I know, the woman is the gardener, and also drives her own car. I also know quite a few men who do the cooking in their marriage. I hate them.

It's funny how these things start, this division of labour, but we've stuck to the same roles since 1960. Just like we lie on the same side of the bed, wherever we are. She always takes the left, looking at the bed from the plan view. I suppose it happens in most partnerships. You take on certain functions, not necessarily because you are good at them, but because someone had to. I do like doing the bills and the finances. If left to Margaret, she would have every penny lying in the bank.

We each of us work all morning, in our own office, in either London or Loweswater. I take a bit of time to get started, have a little walk, and I don't mind interruptions. Margaret is straight to her desk and she never answers the phone or breaks for coffee.

I write on an old Amstrad word processor – PCW 9512, the same model in each house, spare no expense. They must be fifteen years old by now and I've done about two million words on them. When they pack up, they're going to the V and A. I have a computer, programmed for me by Caitlin, but I never use it, so it just lies there. I don't use e-mail either. I have a mobile phone, but never use it. I don't know its number. But I do have a fax machine and photocopier in each house.

Margaret's office is bare of all modern devices. She could well be in the nineteenth century. She writes by hand in ink, immaculately, with her Waterman fountain pen. It's just her, and a pile of blank pages. She sits for the same time each day, two hours, and if she is on a novel, ten pages appear, as if by magic. Next day, she doesn't look at them, just glides on. She makes no notes, no plans, writing a novel for her is a path of discovery. She never discusses it with me, or anyone, won't even tell me what it's about, or even how it's going. With non-fiction, that's a bit different. She is more than willing to discuss it. In fact she'll drag every conversation round to it. I'm having a glass of water and she'll say, 'Daphne du Maurier liked glasses of water,' and she's away. She sees non-fiction as a public act while to her, fiction is private.

In Loweswater after lunch, we go round the lake, Crummock Water. In London, we go round the Heath. I usually go back to some sort of work, or articles, for a couple of hours before supper. Unless there is football on TV, I usually work in the evenings as well, till five minutes to ten, when I race up to bed for the ten o'clock news on Radio 4. Margaret only works in the mornings. During the rest of the day, she reads a novel, normally getting through one a day.

We never feel like rivals, or in competition in any way, despite each of us working at home, writing books. We write such different things. We enjoy any bits of success or news or excitements the other may have, big or small, just as much as our own. I feel it's like having two careers, mine and Margaret's, just as dividing our year between London and Loweswater is like living twice.

We used to scream and shout at each other a lot when we were younger. I didn't like it, going bitter and twisted, but it seems to have got less with age. Either I have learned to avoid upsetting her by saying or doing stupid things, or she has become more tolerant and calm. Our roughest patches were when the children were young, driving us both mad, exhausting Margaret totally so she never had the energy for me, or so I thought. It all seems so long ago now.

We have always talked, all the time, never seem to be bored by the other's company, though I am told to shut up, when I grind on and repeat myself on the same old topics. We still never go to sleep on a quarrel. Each new day the slate is clean. Although we are different personalities, with different characters, we do seem to share many of the same values and attitudes.

It's been a help, or at least an extra source of interest and amusement, to have known each other for so long and to have come from exactly the same place and same social background. We now have so many memories and experiences in common. When the children were young, we often talked in Carlisle slang, so that they wouldn't know what we were saying. We talk about Arthur, her father, as if he were still alive, and also about my mother and her sayings. Our children remember both of them clearly as well. Everyone who has lived lives on in family folk memories for at least two generations. As long of course as you have had a family.

Caitlin now appears settled into her London life, doing some journalism and writing. Her book about her life in Africa got good reviews and has been sold in France and Germany. She's now been commissioned by Simon and Schuster to do two novels. Ruby is at Brookfield Primary, the school all our three went to, so we can see life repeating itself. Her epilepsy never returned, so perhaps it wasn't that, but just the trauma of coming from Africa. Ron, Caitlin's ex-husband, has become an MP in Botswana.

Jake appears happy in his chambers at 5 Paper Buildings in the Inner Temple. He specialises in employment law, people complaining about discrimination and dismissal. Flora, now married to Richard, is still in television, as an associate producer. She is still doing serious documentaries, which is what she wanted.

I've always felt fortunate, since my first day at work, and even more so now, still here, still turning it out, with my dear family around me. Shame about the knee, but I try not to talk about that except to my contemporaries. The young don't want to hear about old age and aches. They think, What do you expect, at your age? But you know your own generation will listen, if only to wait for a break and dive in with the latest on their bad back.

So what's the future? Another ten years on this planet, I hope. My mother did get to seventy-nine, so I'd like to equal that at least. Or I'll be furious. There are so many things about which I want to know – what happened next? My pension plans, will they turn out to be a complete waste of money? Spurs and Carlisle United, and the England team, are they going to be rubbish for ever?

Most of all, I so want to know what happens to my grandchildren, to see them on to the next stage in the narrative, how they'll change and develop. Their story is to come. This is mine, such as it is, so far. Thanks for listening.

Appendix I

Journalism, Jobs, Positions

Journalistic Jobs
- *Palatinate* editor, Durham University student newspaper, 1957–8
- *Manchester Evening Chronicle*, reporter (Kemsley/Thomson graduate trainee) 1958–9
- *Sunday Graphic*, London, reporter, feature writer, 1959–60
- *Sunday Times*, 1960–80
  Atticus Assistant, 1960–4
  Atticus, 1964–7
  Chief Feature writer, 1967
  Editor, Look Pages, 1970
  Editor, Scene pages, 1975
  Editor, Colour Magazine, 1975–7

Freelance Journalism
- Columnist, *Punch*, 1979–89
- Columnist, *Stamp News*, 1981–6
- Columnist, London *Evening Standard*, 1987
- Football columnist, *Independent*, 1989–92
- Interviewer, *Independent*, 1990–3
- Columnist, *Independent on Sunday*, 1991
- TV Critic, Night and Day, *Mail on Sunday*, 1993–4

– Football columnist, *New Statesman,* 1996–
– Money columnist, *Sunday Times,* 1998–

TV
Writer, Wednesday play, *The Playground,* BBC TV, 1967
Writer, presenter, 'The Living Wall' (Hadrian's Wall), ITV 1974
Writer, presenter, 'George Stephenson', ITV, 1975
Writer, presenter, 'A Walk in the Lakes', ITV, 1979
Writer, presenter, 'Beatrix Potter', BBC, 1988

RADIO 4s GOOD BOOK PROGRAMME
BOOKSHELF
PRESENTED BY
HUNTER DAVIES
Sundays 7.30 pm, repeated Thursdays 4.10 pm
BBC Radio 4
1500m/200kHz · 92-95 VHF

Illustration:
David Smith

Radio
Presenter, Bookshelf, BBC Radio 4, 1983–6
Presenter, Radio 2 Arts Programme, BBC Radio 2, 1990
Presenter, I Was That Teenager, BBC Radio 4 series, 1996
Presenter, When I'm Sixty-Four, BBC Radio 4 series, 2001

Films
Screenplay writer, *Here we Go, Round the Mulberry Bush,* 1968

Positions
– Founder and Judge, Lakeland Book of the Year Awards, 1984–
– Governor, Chairman, Brookfield Primary School, 1984–8
– Member, British Library Consultative Group on Newspapers,
  1987–9
– Board of Directors, Edinburgh Book Festival, 1990–5
– President, Cumbria Wildlife Trust, 1995–
– Pro-Vice Chancellor, Lancaster University, 1998–9

Appendix II

Books Published

Novels
- *Here we Go, Round the Mulberry Bush,* Heinemann, 1965
- *The Rise and Fall of Jake Sullivan,* Weidenfeld, 1970
- *A Very Loving Couple,* Weidenfeld, 1971
- *Body Charge,* Weidenfeld, 1972
- *Striker,* Bloomsbury, 1992

Biographies
- *The Beatles,* Heinemann, 1968
    New edition, Cape, 1985, Illustrated edition, Cassells, 2002
- *George Stephenson,* Weidenfeld, 1975
    New edition, Sutton, 2004
- *William Wordsworth,* Weidenfeld, 1980
    New editions, Sutton, 1997, 2002
- *The Grades,* Weidenfeld, 1981
- *Beatrix Potter's Lakeland,* Warne, 1988
    New edition, Warne, 1999
- *In Search of Columbus,* Hamish Hamilton, 1991
- *Teller of Tales, in search of R. L. Stevenson,* Hamish Hamilton, 1994

- *Wainwright,* Michael Joseph, 1995
  New edition, Orion, 2002
- *Dwight Yorke,* Deutsch, 1999
- *Joe Kinnear – Still Crazy,* Deutsch, 2000
- *The Quarrymen,* Omnibus, 2001
- *The Eddie Stobart Story,* HarperCollins, 2001
- *Gazza: My Story,* Headline, 2004
- *Strong Lad Wanted for Strong Lass* (memoir), Bookcase, Carlisle, 2004
- *The Beatles, Football and Me* (autobiography), Headline, 2006
- *Being Gazza* (joint author), Headline, 2006
- *Wayne Rooney,* HarperCollins, 2006

Football

- *The Glory Game,* Weidenfeld, 1972
  New editions, Mainstream, 1990, 1994, 1996, 1999, 2001
- *England! The 1982 World Cup Squad,* Futura, 1982
- *Boots, Balls and Haircuts,* illustrated history of football, Cassells, 2002
- *I Love Football,* Headline, 2006

[Plus novel, *Striker,* and biogs of D. Yorke, J. Kinnear, Gazza, Rooney]

Social History

- *The Other Half* (on new poor, new rich), Heinemann, 1966
- *The Creighton Report* (year in life of a comprehensive), Hamish Hamilton, 1976

Photo: Richard Davis

- *Great Britain, a Celebration*, Hamish Hamilton, 1982
- *Living on the Lottery*, Little, Brown, 1996
- *Born 1900* (people and things born 1900), Little, Brown, 1998
- *Hurry, Hurry while Stocks Last* (Cumbrian history), Bookcase, 2000
- *Relative Strangers* (triplets, adoption), Time Warner, 2003

Travel, Walking Books, Guides

- *A Walk Along the Wall* (Hadrian's Wall), Weidenfeld, 1974
  New editions, Orion 1993, 2000
- *A Walk Around the Lakes*, Weidenfeld, 1979
  New editions, Orion, 1989, 1993, 2001
- *A Walk Along the Tracks* (disused railways), Weidenfeld, 1982
  New edition, Orion, 2002
- *A Walk Around the Parks*, Hamish Hamilton, 1983
- *London at its Best*, Pan, 1984
- *The Grand Tour*, Hamish Hamilton, 1986
- *Back in the USSR*, Hamish Hamilton, 1987
- *London to Loweswater*, Mainstream, 1999
- *A Walk Around the West Indies*, Weidenfeld, 2000
- *The Best of Lakeland*, Dalesman, 2002
- *The Best of Wainwright*, Frances Lincoln, 2003

Publisher and Author

- *The Good Guide to the Lakes*, Forster Davies, 1984
  New editions, 1986, 1989, 1993, 1997, 2003
- *The Good Quiz Book to the Lakes*, Forster Davies, 1987

Other Non-fiction

- *Book of British Lists*, Hamlyn, 1980

- *Beaver Book of Lists* (for children), Hamlyn, 1981
- *Hunter Davies' Lists*, Cassells, 2004

Children's Books
For 8–12-year-olds
- *Flossie Teacake's Fur Coat*, Bodley Head, 1982
- *Flossie Teacake – Again!*, Bodley Head, 1983
- *Flossie Teacake Strikes Back*, Bodley Head, 1984
- *Flossie Teacake Wins the Lottery*, Bodley Head, 1996
- *Flossie Teacake's Holiday*, Bodley Head, 2000

- *Come on, Ossie!*, Bodley Head, 1985
- *Ossie Goes Supersonic*, Bodley Head, 1986
- *Ossie the Millionaire*, Bodley Head, 1987

- *Snotty Bumstead*, Bodley Head, 1991
- *Snotty Bumstead and the Rent-a-Mum*, Bodley Head, 1993
- *Snotty the Hostage*, Bodley Head, 1995

For Teenagers
- *Saturday Night*, Viking Kestrel, Penguin, 1989

S.T.A.R.S series, 12 novels set in a comprehensive Sixth Form, Penguin, 1989–90
- *Fit for the Sixth*
- *Rapping with Raffy*
- *She's Leaving Home*
- *Party, Party*
- *Ice Queen*
- *When Will I Be Famous?*
- *Who Dunnit?*
- *A Case of Sam and Ella*
- *The French Connection*
- *Playing Away*
- *Let's Stick Together*
- *Summer Daze*

Books Edited
– *The New London Spy* (London guide), Anthony Blond, 1966
– *I Knew Daisy Smuten* (group novel), Weidenfeld, 1970
– *Sunday Times Book of Jubilee Year*, Michael Joseph, 1977

Collections
– *Father's Day* (*Punch* columns), 1981
– *The Joy of Stamps* (*Stamp News* columns), Robson, 1983
– *My Life in Football* (football articles), Mainstream, 1990
– *Hunting People* (interviews with the famous), Mainstream, 1994
– *The Fan* (*New Statesman* football columns), Pomona, 2004
– *Mean with Money* (*Sunday Times* money columns), Pomona, 2006

Index

Index

Index

Index

Index